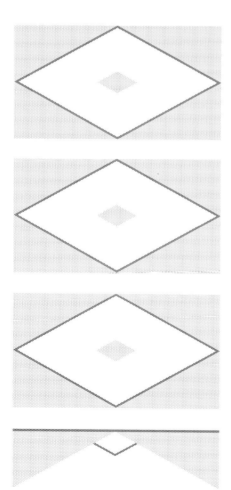

Nez Perce Women
in Transition

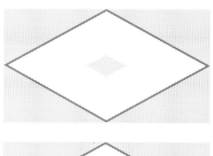

Nez Perce Women
in Transition
1877-1990

Caroline James

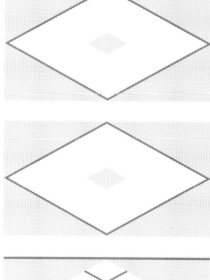

University of Idaho Press
Moscow, Idaho
1996

Published by the University of Idaho Press,
Moscow, Idaho 83844-1107

Printed in the United States of America

Design by Joanne Poon   00 99 98 97 96   5 4 3 2 1

LIBRARY OF CONGRESS CATALOGING-IN-PUBLICATION DATA

James, Caroline.
    Nez Perce women in transition, 1877–1990 / Caroline
James.
      p. cm.
    Includes bibliographical references and index.
    ISBN 0-89301-188-6 (cloth)
    1. Nez Perce women—History.   2. Nez Perce
women—Social conditions.   3. Nez Perce women—
Politics and government.
    I. Title.
E99.N5J36 1996
305.48′8970796′85—dc20   95–49234
                                                          CIP

▲▲▲▲▲▲▲▲▲▲▲▲▲▲▲▲▲▲▲▲▲ TO THE Nez Perce Women
and the Tribe

Contents

▲▲▲▲▲▲▲▲▲▲▲▲▲▲▲▲▲▲▲▲▲▲▲▲▲▲▲▲▲▲▲▲▲▲▲▲

List of Figures

▲▲▲▲▲▲▲▲▲▲▲▲▲▲▲▲▲▲▲▲▲▲▲▲▲▲▲▲▲▲▲▲

Individuals Interviewed

The late Susan Broncheau
The late Julia Pablo
Esther McAtty
Esther McAtty
Nancy Halfmoon
The late Lottie Moody
The late Lottie Moody
Edna Thomas
Lavinia Williams
Iva Wilson (Too-my-o-chuw-my)
Rena Katherine Ramsey
Rena Katherine Ramsey
Josephine C. Hayes
Marguerita Broncheau
Rachel Aripa
Delores L. Wheeler
Louise High Eagle
Mylie Lawyer
Elsie M. Frank
Rose Frank
Beatrice Miles
Gladys Allen
Dorothy Jackson
Alta Guzman
Bessie Greene Scott

Ethel M. Seubert and her daughter, Andra
The late Marie Watters
Patricia High Eagle (Ee-u-weehu-lakh-my)
Nellie Axtell (Its-quoy-malks)
Julia A. Davis
Jackie Wapato
Connie Evans
Beverly J. Penney
Lucinda Pinkham
Hattie Kauffman
Sherri Lozon
Janice J. Smith
JoAnn Kauffman
Ann McCormack
Carlotta Kauffman
Anna M. Ziegler
Jean Bohnee
Carla High Eagle
Yolanda Guzman and her daughter, Britney
Mary Ellenwood
Paulette Smith
Paulette Smith
Trulin J. Ellenwood
Helene Adams
Priscilla Arthur

The late
Susan
Broncheau

The late Julia Pablo (Courtesy,
Lewiston Morning Tribune)

Esther McAtty

Esther McAtty with
her own cradleboard,
made by her mother

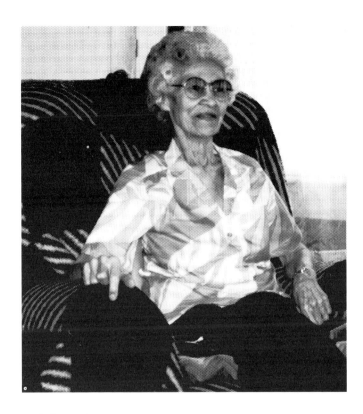

◀ Edna Thomas

▼ Nancy Halfmoon

▲ The late Lottie
Moody ▶

Lavinia Williams

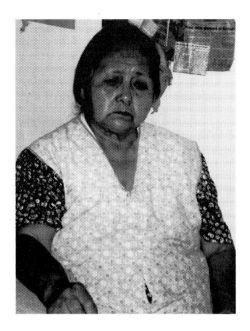

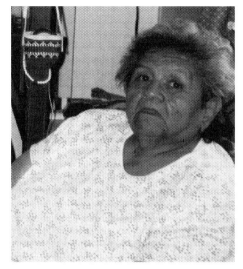

Iva Wilson (Too-my-o-chuw-my)

Josephine
C. Hayes

Marguerita
Broncheau

▲ Rena Katherine Ramsey, working for Head Start

Rena Katherine Ramsey, elected whip woman ▶

Rachel Aripa

Delores L. Wheeler

Mylie Lawyer ▲

Louise Higheagle ▶

Elsie M. Frank, hereditary whip woman

Rose Frank, who was honored with a National Heritage Award for her corn-husk weaving

Gladys Allen, the first woman on the Nez Perce Tribal Executive Committee (Courtesy, Gladys Allen)

Beatrice Miles ▲

Alta Guzman ▶

Dorothy Jackson

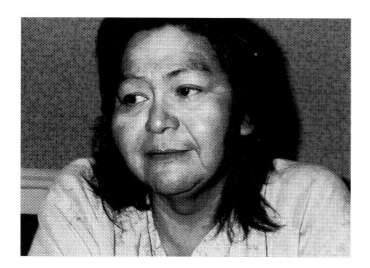

Ethel M. Seubert and her daughter, Andra

The late Mari Watters ▲

Patricia Higheagle (Ee-u-weehu-lakh-my) ▶

Bessie Greene Scott (Courtesy, Bessie Greene Scott)

Nellie Axtell (Its-
quoy-malks) (Cour-
tesy, Nellie Axtell)

Jackie Wapato, for-
mer Nez Perce
Tribal Executive
Committee member

Connie Evans, who
served as a nurse
in Vietnam and
now teaches the
Nez Perce lan-
guage at Lewis-Clark
State College

Julia A. Davis, the
second woman to
be appointed to the
Nez Perce Tribal
Executive Commit-
tee

Beverly J. Penney, graduate student

Lucinda Pinkham

Hattie Kauffman, reporter for CBS (Courtesy, Hattie Kauffman)

Ann McCormack
(Courtesy, Ann
McCormack)

JoAnn Kauffman ▲
(Photographers:
Ankers, Anderson,
and CUHS, 1993.)

Sherri Lozon, work-
ing for the tribe   ▶

Janice J. Smith

Carla Higheagle
(Courtesy, Carla
High Eagle)

Jean Bohnee,
working at the University of Idaho

Carlotta Kauffman,
bringing alive the
coyote legends
(Courtesy, Carlotta
Kauffman)

Yolanda Guzman and her daughter, Britney; Yolanda works for Upward Bound at the University of Idaho

◄ Anna M. Ziegler, left, with her daughter, Christina

Paulette Smith, working as a nurse ▼

Paulette Smith, working for the tribe

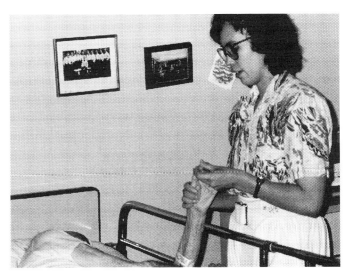

Trulin J. Ellenwood

Mary Ellenwood ▶

Helene Adams ▼

Priscilla Arthur

▲▲▲▲▲▲▲▲▲▲▲▲▲▲▲▲▲▲▲▲▲▲▲▲▲▲▲▲▲▲▲▲▲▲

Acknowledgments

THIS BOOK WAS FUNDED mainly through a grant from the John Calhoun Smith Memorial Fund, College of Letters and Science, University of Idaho and grew out of a photographic exhibit ("Nez Perce Women in Transition 1877-1990") funded by the Idaho Humanities Council. The late Daniel A. Aherin, Genesee, Idaho, generously assisted in the purchase of photographs; without his financial and moral support, this project would not have been possible. Funding was also received from the Alfred W. Bowers Laboratory of Anthropology at the University of Idaho.

Many others have helped make this book possible. First, much is owed to the Nez Perce Nation, especially the women, whose knowledge and experience played an enormous role in the creation of this book. Thanks are due to all my interviewees: the late Susan J. Broncheau, the late Julia Pablo, Esther McAtty, Nancy J. Halfmoon, the late Lotty Moody, Edna Thomas, Lavinia Williams, Iva Wilson (Too-my-o-chuw-my), Rena Katherine Ramsey, Josephine C. Hayes, Marguerita Broncheau, Rachel M. Aripa, Delores L. Wheeler, Louise Higheagle, Mylie Lawyer, Elsie M. Frank, Rose Frank, Beatrice Miles, Gladys Allen, Dorothy Jackson, Alta Guzman, Bessie Greene Scott, Ethel M. Seubert, the late Mari Watters, Patricia L. Higheagle (Ee-u-weehu-lakh-my), Nellie Axtell (Its-quoy-malks), Julia A. Davis, Jackie Wapato, Connie Evans, Beverly J. Penney, Lucinda Pinkham, Hattie Kauffman, Sherri Lozon, Janice J.

Smith, JoAnn Kauffman, Ann McCormack, Carlotta Kauffman, Anna M. Ziegler, Jean Bohnee, Carla Higheagle, Yolanda Guzman, Mary Ellenwood, Paulette Smith, Trulin J. Ellenwood, Helene Adams, and Priscilla Arthur. They gave unselfishly of their time, hospitality, and friendship. Appreciation goes also to June Greene, who provided a list of names of Nez Perce women.

Special thanks are due to Horace Axtell, leader of the Seven Drums religion; LeRoy Seth; Ken Frank; Richard Halfmoon; the late Elmer Paul; Levi Holt; Diane Miles; Andrea Axtell; Clifford Allen; and Allen Pinkham for their invaluable individual contributions. Herman Reuben, Cultural Specialist, and Sherri Lozon, Environmental Health Specialist, both of Environmental Restoration and Waste Management, Nez Perce Tribe, Lapwai, Idaho, provided demographic data for my research. Also, I would like to thank Jack H. Bell, Director of the Nez Perce Land Services Program for the map which depicts the ownership and reservation boundary of the Nez Perce Tribe.

Phil and Donna Wardell, Gene McVey, Sandy Russell, Sylvia and Dr. Joe Brisbane, Kenneth and Irene Aherin, Clytus Morgan, and Ruby Lilian Hobson gave generously to support this project.

For their friendliness and helpfulness, I am indebted to the staff of all the institutions which so willingly provided photographs for the exhibition (and for this book), especially Susan Buchel,

Elizabeth P. Jacox, and Carol Lichtenberg. Photographs were also donated from collections of the following individuals: Nan Rick, Richard Storch, Carmelita Spencer, Mary Banks, Alta Guzman, JoAnn Kauffman, Carla Higheagle, the Rev. Henry L. Sugden, and the late Steve Shawley. Lorna and Doug Marsh not only donated photographs but graciously offered encouragement. Carmelita Spencer, Lorna and Doug Marsh, and Connie Evans lent Nez Perce artifacts from their private collections to the photo exhibit.

I want to convey my deep appreciation to the people of the Nez Perce Tribe for the time and effort they devoted to the photographic exhibit, providing information and help with photo selection. Mary Reed and the staff at the Latah County Historical Society also deserve recognition for their cooperation. A special thanks to Mr. C. M. Ott for copying the photographs and to C. Scheer of Boise State University for dry-mounting them. I express heartfelt thanks to my friend and colleague, Dale Barsness, for copying and transporting the photographs and for his continuous help on this project. His technical assistance, his many editorial suggestions, and his encouragement were invaluable. I am grateful to the Idaho Commission on the Arts who enthusiastically offered to host the photo exhibition. Also, I would like to thank several other organizations for their staffs' cooperation and support of the exhibit, including the Nez Perce National Historical Park; the University of Idaho; the Bicentennial County Museum of Grangeville; the Latah County Historical Society; the Wallowa Mountains Visitor Center, Enterprise, Oregon; and the Lewis-Clark State College Center for Art and History. The Latah County Art and Cultural Committee funded the slide show, "Nez Perce Women in Transition 1877-1990." Thanks to Carla Higheagle for narrating the slide show and for her enthusiastic participation.

I owe a great debt to my friends, Dr. Tara Mehta and Mr. S. G. Mehta, who brought me to this country from India and who aided me in my educational endeavors. Thanks to the international philanthropic and educational organization, P.E.O., especially Delight Maughan and Betty Clark, for their assistance. My deep gratitude goes to my friends Karen Davis and David Talbott; without their support in the final stages of my manuscript, I would not have been able to accomplish this task. JoAnne and Edward Barton, Uniontown, Washington, provided a peaceful place to write and a loving and caring atmosphere, and Jeanette Talbott, Connie Hatch, and Linda Steigers gave me support and encouragement.

Isabel Bond, director of Upward Bound, University of Idaho, and her husband, John Bond, provided help and guidance. The late Mrs. Lola Ann Clyde, Isabel Bond's mother, gave me many valuable insights into the time period through her own experience. Thanks also to Deanna Vickers for all of her support and assistance, Alvin M. Josephy Jr. and his wife, Betty, for their encouragement in my work, and Grace Bartlett, historian, for her helpful information.

I am deeply indebted to anthropologist Dr. Joyce Wike, Cusick, Washington, professor emeritus of sociology and anthropology at Nebraska Wesleyan University, for her painstaking editing of various drafts and for her constructive insight and ideas, and to anthropologist Dr. Nancy McKee of Washington State University, for her useful comments and her aid in editing my manuscript. Kevin Harvey-Marose advised me during the research project and also offered perceptive suggestions on the manuscript. My appreciation also goes to Alan Marshal, professor of anthropology, Lewis-Clark State College, and to Diana Ames for their helpful editing comments, and to Allan H. Smith, professor emeritus of anthropology, Washington State University, and

Steve Evans, professor of social science, Lewis-Clark State College, for their contributions. Esther McAtty and Mylie Lawyer read the manuscript and made many constructive comments. Thanks to Beatrice Miles for her help in clarifying certain issues for my research.

Many thanks must go to Dr. Roderick Sprague, Director, Alfred W. Bowers Laboratory of Anthropology at the University of Idaho, to my project committee members—Keith Peterson, Alan Marshall, Katherine Aiken, and LeRoy Seth—to Professor Sue Armitage of the Washington State University history department, to my Ph.D. chairwoman Dr. Linda Stone of the Washington State University anthropology department, and to Dr. Thomas Trail, the chairman of my Master's committee. Thanks also to the Department of Sociology/Anthropology at the University of Idaho and to all my typists, Rodger Stevens, Linda Carrolle, Heidi Hill, and Karen Wethered Niskanen, for their cheerfulness, careful work, patience, and inventiveness.

Minerva Halvorson, Rachael Farrier, Verla Hall, Elsie Lanahan, Mary Hughes and Dan Brownie, Harry and Hettie Farris, Guy Marden, Laurel Ruben, Karen Young, and Lee Sappington gave me their supportive friendship. Thanks to my friends the Kalove family; Viva Upadhayaya and family; my cousin Kusum Firoz and family, my sister Monica George—who came all the way from India to give me encouragement—and my friend Ramesh Mehta. Many thanks to my mother for her patience and understanding.

Finally, I would like to offer thanks to the University of Idaho Press, especially to Peggy Pace, Toni Smith for her unstinting editorial guidance, and the entire staff.

There are many other organizations and individuals who believe in the aims of this book and who have come to view it as their own. They are so numerous that it is not possible to acknowledge them except in this collective manner. Their generous commitments of time and energy continue to sustain this process and help to convey the reality of the women's lives recorded in this book. In truth, this book is the fruit of a *collective effort* by the few I have named and the many I have not. Nevertheless, I expect everyone will find parts with which they disagree, and the responsibility for errors of fact and judgment is mine alone. If in this process I have unknowingly offended or hurt anyone, particularly my Nez Perce women mentors and other members of the tribe, here with my folded hands I ask forgiveness.

ONE▲▲▲▲▲▲▲▲▲▲▲▲▲▲▲▲▲▲▲▲▲▲▲▲▲▲▲▲▲▲▲▲▲▲▲▲▲▲▲

Introduction

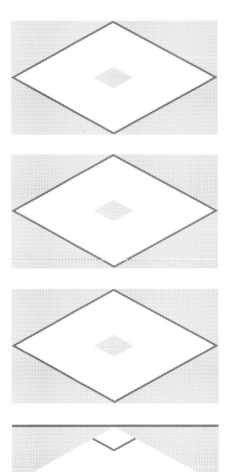

THE FOCUS OF THIS BOOK is Nez Perce Indian women, about whom very little has previously been written. A review of the literature reveals substantial concern for the exploits and activities of Nez Perce men—particularly chiefs, warriors, scouts, and hunters. However, recognition must also be given to Nez Perce women and the important role they played in tribal welfare. They conducted vital, routine, day in and day out domestic chores while maintaining a strong influence in tribal community culture and traditions.

Although the primary audience of this book is adults, the wealth of photographs makes it an ideal way to bring the culture of the Nez Perce, past and present, to both Native and non-Native children. Through this book, I hope to add the history of Nez Perce women to existing information on the Nez Perce Tribe and provide a photographic and written record for future generations.

Anthropologists have studied Nez Perce history, cultural beliefs, social practices, religion, economics, and politics, analyzing past and present Nez Perce lifestyles and specific aspects of their culture and society. However, the role of Nez Perce Indian women and their status from pre-agricultural times until today has not been examined, except as a part of Lillian Ackerman's general treatment of Plateau Indian women (1982) and, very briefly, by Kathryn Arneson (1993, 49-51). Learning more about the lives of these women has the potential of adding tremendously to our

1

knowledge of the indigenous Nez Perce culture. Women's role and influence are today recognized and appreciated by other females and most males of the Nez Perce Tribe. However, in aboriginal Nez Perce society, women were not included in the decision-making process in the village council because such leadership was a male role. Only since the early 1950s have women been active members of the Nez Perce Tribal Executive Committee (NPTEC). Women have always been leaders in other areas of the Nez Perce culture, as they are in the present.

In many of the early accounts, official reports, and other historical documents, Native American women were portrayed only in relationship to men, both Indian and non-Indian. Terms such as captive, wife, or squaw were used to describe women. *Squaw*, an Algonquian word for a married or mature woman, later became a demeaning label applied to all Indian women. This practice of devaluing women and their accomplishments persists today (Green 1992). However, in the Nez Perce culture, "*ahtwy*" was added after the name of a woman to indicate respect.

Said one Nez Perce man, age fifty-seven, a former NPTEC chairman, "*Iyet* ... that means woman, and *ahtwy* is the one that has all the knowledge, is the grandmother. And she has all the knowledge of her years. She probably has more experience than anyone else. And the grandmother was really, I think she was the core of the whole family group. She was the one who kept the family together, probably the one that had the most influence and directed the family, how that family acted. She probably had more effect on the family group than any other person, the grandmother, the *ahtwy*."

The intent in writing this book is not to segregate women and men, but to balance and make more complete the record of the Nez Perce women and, by inference, of the entire Native American community. I hope that this book, combined with the existing literature on the Nez Perce Tribe, will give a more holistic picture and a better understanding of the Nez Perce Nation.

This book contains material that is extremely important in understanding how Nez Perce women survived the challenges of adapting to the predicament of acculturation. These findings are beneficial, not only for Nez Perce Indian women and the Tribe, but for women as a whole and for the American historical record. They provide an impetus to rethink the role and status of women.

The time period chosen, 1877 to 1990, spans many rapid historical, political, and cultural changes. The narratives, reminiscences, and information presented in this book were inspired by hundreds of photographs of Nez Perce life covering this period. The photographs and narratives of Nez Perce women demonstrate individual factors that have affected them and their culture, and they provide an opportunity to view the Nez Perce making these dramatic transitions. These photographs were selected as representative and accurate from a larger body of five hundred which I accumulated as a first step in the organization of a traveling exhibit, "Nez Perce Women in Transition: 1877-1990." Not all of the photographs were accompanied by dates. Presently, some dates are valid, but many others are careful estimates provided by Tim Nitz, research librarian of the National Park Service at the Nez Perce National Historical Park in Spalding, Idaho.

My choice of photographs rested primarily on the following criteria: relevance to the focus upon women; a natural, relatively unposed depiction; variety; presentation of the cultural setting; the depiction of an activity or the portrayal of traditional techniques and objects; the portrayal of significant elements of acculturation; group pictures/complete families; and the illustration of traditional values.

Prior to the photographic exhibits, the Nez Perce Tribal Executive Committee and members of the General Council were shown the photos en masse; they gave their permission for the project. The pictures were then shown to individual elderly women on and off the reservation. An eighty-two-year-old woman, after viewing all the photographs, said, *"It's funny how you can get memories seeing all these old photos like this."* These elders were able to supply invaluable correction and amplification of the captions. Friends and relatives were recognized and details were remembered. Most of these photographs had been inaccessible to the Nez Perce people because they were scattered among various libraries, educational institutions, museums, and personal collections throughout the Pacific Northwest. Viewers spoke regretfully of the practice of many photographers not to give copies to their subjects, even in the case of individual or family portraits.

This exhibit was shown in Boise as part of the Idaho Centennial Program during the second week of May, 1990. Approximately three thousand visitors attended; more than two hundred were of Nez Perce background. Their enthusiasm and interest led directly to this publication. The visual and emotional impact of the photographs provoked a flood of comments and memories that I captured on audiotape for these pages.

This photographic collection began as a part of an initial research project, "Effect of Socio-Economic Factors on the Role and Status of Nez Perce Indian Women," funded by the Idaho Humanities Council, for which I conducted in-depth interviews of fifteen women aged twenty to ninety living on or near the reservation. Thirty-one additional women were interviewed in the process of writing this book. These women are housewives and single parents; employees of tribal, state, and federal governments; secretaries; counselors; nurses' aides; teachers; artists; and executives. Some women are students getting their degrees at colleges and universities. The elderly women are volunteers in community development programs and cultural activities. Some are widows who continue to manage their households and often contribute their experience to the community directly by their involvement in different cultural activities. This spectrum of activities includes Nez Perce language, powwow conduct, dances and songs, native crafts, church activities, dinners, sales, and memorials. All of these women are trying hard to eradicate health problems, alcohol and drug abuse, child abuse, and domestic violence against women. Through community participation and education, they are working toward a better future for themselves and their children.

A total of forty-six women have contributed their experiences to this book in interviews conducted in their homes and recorded with their permission. The use of a tape recorder and camera provided a permanent record of the interviewees. Some information was collected by informal visiting, some by participant observation. One interview was done by telephone. Some women volunteered in response to an announcement published in the *Lewiston Morning Tribune* asking for participants for the original project. Some were contacted by telephone from a list of women on the tribal rolls obtained from June Greene in the tribal office. Questions used in personal interviews varied with each individual, as circumstances in each case were different. Direct quotes from the interviews are italicized in the text. Botanical names and Nez Perce language terms are adapted from studies by Lucy J. Harbinger (1964) and Alan G. Marshall (1977). In addition, the elderly interviewees were consulted as to the accuracy of the Nez Perce pronunciation.

▲ ▲ ▲ ▲ ▲ ▲ ▲ ▲ ▲ ▲ ▲ ▲ ▲ ▲ ▲ ▲ ▲ ▲

THE DOMESTIC ROLE and status of Nez Perce Indian women was altered drastically by nineteenth-century missionary activities (the introduction of Christianity, the imposition of formal education, and the move toward European agricultural practices) and by loss of territory. There was a rapid transition from a fishing, hunting, and gathering society to sedentary agriculture, from a subsistence economy to a monetary economy, from tipis to permanent houses, from native garments to Euro-American clothing, from an oral tradition to books and written language, from the original Nez Perce language to (primarily) English, and from traditional education to institutional schooling. Transportation shifted from canoes and horses to stagecoaches and railroads. Traditional handwork construction materials changed from natural dyes to synthetic paints and from bear grass to corn husk and later to yarn.

Further, due to missionary influence, religion moved from sweat houses to churches and from rock chamber burials to cemeteries. The missionaries prohibited the use of native language, the wearing of native clothing and long hair, beadwork, decorated horses, horse races, gambling, drumming, dancing, singing, and shamanism. They disapproved of both native religion and ancient patterns of family interaction and residence. The missionaries and the government worked hand in hand to "civilize" the Nez Perce, breaking down the tribal culture and language and assimilating the Indians into the mainstream of Euro-American culture.

Missionary instruction forced major adjustments in women's lives, such as changes in dwellings, households, and extended family membership, apparel, and marriage (polygamy was outlawed). The extended family was weakened by the change in residence to single-family dwellings, at which time only a very few households continued to reside together. Nuclear family homes were even more predominant off the reservation (still, some households have been able to continue the Native extended family home).

Of course, one can over-generalize about these changes. Certainly, those Nez Perce who converted to Christianity experienced it as a benefit. But not all Nez Perce converted; missionaries did not change everyone. Some Indians resisted acculturation in whole or in part. Non-Christian Nez Perce continued to practice their native culture, as do some who now are Christians. It is important to understand that past practices currently exist in varying degrees in spite of acculturation.

The repercussions of acculturation, such as alcohol abuse and dietary illnesses, are still affecting the Nez Perce population, creating mental and physical health-related problems. Diabetes has become the number one cause of death among the Nez Perce and heart disease and arthritis, the main health problems.

As destructive as missionary activities were to the culture of the Nez Perce, another devastating process assaulted their traditional ways, the reduction of the Nez Perce territory. Before 1855, the Nez Perce hunted, gathered, and fished without restriction on territory now estimated to have been in excess of thirteen million acres. The Treaty of 1855 confined them to a reservation. Following the discovery of gold on Nez Perce land, another treaty in 1863 reduced the reservation by six million acres.

Allotment reduced the land still further, until the Nez Perce holdings came to less than 200,000 acres (see Fig. 1.3). (At present, total holdings are 112,409 acres [Nez Perce Land Services]. See Fig. 1.4.) Following the 1863 treaty, the Dawes and Severalty Acts of 1887 and 1893 opened nonallotted lands on the reservation to non-Indian settlers for homesteading. Under these acts, each Nez Perce man, woman, and child received an allotment of

1.1. Consultation on land allotment, Alice Fletcher, in shelter; Charley Adams; Louise Kipp, seated with baby; Mary Kipp, next to Louise; other children are unidentified. Idaho State Historical Society 63-221-71, Jane Gay Collection, c. 1890.

1.2. Tribe receiving first payment for surplus lands at Lapwai Agency, August 1895. Idaho State Historical Society 78-203-61.

land. Different categories of people received different amounts (e.g. heads of households 160 acres, unmarried adults and all orphans 80 acres, children 40 acres). The "surplus" land on the reservation was then open for settlement by white people. Much of the remaining land later passed out of Nez Perce ownership because of leasing to settlers, debt, and complex problems with inheritance. Furthermore, the land was held in trust, and the Nez Perce had no legal control over it. Alice Fletcher (see Fig. 1.1) was the anthropologist assigned by the government to allot the lands.

At the present time, tribal land holdings comprise only a small percentage of the reservation land base; the federal government, the state of Idaho, and non-Indians own about 80 percent of the 7.5 million acres. The present Nez Perce population is approximately 3,500. The population of Nez Perce living on or near the reservation is estimated at 1,900, while the non-Indian population on the same land is about 16,000 (Meyers 1993, 35-37). Of the 1,863 Nez Perce who reside on the reservation, 953 are women (U.S. Census 1990, 68).

The Nez Perce depended on the land of their ancestors for their food, shelter, clothing, and comfort of spirit. To the Nez Perce, land was and is the everlasting source of life. The cyclic nature of the weather dictated the patterns of their lives. In the summer, they moved up to the mountains to escape the heat and also to hunt, gather, and collect plants and berries as they ripened at different elevations. From spring through fall, roots were gathered, and in the winter, steelhead, salmon, and white fish were caught and cooked over fires. People's lives revolved around the land; their livelihood came from nature. They neither owned land nor wanted other tribal lands. Yet land was at the center of their most significant ceremonies (e.g., medicine dances, celebrations, and rituals).

The introduction of agriculture and a sedentary lifestyle dramatically and everlastingly affected the Nez Perce Nation. The consequent shift from native foods resulted in increased cases of diabetes, arthritis, and heart disease. Smallpox, tuberculosis, and other contagious diseases, carried to the Nez Perce Nation directly and indirectly by the fur traders and settlers and probably also by contact with other native groups, decimated the tribe. The native people had no immunity to these imported diseases.

As previously noted, the photographs cover the period from 1877 to 1990. These photographs and the narratives and explanations they inspired shed light on the process of Nez Perce acculturation and the shifting, dynamic role of women. The interviewees focus on these changes: the early shift from aspects of traditional culture, the postmissionary era through which many of them lived, and the repercussions of these many changes and the adaptations in the present day.

Since my interviewees ranged in age from twenty to ninety, the oldest were children when the first photographs of this century were taken. This means that the oldest generation, through their grandparents, always the source of most traditional knowledge, could have been witness to the major part of the nineteenth century. Their grandparents' elder mentors, in turn, may have experienced directly many events and a significant part of the preceding one, the eighteenth. For a published account that gives some base for the pre-contact society, we have only H. J. Spinden's 1908 study.

Through intermarriage and travel, the interviewees have various personal histories; therefore, their observations may not be identical on a given topic. Due to the variety of experience brought by family members from other tribes, each individual extended family had their own "traditions," which may or may not have been the same throughout the community.

Women have played and are still playing a major role in the Nez Perce culture and in the history of the Northwest. Nez Perce women now realize that they must assume an even stronger leadership role, that education is an essential tool for the present and the future, and that they must retain their cultural identity. Today the tribe is working hard to preserve this cultural identity through a return to the Nez Perce language, traditional clothing, singing and drumming, and, perhaps most important, the telling of Nez Perce lore.

▲ ▲ ▲ ▲ ▲ ▲ ▲ ▲ ▲ ▲ ▲ ▲ ▲ ▲ ▲

ABORIGINALLY, THE NEZ PERCE roamed a huge area of what is now north-central Idaho, southeastern Washington, and northeastern Oregon; it is bounded by the Blue Mountains to the west and the Bitterroot Mountains to the east and lies between the latitudes forty-five and forty-seven degrees north. (Spinden 1908, 172). The Nez Perce land areas are mountainous, rough, and hilly. The altitude ranges from about five hundred feet to over ten thousand feet in elevation. Both precipitation and temperature vary with elevation, which has important effects on local climate. Most reservation land is situated on a high, rolling plateau, a little more than three thousand feet high. The plateau land is adjacent to deep canyons of the Clearwater River and its tributaries, Lawyer's Creek, Big Creek, and Lapwai Creek. These canyons are deep and very narrow.

The high plateau's soil is fertile and of high quality; it is the site of some of the most productive wheat land in the United States. The narrow canyons are for the most part rocky, but where soil is free from rocks, the valleys are very productive. In the forest land, yellow pine, Douglas fir, and tamarack predominate.

In the mountainous and the higher plateau areas, the climate is colder and the seasons shorter than in the valleys, which have a much milder

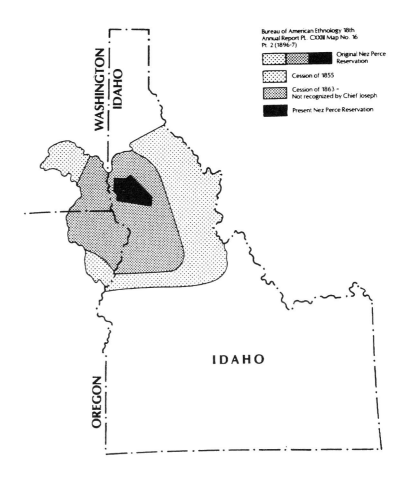

1.3. This map shows the area of the present states of Washington, Oregon, and Idaho. The area in black illustrates the present-day Nez Perce Indian Reservation as defined by the Treaty of 1863; it covers 7.5 million acres. The area in gray is the Nez Perce land which was reserved in the Treaty of 1855 and extended into Oregon and southeastern Washington. The outer boundary in light gray marks the original Nez Perce territory, which covered 13 million acres. Treaty Reduction of Nez Perce Territory. Courtesy, Alfred W. Bowers Laboratory of Anthropology, University of Idaho.

1.4. This map shows the reservation's checkerboard of land ownership and the reservation boundary of the Nez Perce Tribe. Map created by the Land Services Program of the tribe with Geographical Information Systems software, 1991. Courtesy, Nez Perce Land Services, Nez Perce Tribe.

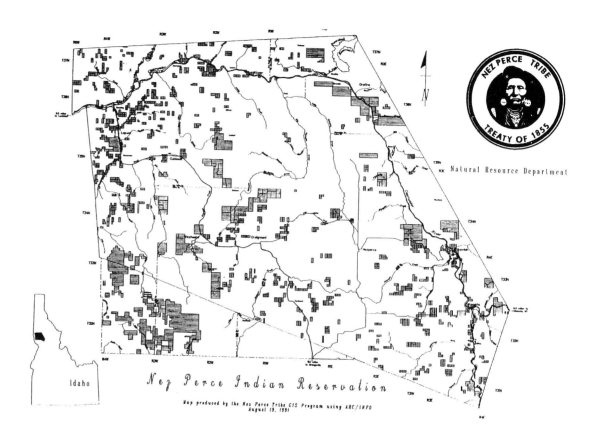

climate in winter, without snow, the temperature seldom dropping below zero. On the plateau, there is frequent rainfall during the winter months, and the summers are cooler than in the valley. These climatic patterns strongly affect regional vegetation.

Some Nez Perce Indian families live on the plateau; however, a majority of them live in the Clearwater Valley near the towns of Kooskia, Kamiah, Ahsahka, Lenore, and Spalding. Another settlement is found along the Lapwai Valley in the vicinity of Lapwai, Sweetwater, and Culdesac.

The location of the present Nez Perce Reservation is in north-central Idaho, to the east of Lewiston (see Fig. 1.3). The three major towns within the reservation are Lapwai, Kamiah, and Kooskia. Lapwai, which means "valley full of many butterflies," *tep-tep* (may also be written as *[xep] xep*), is southeast of Lewiston on Lapwai Creek. As the name suggests, in earlier times the valley was filled with butterflies. Kamiah, nestled on the banks of the Clearwater River, was the camping ground for the Indians who gathered at the river before the coming of Lewis and Clark. It was called Kamuckp, *qemyexp*, by the Nez Perce. Kooskia is situated on the Clearwater River at the mouth of the South Fork of the Clearwater River. The Nez Perce name for themselves is *Numipu* or Noon-nee-me-poo, "the people." The designation "pierced nose," evidently given by the French fur traders, is probably a misnomer.

"Lapwai is derived from the word . . . the first two syllables are tep-tep, means butterfly," an elderly woman of eighty-two explained. *"And they say originally the Lapwai Creek ran full and clear. There were eels and salmon going up the river, this creek, and people lived along it and along these edges of the river. There is a little bit of sand or damp soil or damp rocks. Hundreds of butterflies would gather together, and stay on these rocks. I don't know whether they were eating or what they were doing. They were the blue-gray butterflies, not quite as big as a moth, and I can remember seeing those when I was a child and we played along the river. We'd see them gather together in huge numbers. This is what the early Nez Perce called this valley was tep-tep, and originally the name Lapwai was given to the place at the mouth of the Lapwai River which is now called Spalding. That is where the agency was, and that's where the main gathering of the Indians was along the river there. Chief Big Thunder was in charge of this big Lapwai Valley. He lived at the foot of Thunder Hill, near the spring there. The spring is still there."*

An eighty-year-old woman reminisced, *"And I lived mostly in Kamiah . . . Kamiah wasn't Kamiah, it was Kamia . . . There used to be a grass down here by the mill, and the Indians used to go there and pick them and dry them out and make ropes out of it; and they were ropes that could not be broken . . . You'd have to take a sharp knife and cut it apart. And that was Kamuckp, qemyexp, it was . . . but [white] people came and decided to call it Kamiah, I guess the way the sound was to them was Kamiah.*

"Kooskia, because there's lots of water there, and koos means 'water' in our native Nez Perce language."

An eighty-two-year-old woman said, *"Up-river and Down-river, you would call the division between the Nez Perce Tribe. Those that lived towards Orofino, Ahshaka, Kamiah, Kooskia, and Stites and up towards the old Lawyer's Canyon towards Grangeville, those people were called the Up-river Indians to distinguish them from the Down-river Indians—which mostly included the people in Lapwai, Spalding, and those that lived along where Lewiston is now and where Asotin is and down along the edge of the Snake River, Clearwater River, and down towards Grand Ronde—those they called the Down-river Indians. They were distinguished through their language. Sometimes there was a slight change in the dialect, mostly on pronouns where they change maybe a letter or two in it. There was a change [in] the way their diet was. The Down-river people were mostly fish people. They liked the salmon: they went to Celilo, they brought the meat (the dried salmon), they dried it, they pounded it, and they mixed it with huckleberries. They called it ton-nut, and that was the most expensive and one of the most cherished of all of the foods because they could carry it. The Up-river people were mostly buffalo people. They tended to go to the plains, and to the buffalo country. They were friendly to the Flathead, and they used the Lolo Trail more often than the Down-river Indians. A few Down-river Indians went [to buffalo country]; for example, Looking Glass came from Asotin, but he married an Up-river Indian woman, so they were familiar with going to the buffalo country. The Up-river Indian would go there and stay maybe a year or more. They'd dry the buffalo meat, bring the buffalo hides, tan the hides and bring them, and there was an exchange between the Up-river and Down-river Indians on both the foods, their salmon and the buffalo. It was kind of an acculturation thing, going there, and the Up-river Indians were instrumental more in taking their salmon and eels, that kind of things, across to the Flatheads or to the Plains people. Sometimes they had a rivalry. I can remember some Indians telling that one time, one of the first fights they ever had between the two groups was on the other side of the Arrow Junction. It was not a very big fight, but they fought, and it was the Up-river from Ah-shaka and Lower people from Hatwai. The Hatwai people lived just across from where the old dam was.*

"The people themselves made this division, . . . Up-river and Down-river. For example, where are you going? I am going down river. So that was down river: that meant you are going to see Down-river people. Where are you going? I am going to see my aunt up the river. So that was the distinguishing name of where you lived. There was a story that was related to it. Coyote stories are either he is going up the river to the buffalo country or he is going down the river to the Celilo, one way or the other. And that means, if he is going down the river, he is going to go to get fish; and, if he is going up the river, he is going to buffalo country. It depended upon food, just like most people of that time, you went where there was food. These people who were down here, mostly they were fish people."

Women as Providers

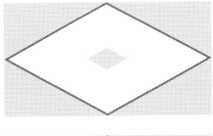

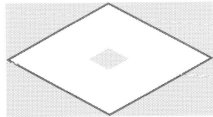

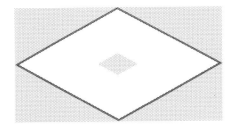

"I think they [anthropologists] are missing out, because they seem to fail to realize that Nez Perce women were the mainstay, that they provided anywhere from 80 to 85 percent of the work to maintain a household. Even in the old days, even today, whether or not they are a single parent, they provide an awful lot of the mainstay to an Indian family life," said one middle-aged woman.

An eighty-two-year-old woman remarked, *"It seems to me they kind of work together because each one had their own role, own responsibilities. It was a man's job to furnish the meat and fish, take care of the horses, and to protect them. Women always provided the roots, berries, and took care of the meat and fish to dry for the winter, fixed up the tipi and took care of the fire. I think women did a lot of hard work. They provided the life, took care of children. I don't think the men would have gotten along without them. I think they are an important part of the whole social setup of the Nez Perce Indians."*

IN THE NEZ PERCE culture, work was assigned according to sex, in a fashion that is common to almost all cultures. Presumably, this division originated from the biological foundation of women's special role in childbirth and lactation in contrast to the naturally greater muscular strength and mobility of the adult male. Nearly universally, women have remained at home, conducting household affairs as they cared for infants and children, while men have ranged more widely.

Nez Perce men hunted, trapped, and speared the living, mobile, sources of food, hides, and oil. While women, too, hunted small game, usually birds and rabbits, they also typically dealt with vegetation: gathering roots, herbs, berries, seeds, firewood, and a variety of plants for medicines, fibers, and dyes. There were exceptions; for example, men cut wood supports for the lodges that women constructed, maintained, and dismantled. To exploit the huge seasonal runs of migratory salmon, men and women worked closely together. Woman handled the processing, maintained the weirs which the men erected, and fished with seine nets themselves.

Food Quest and Processing

Many of the traditional foods are not remembered anymore, partly because some of the species of plants were wiped out by agricultural development of the land. Furthermore, in modern Indian society, there has been a demise in the original, traditional food gathering techniques. (See Hunn [1990], Marshall [1977], Scrimsher [1967], Harbinger [1964], and Spinden [1908] for information on traditional foods and plant species.)

As food gatherers, the women were responsible for collecting the major food staple, camas roots (*Camassia quamash*), or *gémes*, from June through September, depending upon site elevations. The bulbs were gathered in the wet upland meadows—the Weippe Meadows and Camas Prairie north of Grangeville, Idaho; the Palouse Prairie near Moscow, Idaho; the Elk City, Idaho, area; and the Grande Ronde Valley of eastern Oregon.

A seventy-year-old woman, remembering her grandmother, recalled: "*Grandmother was a strong woman. She would go and dig all the roots, and she would go over and camp over to Weippe*

back there, and she dug this camas. She always went to dig. They are like little onion balls."

The crutch-handled camas digging stick, the *tùk'es*, was a wooden shaft about two and one-half feet long with a fire-hardened point bent slightly forward. The crosspiece handle, from five to eight inches long, was made of bone, horn, wood, or stone and in later times, metal. To operate the stick, both hands were placed on the handle, and body weight was applied until the point reached a depth of about six inches (Spinden 1908, 200). Cylindrical carrying baskets were used to transport the roots to camp where they were cleaned by the women and children prior to baking.

Young girls began to dig as a form of play and later helped with the harvest. They were rewarded for their first root digging.

According to one young interviewee who grew up in a longhouse on Nespelem Reservation, "*When I was fourteen years old, my mother brought me to Mrs. Cleveland's house in Nespelem. Mrs. Cleveland, Mrs. Red Star, and Mrs. Owhi were there. I drove my mother to Nespelem to their house, and we went out root digging. We drove a little ways away from Nespelem, and crossed over the fence, and I helped them go through the fence. We dug roots that day. That was the first time I had dug roots with these people, that certain people from the long house. Previously, I had dug roots with my great-grandmother, Carrie Innes, but never with these people before. When we returned back to Mrs. Cleveland's house, Ann George measured the size of my foot, and I did not know the reason. Shortly after that, she had given me a pair of white buckskin moccasins that had fit me just perfectly.*"

"*Women cleaned the roots with their hands,*" according to an eighty-two-year-old woman. "*Most of the roots have covering on them. There was an old lady who lived in this area, and she used a little rock like a knife to peel off the skin or the covering.*"

2.1. Ah-yah-toe-tuhn-my (Mrs. Lizzie Pablo) of Kooskia, Idaho, mother of Mabel Lowry, Black Eagle, and Delia Lowry, shown gathering camas roots on the eastern part of the Nez Perce Reservation, with her root digger, *tùk'es*, and ancient corn husk bag and another bag on the ground already filled. Idaho State Historical Society 3793.11, c. 1910.

2.2. Mrs. Elizabeth Wilson (left) and Agnes Moses digging roots. Lewiston Morning Tribune, c. 1970.

An article in the *Lewiston Morning Tribune* of March 26, 1967, described the roots which made up such an important part of the Nez Perces' diet. Camas was never eaten raw. Large quantities of roots were baked and steamed in a large pit for a few days. The cooked roots turned from white to brown, and the taste became much sweeter. For immediate consumption, the cooked roots could then be made into a porridge or boiled in water. Camas was a perfect food for winter, complementing the dried fish.

Baked camas did not keep well, so the cooked roots were pounded and dried as a meal called *kom'es'es*, then formed into loaves, rolled in bunch grass (*Agropyron sp.*), and again steamed. After cooking, the loaves were made into smaller cakes, known as *ep'ine*, and dried in the sun or over a campfire. These were stored for winter use.

This account of camas preparation was provided by an eighty-four-year-old woman: "*In the fall season, camas is gathered. We went to*

14

2.3. Jane Smith, at ninety-six years of age, demonstrating the use of a digging stick. *Lewiston Morning Tribune*, June 20, 1972.

2.4. Digging sticks, *tùk'es*, owned by Mrs. Elizabeth Wilson of Kamiah, photographed in 1960. Idaho State Historical Society 60-179-8.

2.5. Agnes Moses cleaning camas roots. *Lewiston Morning Tribune*, c. 1960.

Weippe. That is the big place. There used to be a big place in Camas Prairie until all was plowed out. . . . Women go for digging just once in a year. I never saw them eating raw camas. First thing they ever think about it before they even start digging, they have to make their own [cooking] pits and get all the stuff ready. . . . As soon as they clean it, they put it down and get it ready to cook."

Another woman, eighty-six years old, adds the following description: *"They dig a big hole, and they lay out red rocks, sprinkle water, put dirt over the rocks and over the dirt, fresh alderwood leaves would be spread on the dirt and then a layer of meadow grass. And then they put this camas on top of that. They covered it up with alder leaves and a thick layer of meadow grass again, then water was sprinkled to make steam, and dirt on top. They built the fire up to heat rocks. The cooking is inside, from the fire on top, for three days or so. My grandmother would dig to check how far along they were cooking and then dig them out. . . . When they are fresh it was just like candy to us . . ."*

An eighty-two-year-old elderly woman said, *"Baking camas, it's a lot of hard work. Only one woman bake the camas. She has most of her grandchildren do for her. She is lucky to have a lot of help. They don't do digging by hands anymore, but they now do it by machine."*

Nez Perce women told the *Lewiston Morning Tribune* that cous (*Lomatium cous*) or *kouse*, also known as biscuitroot and called *gámsit* before drying, was similar to a carrot in shape and was dug from April to July from the dry, rocky soil on the hills around Lewiston, Idaho. At the time of the interview, cous was served as a delicacy with sugar or sugar and cream. Rich and filling, it was almost as important a staple as camas in earlier times. It was eaten fresh or dried and was cooked whole.

One eighty-year-old interviewee explained how cous was prepared: *"Then there's cous that*

you had to go out and dig among the hillsides. And they'd peel the skin off them, wash them, and sun dry them. Then they look white. And in the wintertime, a lot of these were served. My grandmother used to pound it to grains the size of oatmeal or cornmeal. Then, she'd put them into . . . a round biscuit . . . or make it into cereal [qóm-sitsí.s.]. In the mornings, they'd have fresh cereal that's made out of cous—a white cereal, kind of cream colored. I used to watch my grandmother. She would grind the fresh cous, make a little ball, and take it in her hand and squeeze it. Her fingerprints would come; that's what they called 'fingerprints' or capk'í·cay, and then it was sun dried. She made a bunch of that, plus she made something that looked like bricks—a long bread called o'ppah—and smoked them. It gave a particular flavor to it. Another bread was called tsa'pu-khm-luct, *and our grandmothers used to tell us, 'That's a food that you have to eat in the springtime. Be thankful that you're living to eat these things . . .' Way back then, they served it, and we're still serving it. I'm sorry to say, sometimes we don't have much time to go out and dig for those foods, but it's really delicious, and it's good for your health. That's the way we were told, so we try to tell that to our children, our grandchildren."*

Said an eighty-four-year-old woman, of her own grandmother, *"My grandmother taught me how to dig roots. We had* tùk'es, *or a digging stick. I don't have it at my place anymore now. My grandmother went to the blacksmith. He made it and put a handle on it. That's what is used to dig with. I was the peeler at home. That was hard. We had to peel, then she washed it up. And she had a big board. Then she put something over it, like a tablecloth, and then dried them. Those were kouse. For camas, we had to go to meadows. Camas baking was very hard work. They had to watch that it didn't get moldy after it dried up. It was pretty good then. She used to trade with some*

2.6. A group of Nez Perce are covering the camas which is being baked inside the pit. From left, Elizabeth Penney Wilson, Agnes Moses, Rachel Aripa, and Ike Wilson. Bicentennial Historical Museum, Grangeville, Idaho, c. 1970.

2.7. A woman pounding the camas roots after they have been baked and spread on the tule mat to sun dry. This is possibly at the upper Clearwater River or the South Fork of the Clearwater River. National Park Service, Nez Perce National Historical Park Collection, Stephen D. Shawley Collection Neg. 0773, c. 1890.

relatives who used to come from Pendleton, Oregon. They would trade with their blankets, very big and nice blankets—very big and nice ones. They were like the ones from the late 1930s."

"Bitterroot [Lewisia rediviva], we don't have it here. They traded with other tribes and got some bitterroot. They get it near Colville, Washington, and is up there near Canada some ways. They all are in one bunch that you get to separate them and you take that black skin off that's on top. Then you wash it and dry it," commented an eighty-year-old Nez Perce woman.

Bitterroot, "*bi·t'a·n*", was dug in the Nespelem area, near Colville, Washington, in August. The plant resembles a crocus with pink flowers. Its yellow root looks like a mass of spaghetti and must be peeled. It was served as a vegetable with dried salmon. The women advised against grinding this root because it turns bitter.

Bitterroot can be found in the highest elevations in Idaho, but not in such quantity as in Montana. Although the Nez Perce did collect this root in the Bitterroot Mountains along the present Idaho-Montana border, as well as in Montana, it was easier to trade for it. Bitterroot was commonly used throughout the Plateau. Women ate bitterroot or drank a tea made from boiling the roots to increase milk flow after childbirth. They also believed the root was good for curing skin problems and diseases caused by impure blood (Harbinger 1964, 14; Hunn 1990, 137).

Wild onions (*Allium spp.*), *Ses'aauh* or *ka-heet* or *se.x*, the first root of the spring, were dug in April. This plant has a green, fernlike top and is four to five inches high. Flowers range from rosy white to deep lavender. About the size of a walnut, it was baked while fresh with the skin on and peeled after cooking. The texture was fibrous, like a sweet potato.

Wild carrot (*Perideridia gairdneri*), *tsa-wetkh* or *cawítx*, or *yampa*, was dug in May. Growing in

2.8. Women digging cous, April 9, 1974. Left to right, Kay Bohnee, Elsie Frank, Helen Pinkham. Idaho State Historical Society 78-203-68.

clusters in damp or wet areas and standing two feet high, its blossoms smell like the food itself. The women described it as finger-sized food. The root has a brown jacket around white meat. It is so sweet and rich, it may be eaten raw. It also can be dried and ground for porridge or boiled fresh like a potato. Dried wild carrots were preserved like the other roots by grinding them into flour, fashioning them into loaves, and smoking them, before storing them in a pit.

During the warm season, mushrooms (*Agaricus sp.*), *hípéw* or *he'puph*, were gathered. This particular mushroom grows on cottonwood trees.

According to the *Lewiston Morning Tribune*, the women described the taste as similar to fried oysters and enjoyed them breaded and fried in butter. Wild celery (*Lomatium salmoniflorium*), *wa'weem*, was harvested in April. Both the tops and the roots were eaten raw.

Roots and herbs, particularly kouse-kouse, were collected also for medicinal purposes. Mountain tea or Labrador tea (*Ledum glandulosum*), *písqo*, gathered during the huckleberry season, was thought to be good for coughs and colds and was described as being strong and having a nice aroma. Knowledge of the location of root fields and medicinal uses of foods and herbs was passed down from generation to generation.

Black moss or pine moss (*Alectoria jubata*), the lichen *hó-pop*, was gathered in the fall and cleaned of all twigs. The *hó-pop* was a starvation food as well as a delicacy when prepared as a dessert. It was baked in the pit along with camas, dried, ground, and made into soup. It has a bitter taste and a texture like gelatin. Camas was mixed in to sweeten it; currently, sugar is added.

An elderly woman of eighty-two said, "*My father told me that his grandmother told him that* hó-pop *was a starvation food. When the Nez Perce did not get any food and the winter was severe, they did not get any deer, they used that and that was starvation food. They would go and get it from the tree. That was like a black soup. Hó-pop* moss . . . *was also baked same way in the pit along with camas.*"

Yellow pine (*Pinus ponderosa*), *cuk'eymit*, was also used by the Nez Perce. They removed the bark with a bone chisel and, later, a knife and ate the soft inner layer, sliced into small pieces. Some very old yellow pine trees still bear the marks of their knives. They used the sap to make chewing gum and droplets, and later, after sugar was introduced, some families added sugar to the process.

The balsam root (*Balsamorhiza sagittata*), *pásx*, was eaten, the outer part of the stalk peeled back to reveal the tender inner part. Seeds of the sunflower (*Helianthus annuus L.*), *wa'wit*, provided nourishment in the spring or in times of famine. When gathered in May, before the flower was in full bloom, the sunflower stems, also were eaten. The taste is similar to celery.

The Nez Perce had a variety of uses for bunch grass (*Agropyron sp.*). A woman in her seventies said, "*Bunch grass was used for many purposes. It was used in baking [like waxed paper]; to wrap fish and wrap food before storing them in caches. It was also used as tissue paper. Another use was in construction of sod houses.*"

The main berries gathered were huckleberry (*Vaccinium globulare*), *cemí.tk*; serviceberry or June berry (*Amelanchier spp.*), *kikéye*; chokecherry (*Prunus demissa*), *tíms*; gooseberry (*Ribes spp.*), *pílus*; black thornberry (*Crataequs douglasii*), *sísnim*; elderberry (*Sambucus cerulea*), *míttip*; thimbleberry (*Rubus parviflorus*), *taxtáx*; blackberry (*Rubus macropetalus dougl.*), *cé.gat*; and red thornberry (*Crataequs columbiana*), *télx*. Often they were sun dried and stored for later use.

According to one elderly woman, eighty-six years old, "*Mostly berries were preserved by drying. Sometimes the women would sit there and watch all the time they were drying. My grandmother said that her grandmother made her sit there and watch. The kids watched, and she would give her a long stick like a whip if the birds come [and] she chased them all.*"

"*We went to collect berries, especially huckleberries,*" reminisced a woman of eighty-two who came from a very big family. "*We went towards Grangeville, mountains, Weippe, and the Pierce area, all along in there, China point. Most of our people went to Mount Adams for huckleberries.*

*We picked the berries by hand. They are a lot big-
ger than our huckleberries. Our huckleberries are
smaller and sour. There are different kinds of berries. We also went for the blackberries. A lot of
blackberries grow up here, Harpster's way, up towards Grangeville. We went up to Northern
Idaho, close to the Canadian border. We drove up
there. We canned a lot of the berries and made jam."*

Another eighty-two-year-old woman said, *"I
have never seen a comb or anything like that to
collect the berries. In modern times, you do it by
hand, and that's the way they have always done
it. They had these big baskets. They carried them,
and put it beside them or tied to their waist. The
berry bushes are low. They just do it by hand and
fill it up. Some are very fast at it."*

Mused an eighty-four-year-old woman, *"A
long time ago when I was growing up, there used
to be two, three families that got together and
went on horse buggy to the mountains to pick
huckleberries. Now, they just go, sneak by themselves. Now, they have cars, and they go by themselves. They don't ask, 'Do you have a ride? Come
with us, we are going berry picking,' as they used to."*

An impressive amount of plant food was handled daily by women throughout the year. In his
1990 study, Eugene S. Hunn conducted time and
motion studies of women digging camas and cous.
He calculated an average hourly rate of return
which turned out to be consistent with early observations of a bushel for a day's work. Hunn's
"day" was the contemporary eight-hour work day
with a bushel's weight given as 60 pounds (27
kilograms). Adding the hypothesis that sixty days'
(or two months') time out of a year might be
devoted to all root digging, he reached an annual
total of 3600 pounds or 1620 kilograms (175-76).

It is probably more germane to consider what
this bulk represented in nutritional terms. Alan G.
Marshall concludes that 30-40 percent of the Nez
Perce diet probably consisted of plant foods and

2.9. Cedar-root berry baskets were obtained in
trade from other tribes.
Women would line these
baskets with fresh leaves
so the fresh berries would
not stain the basket. Na-
tional Park Service, Nez
Perce National Historical
Park Collection 64,
c. 1890.

2.10. Cowlitz cedar-root
baskets were obtained in
trade from the coastal
tribes. National Park Service, Nez Perce National
Historical Park Collection
2351, c. 1870.

2.11. Klickitat cedar-root huckleberry baskets were obtained in trade with the Yakima Indians. National Park Service, Nez Perce National Historical Park Collection 2345, c. 1870-1880.

that 10-25 percent was game (1977, 37-38). Salmon may have accounted for as much as 50 percent of the food consumed by some Nez Perce.

Hunn constructed a representative or ideal diet on the basis of the nutritional values of the most common staples in the Middle Columbia region. The bulk of this diet, 66 percent, was vegetal, accounting for some 55 percent of the total calories consumed. Salmon, with 23 percent of the bulk, supplied 64 percent of the total protein and was the main source of calcium. Various roots also contained some calcium as well as iron. Vitamin C was obtained from berries (1990, 177).

On the basis of this construct, one can conclude that the Middle Columbia diet was well balanced and healthful, and women's efforts contributed significantly to their families' well being. In fact, more than half of the food for the extended family was provided by women. Through their customary role as food gatherer, women provided nutritious food which was at least equal in importance to the men's contribution of meat and fish.

By tradition, hunting was a man's domain, although in recent times there has been a shift away from such strict role definition. Some of the interviewees, particularly the single parents, have assumed the role of hunter.

One forty-four-year-old woman observed, *"I was allowed to go for hunting as a woman. That started out when I was ten or eleven years old. My brothers were going hunting. That was the first time I was asked to go, and my brothers told me, 'No! You cannot go with us, you are a woman.' My mother told us a story of how she would go out and take her horse above Arrow Junction at Potlatch Creek, go up in hills and shoot a deer, put it on back of her horse, and ride home with it—and she would be by herself. We had pictures of our mother with her horse and a four-point deer that she had shot. So we knew that this was acceptable, and so I started hunting with my brothers at that time. The first time I went with them, I was not sure of what to expect. But my father shot a deer, and we took a piece of the raw heart and ate that. They told that this was the traditional way you show thanks for the things you do, so I ate the piece of heart, which I'd never had before. It was a different experience for me. Then after that, I have gone hunting several times."*

"You are the sole bread winner; you've got to put meat on the table," remarked a very young single parent of two. *"You have to get out there and do it. You cannot afford to buy meat from a grocery store every day. I think you have to do what you have to do. Just as roles have changed, the men did this and the women did that. You can still respect each other, but still, like me as a single parent, I have to provide for my children."*

According to the *Lewiston Morning Tribune* article of March 26, 1967, all parts of the animal were used by the Nez Perce; nothing was wasted. Meat was cooked, smoked, and dried in a traditional way on a slow open fire—a good method of preservation. The tongue and liver were eaten raw. Ears were used for seasoning. The fat from the stone-boiling broth was skimmed and used to cook fry bread, and bear meat was barbecued.

An eighty-four-year-old woman described the making of pemmican: *"My grandmother used to pound deer meat . . . She had a deep mortar, and she said they used that mostly for meat because, you know, their meat was in long strips and hard and dried. She said we kind of break them up and put them in there, and when one woman gets tired, then the other woman would get in there, and they pound them up . . . They put in dried intestine . . . mixed it with meat fat . . . Apparently that is what preserved the meat. It sure tastes good!"*

Hides were used for many purposes, and preparation of hides was a complex and time-consuming process. Women skinned and dressed the animals. After skinning, if the hides could not be dressed right away, they were cleaned and dried to be dressed and tanned later. Scraping, graining, stretching, and curing the hides was done arduously by one woman, but festively by more. The communal process familiarized the women with the characteristics of various animal hides. Women collected pinecones for smoking the hides, the last step in preservation.

The brain-solution method of tanning was described by an interviewee, thirty-seven years old: *"My great aunt taught me how to tan deer hide using the brain-solution method. The method of brain tanning she taught me was: you have the hide from the fresh deer, or it can be one that's been hanging out to dry it. You have to soak it for about five days in the water . . . with the*

2.12. Skin lodges in a temporary encampment of a small hunting party on the Yellowstone River. The Nez Perce woman in the foreground is making pemmican, a form of dried meat, using a piece of buckskin or tule mat for drying the pemmican and watching it to keep birds and animals away. Sticks were put at the edges of the hide or tule mat to hold it down. Smithsonian Institute 2978-B, Jackson Photo, 1871.

2.13. Roasting beef to feed funeral guests at old Chief Joseph's reburial. The meat is cooking on a frame similar to a sweat lodge frame. Idaho State Historical Society 77-60-14, Stephen D. Shawley Collection, 1926.

hair on, and you change the water every day so it does not get very smelly. After five days, you check when you are able to pull out hair from it with your hands. Pretty easy. Then, go ahead and hang it on a log or a board or a post. You have this scraping tool which has two handles and the blade in the middle. The blade is not very sharp; it's kind of a dull blade. You scrape it down [in the direction] . . . the hair lies down. It scrapes the hair off the inside which would be like the muscles and the fat. Scrape all that off. Then, you turn it over again on the hair side, where there is really a thin layer of skin, and you have to make sure to get that off—otherwise it ends up that when you get the brain solution, it won't soften up. But once you have it good and clean that way, you have one

deer brain for each hide. That's how we're supposed to do it, so you should save some brain. If you can't get that, then you can use cow brain or buck brain. You take the brain and boil it until it becomes mushy and so soft that you can squeeze it. Then, you put the solution in a container and put the hide in it. Put the brain in it. Mix it real good, that brain solution, and leave it there for five days again. This time, when you pick the hide up and pull it, it should be really elastic. And when it is real soft and elastic, then you take it out. Rinse it with cold water. Then, you hang it up on a board where you can stretch it out. You start scraping with a hand-held scraper. You just go back and forth on it, and you let it dry and keep stretching it and pulling it until it is all the

2.14. Viola Morris tanning a hide. National Park Service, Nez Perce National Historical Park Collection 1301, c. 1970.

way dry. When it is dry, it should be nice, soft, and off-white.

"One-person stretching was done by pulling a small section in opposite directions by both hands or between the feet and hands. In an extended family, it was done by two women, each holding opposite ends and pulling the hide in all directions. The more you work on it, the more it becomes soft and white. Sometimes it needed to be done two or three times before it would become soft and off white.

"If you want to smoke it with some hard wood, you get the kind that gives real smoke. You can smoke it in a smoker like a square box, with the smoke fire underneath it, or in a small tipi. You hang it on a rock inside, spread it out and let the smoke come. You smoke both sides. It depends on how well the smoke keeps going. It depends on the type of wood and how dark you want it. Sometimes you have to sprinkle water on the fire to make more smoke. Smoking a hide makes it water resistant."

At eighty-six, one woman recalls her grandmother's and mother's tanning handwork: "My grandmother used to fix hides and tan them, and my mother did the same; she'd tan hides. And when they'd scrape it, it would make it really nice. They'd use one of those stone scrapers with [the right grooves/texture] . . . on it. That's what makes the hide . . . really soft and white—to work it two or three times."

In the spring and fall, women cleaned, dried, and pounded salmon for preservation. At other times, after cleaning, it was simply sun-dried or smoked. Fresh salmon was baked, broiled, boiled, or occasionally smoked. The broth from boiling was saved for soup.

"Salmon feast, yes!" reminisced an eighty-four-year-old interviewee. "From the beginning when the salmon start running up the river and everybody knows it is going to be a good salmon runway. They catch them and they would decide to put on their salmon feast. The women get ready. The men would catch the salmon and the women cooked them and they all get there. It comes about the same time that the roots are ready. The women prepared it all and they all come. In a way, it's a prayer for thanksgiving, for the Creator to give them this food, and it's a blessing."

A woman, age forty-seven, said, "My mother knew how to make fishing nets. She never taught that to any of her children. She would go down to Columbia with her dad when she was a young girl. They would go to Celilo and fish for salmon. . . ."

"We used to go down in [the] 1950s, and we would have those big blocks of ice in the pickup; and, after the catch, they threw all the salmon in. I remember distinctly them going to the grocery stores. It was covered with canvas and smelled like fish because it was summertime. They go to the grocery stores, and they would sell the fish to the grocery store."

An eighty-two-year-old interviewee related the following memory: "Nez Perce went to Celilo when I lived there. The whole family would travel to Celilo to fish. They made fish fillets and used little tiny willow sticks to support them while being dried. Every woman had her own bundle of willow sticks so wide like this [a 16-24" diameter]. They fillet them and lay them up putting willow sticks through the part of the flesh to hold them in the space quite straight. I have seen a lot of them. They have racks and racks down in Celilo."

An eighty-four-year-old Nez Perce woman described night fishing for salmon: "My dad always told me that when it was time the salmon was running, they'd have these long dugout canoes, and they'd get out in the water. They'd have a fire at one end at nighttime, and the salmon would come in, and they would spear them. He

2.15. Salmon fishing at Celilo Falls, The Dalles. University of Oregon Library M2380, Moorehouse Collection, c. 1910.

2.16. Drying eels at the Snake River. Courtesy, Richard Storch, c. 1907.

was a boy. He was right there. His job was to catch them and get them into the boat, and the women would be right at the shore, and they'd take care of them. They'd clean them and get them ready.

"They used as a torch these long poles like a cedar pole. And they used a pole because it burns better for light. And they [the poles] stuck up at the back end of the boat like this; and it would light [their way]. He would be this side, and the other would be on the other side. And when the salmon would come up, the men would stand over them and spear them."

One woman, age seventy-nine, recalled: *"A long time ago, they did have lots of eels [lamprey, Entosphenus tridentatus] . . . Asotin is an Indian place of collection . . . where there were eels. A long time before they put up that Lewiston dam, there used to be a lot of Indians who'd go and get it from there, the fish ladder; they used to get eels."*

According to an eighty-two-year-old interviewee, *"Lots of them used to catch eels on the mouth of Lapwai Creek going down. They would have a wire with which they caught them. Then, they'd pick them up, and they'd take them where the people were living, and they'd have to cook these eels on sticks. They had a lot of willows [with] string through the sticks. They made a place outside for a fire; then they cooked them over the fire to eat. Nez Perce eat eels. My husband said that his grandfather would get some and my grandmother cooked it up. You don't get eels anymore because the creek dried out."*

A woman in her sixties said, *"I remember, as a young girl, we used to have eels. Someone would bring us eels, usually my grandfather. He would bring eels and salmon. Whenever we had fresh eels, my mother would go to the creek close to our house, and this would be early in the morning. She would go there and clean them, and build the fire. She had her sticks ready and she would put*

the eels on them like skewers, wrapped the eel around that stick in the circle. Then, she would put the stick in the ground close to the fire, open fire, bake the eels that way. In the morning, when we got up, we'd go down by the creek and eat our eels, . . . the whole thing, that way. Salmon [was] always dried and [sometimes] eels, too. My grandmother and my mother did [that] too."

Women made the tools used in harvesting and food preparation—baskets for carrying, utensils for eating, mortars and pestles for grinding and pounding, and the pots used for cooking and preserving not only vegetable foods but also the meat and fish the men contributed. Women became skilled producers of their own tools: stone scrapers, bone grainers, and bone or antler fleshers. They became expert at sharpening the working edges. Later, they continued to sharpen the scrapers and knives of metal which were introduced during the nineteenth century.

Mortars and pestles were valuable property, passed down within the families. Selected river boulders were pecked with the sharp edge of another stone to shape these implements. A long pestle was used to pulverize meat, fish, and berries in a mortar or stone-basket (hopper). These funnel-shaped baskets, made by coiling, were secured by pegs to a flat stone slab base. The stone pestles were also employed with wooden mortars.

Women cooked and served food to the extended family and guests, who were seated on mats in the tipi. Men and older children ate first. The food was served in wooden bowls and bowl-shaped baskets with either short- or long-handled spoons and ladles of carved wood or buffalo or mountain sheep horn or carved wood, a traditional woman's wedding gift. A variety of elaborate dishes was made by combining several ingredients. The women passed on recipes for preparation, including spicing, and the best ways to store different foods under diverse weather conditions.

2.17. Mrs. So Happy (Rachel Aripa), daughter of Elizabeth Wilson of Kamiah, crushing roots and bulbs with a stone pestle in a wooden mortar. Idaho State Historical Society 60-179-4, c. 1930.

2.18. Mrs. Yellow Bear (Wah-win-tee-lokt) is sitting inside her tipi and pounding roots using a hopper. National Park Service, Nez Perce National Historical Park Collection 217, c. 1910.

2.19. At mealtime inside the tipi. Idaho State Historical Society 77-60-3, Stephen D. Shawley Collection, c. 1900.

2.20. Left to right: Ida Wheeler, Edith Strombeck, Sarah Jackson, Helen Eneas, John Moffett, Dave Arthur, Valarie Stelljes, Mrs. Allen Durr. In modern times, public feasts are held inside buildings, and modern furniture and utensils are used, unlike traditional root, salmon, and berry feasts. University of Idaho, Alfred W. Bowers Laboratory of Anthropology, Stephen D. Shawley Collection, c. 1960.

An eighty-two-year-old woman recollected: *"Men ate first, then children and women. A lot of times, the children and women ate together. Of course, the mothers look after their own kids. It was carried out, these places you go, like a wedding trade, anything like that, a long time ago. Ever since I have been here, men always ate first. They got the best. If you are smart enough, save some for yourself; otherwise, they would eat all."*

Food was stone-boiled in coiled willow baskets or rawhide containers. For variety, some foods were steamed in pits or roasted in ashes. Women also dug holes in the ground and lined them with rawhide or used containers as shown in Figure 2.6. The hole was then filled with water, and large stones were heated red hot in the fire and then dropped into the water. When the water reached the boiling point, meat, roots, or fish were added and the cooled stones replaced until the food was cooked.

Knowing how to store and cache food was all-important, and this knowledge was passed down from great antiquity by Nez Perce women. Food was stored in baskets and hide bags. Women made caches by digging a pit, which they lined with leaves, bark, and grasses. Baskets and hide bags full of dried roots, meat, fish, and berries were

2.21. A family sitting in front of a mat lodge. Woven mat lodges such as this were all but abandoned in favor of the conical hide tipis. Oregon Historical Society 4466, c. 1910.

then placed in the pit, and it was filled with more leaves, bark, and grasses and finally covered with dirt. Afterward, some rocks were placed on the top of the pit to mark the location of the cache.

A seventy-four-year-old woman (now deceased) considered Indians' eating habits to have deteriorated: *"Women in my grandmother's and mother's time, they stayed at home and took care of children. They stayed and took care of the house. They stayed at home and took care of the food, the preparation of the foods for the coming winter. Today you don't see that. It's fast food things, junk food, and we don't have time for all that preparation any more."*

Shelter

Many families lived communally in longhouses, elongated dwellings which were constructed and maintained by the women. Above a shallow excavation, two separate, parallel ridge poles were tied to upright supports, leaving a space the length of the house to serve as a smoke flue. Other poles were laid against the ridge poles to form an A-frame on which tule, or *túk'o*, and skins were tied. Eventually, skins and hides completely replaced the tule. These covers had to be cared for and adjusted. Usually, more poles were laid on top to hold them down during a heavy wind. During the cold season, women were busy arranging and at-

32

tending fires placed about twelve feet apart down the center of the house, each fire usually serving two families.

Temporary dwellings served for specific purposes, such as at root-digging locations. Semi-subterranean circular structures were constructed for menstrual isolation and childbirth; large ones were used as separate sleeping shelters for the unmarried of each sex over fourteen years of age.

An eighty-two-year-old interviewee said, *"Tule is a kind of a reed that grows in swamps or mushy places. They grow at the edge of a creek or edge of a river or edge of a lake or a pond. Women would go and collect tule from different places, for example, Walponat Pond. Tule was harvested in a certain month. Then the women would dry it in the sunlight so it bleached out and became lighter in color. Then it was split into two parts, twisted, and laced or sewn together with kamo, that kind of material they . . . used before they had corn husk."*

An elderly woman, eighty-two years old, tells of the housing during her early years: *"This is the kind of tipi, a tule mat tipi, my father was raised in across from First Church in Kamiah where a lot of them lived. He was raised in the kind his grandmother had that I asked, 'Did it leak?' She said, 'No, when the water come down, those reeds swelled.' He said, 'It's waterproof. No rain, no nothing got in it.' Yes, they used tule. A lot of them used tule on the floor, too, when they could get them."*

"Another use of tule mat was . . . on the floor when they would eat. They laid them a lot of times inside the tipi. They lined the floor . . . with the tule mats . . . fixed their beds. That's how his parents put [their mat] . . . down there, and then they rolled it up in the morning and put it away, and in the evening untied it."

". . . Mostly, they used it for their tipis and for inside their tipis. If they did use new ones, newer

and better ones, they would save and repair the old ones and renew them. [The new mats] would be added I'll say in the summer, because a lot of times they rolled up the edges of their tipis and then put tule mats a little bit up . . . [for] better ventilation. A lot of times, in real hot weather, they would not even put the tule mats down. They would be just rolled up and leave them there."

Sokoy, tipi making, was a woman's job. A skin or hide tipi was readied in less than a day, the hides sewn together by hand using sinew. Women were also responsible for pitching and maintaining the

2.22 A view of a summer tipi (women and children unidentified). During the summer the tipi cover would be opened to allow air to circulate. Idaho State Historical Society 63-221-149, Jane Gay Collection, c. 1890.

2.23. Buffalo-hide tipi at Cottonwood Creek. Mr. and Mrs. Jesse James and Susie Broncheau, the little girl holding a pony, who was ninety-six or ninety-eight years old in 1993. National Park Service, Nez Perce National Historical Park Collection 6942, c. 1890.

2.24. Canvas tipi (long-house) at Chief Joseph's funeral feast. Canvas tipis eventually replaced tule and hide tipis. Long-houses were used not only for communal living, but also for ceremonial purposes. University of Idaho, Alfred W. Bowers Laboratory of Anthropology, c. 1904.

tipi or camp. They kept the fire going day and night for warmth in winter and opened the tipi covering for ventilation in summer. The top of the tipi had a hole or outlet for the smoke from the fire which was positioned in the center below. Beds of grass, tule mats, or hide were spread out at night and rolled up in the morning and stored inside along the wall of the tipi. Branches of trees were put against the tipis for shade in the summer.

"My grandmother had a rawhide [tipi]; one of the pieces looked like buffalo. You know, when hair are on it, like rawhide," related one interviewee, age eighty-two. *"And then she had other small pieces that they put down on the floor of the tipi. She had two covers: one was buffalo hide, and one was cougar; and that's what she covered with. My grandmother had one buffalo-hide tipi; it had fifteen to twenty hides depending on the size of the buffalo. The weight of the buffalo hide also depended on the size of the buffalo. Some of the hides were big. They always tried to put big ones up at the top—the big, thick ones—so it wouldn't leak, and then they filled in all around. Buffalo tipis are rare, especially here now."*

When canvas was introduced by the Euro-Americans, it replaced hides for tipis. Like hide, canvas is water repellent, although buffalo hide is somewhat heavier than canvas. Women started using canvas cloth to make tipis and patched torn tipis with canvas, as they had previously done with hide or tule mats.

Another woman, age eighty, stated, *"Even when canvas was introduced, women would make tipis in one or two days, sewing by hand. They would cut strips into a circle shape and then join the strips together. It is more round at the back than in front where the door is. The front [twenty yards] takes more cloth than the back [fifteen yards] because the front has the opening or a hole for the smoke to go out and also the lower front*

2.25. Women in front of a canvas tipi. From left, Jeanette Jackson, holding a doll; Lizzie Fairfield, part Yakima; and Maggie Jackson, sister of Tom Hill, a Delaware/Nez Perce. Idaho State Historical Society 63-221-125a, Jane Gay Collection, c. 1890.

2.26. Young Nez Perce woman seated in front of a tipi or a menstruation lodge. University of Idaho Library, Historical Photograph Collection MG-18, c. 1910.

was a door. . . . The number of poles used in the tipi depended on the size of the tipi. When they start the tipi, they start with four poles. Some tipis have fifteen or eighteen poles, whereas the larger tipi would have twenty-two."

During their menstrual period, as well as during labor and childbirth, women used a special tipi. Cooking their own meals there, they were not permitted to touch anything outside of the tipi, nor did they attend any ceremonies. From the women's standpoint, isolation in these lodges served a social purpose, as they were able privately to discuss personal problems and conditions of health, exchange views on herbal medicines, compose songs, and so forth.

One elder Nez Perce woman, age seventy-nine, says, *"Not too many women nowadays realize that, when the women in the old days had their menstruation, they stayed in a special tipi and a hole was dug, and they did their whole cycle through, and it was buried in that hole so that their power wouldn't affect any of the men. Childbirth was another thing in which they were restricted to another tipi. The women went there when they were having their children, and their midwives went with them, and they leaned back, and all of the blood and the afterbirth and everything was buried in this hole after the child was born."*

Sweat houses, temporary or permanent, were constructed and used separately by both women and men, although in Nez Perce mythology, a female character was directed to prepare the sweat house for a man (Phinney 1934, 483-488). If there is only one sweat house, the men always use it first.

2.27. Old temporary sweat house in a remote area (right foreground). Washington State University Libraries 90-048, c. 1890-1900.

2.28. Use of the sweat lodge has continued into the present. National Park Service, Nez Perce National Historical Park Collection. Photographer, Bob Burns, 1968.

2.29. Family on the porch of a dwelling. Seated, John Seven Wilson and Mrs. Wilson; standing, Jane Wilson, Mary Wilson and an unidentified boy. Idaho State Historical Society 63-221-240, c. 1905.

2.30. Woman sitting on the porch cooking and taking care of a child. Courtesy, Richard Storch, c. 1909.

2.31. Eddie Conner, a Methodist minister; his wife, Sarah; baby, Elizabeth Blanche Conner, who later became Mrs. Sam Watters and whose second married name was Hung; David Conner; and Joe Conner on the porch of a frame dwelling. Bicentennial Historical Museum, Grangeville, Idaho, c. 1890.

According to several interviewees, the frame of the willow sweat house was covered with hides. The more permanent sweat houses were made with an identical framework but were covered with grass, sod, and again, grass. The preceding information on sweat lodge construction was provided by several interviewees.

Said one interviewee, age eighty-six, *"Now, the children of today, now and then, they'll talk about sweat baths. Everything has to be rushed through, so it's a shower or a tub. But I wish that those days would come back. It used to be a big help to people, like, if you had arthritis or rheumatism, they'd make you go take a sweat bath every day until it went away."*

"Now, nobody has time for that: it's medicine, or else we have to go to the doctor; there's no more medicine women or medicine men. Sweat baths, they have it, but just now and then, not all the time, because they had to upkeep the wood, they had to upkeep the rocks. And we certainly have changed a lot. Our days are different from the way our grandparents were."

When missionaries introduced frame houses, women lost their traditional role as provider of housing—tipi builder. By this time, the Nez Perce were mainly confined to the reservation area. Traditional longhouses were abandoned, so in order for the natives to lead sedentary lives, houses needed to be constructed. The new houses were

2.32. Martha Morris of Stites, Idaho. Nez Perce women were famous for their excellent workmanship in traditional handwork. University of Idaho, Alfred W. Bowers Laboratory of Anthropology, Stephen D. Shawley Collection, c. 1965.

small, accommodating only nuclear families, rather than the large, traditional extended families. This represented a radical shift from the social and economic ties of the past, but the missionaries failed to understand the disruption this change brought to the lives of the Nez Perce people.

Clothing

The complete construction of clothing, including preparation of the material, was another of the tasks women performed for the welfare of their extended families. Sewing with an awl and sinew or buckskin string, women fashioned clothing without patterns or outlines. A buckskin strip was moistened with saliva, then shaped and tightened by rolling it on the thigh. Sometimes one end of the string or sinew was moistened further with saliva so that it could be easily threaded through the punched hole after it had dried stiff.

Apparel for special occasions differed greatly from the simpler garments worn in the course of everyday work, but all of the garments worn by men, women, or children were made by these skillful, knowledgeable artisans. (The various descriptions of ornamentation and decoration below refer to special occasion clothing.) Artistic skill and a concept of beauty are strikingly evident in their clothing, arts, and handwork, as women imaginatively adapted to new materials and other changes through time. They were and still are resourceful and creative.

A simple dress with cape sleeves, the traditional buckskin gown hung straight down from shoulder to ankle. Two deer skins formed front and back, oriented with the posteriors at the top. The hide of the rear legs was sewn together to form sleeves, never longer than elbow length. The remainder of the top (tail end) was folded down to form a false yoke. If too short, the skin was cut straight across and a yoke later suggested by ornamenta-

40

2.33. Maggie Hill, shown with her daughter, Jeanette Jackson. Women made a majority of the clothing and handwork, including cornhusk bags and wallets, beadwork, and toys for children. Idaho State Historical Society 63-221-178, Jane Gay Collection, c. 1890.

2.34. Family dressed in traditional "good clothes." National Park Service, Nez Perce National Historical Park Collection, c. 1905.

2.35. Stephen Reuben, wearing beaded hide clothing, beaded moccasins, beaded belt and belt pouch, and beadwork jewelry. University of Oregon Library M4523, Moorehouse Collection, c. 1910.

2.36. Delia Lowry, wearing a skin dress with a traditional Nez Perce pattern beaded in "seed" beads. The cape-like sleeves were made to cover the elbows and were fringed at the end. National Park Service, Nez Perce National Park Service Collection 0244. Photographer, J. W. Webster, c. 1915.

tion. In the former case, the tail piece was left on for ornamentation, with its hair trimmed in parallel horizontal lines. In later times, a diamond-shaped beaded patch covered the spot on the dress front where the tail had been. The most prominent design on women's clothing became the diamond-shaped design on the neck, both front and back, on women's dresses (Gunther 1950, 75).

At the bottom of the dress, four half-circular pieces were added between the neck and leg extensions of the hide in order to even up the hem and to provide a graceful fullness for walking and riding. The side of the skin that formerly carried the hair was next to the wearer's body for softness and warmth.

For ornamentation, fringes were added to the bottom of the skirt, at the ends of the sleeves, and along the side seams, either from the material itself or added strips. Usually the yoke and sleeves were solidly beaded in variegated, horizontal bands. Other decorative materials—shells, seeds, elk teeth, or porcupine quills, for example—were used prior to the fur trade. Various trinkets adorned the dresses in styles depending only upon the ingenuity and artistry of the maker.

With the introduction of Euro-American fabric, the buckskin dress was slowly replaced by the wing dress. The trading companies offered such cloth as woolen felt, flannel, corduroy, and velvet, which were in great demand by Indian women, who preferred their color and light weight. Also, much less labor was involved in their use in comparison to buckskin clothing. Women adapted the new materials to the aboriginal buckskin style and thus created the wing dress.

The wing dress was so named because the underarm was left open, allowing the sleeves to flop like wings. Two large rectangular pieces were used for the front and back; the size depended on the height of the wearer. Another style used one rec-

2.37. On the left is Susie Looking Glass (Ip-naw-tomh-we-tah-kit, or Op-graw-tom-moi-tah-kichkt), daughter of Chief Looking Glass of the 1877 War. Susie is wearing a traditional Nez Perce buckskin dress, beaded belt, and beaded belt pouch with a hand-print design (women sometimes used their own handprints as their design) and a cloth dress under her buckskin dress, a practice begun when woven cloth was introduced. On the right, her unidentified cousin is wearing a beaded Hudson's Bay Company woolen-felt wing dress. Idaho State Historical Society 77-60-29, Stephen D. Shawley Collection, c. 1899.

2.38. Two young girls, unidentified, during the filming of the movie *Told in the Hills*. The girl on the left is wearing a trade-cloth decorated wing dress, and the one on the right is wearing a traditional beaded skin dress. Courtesy, Richard Storch, c. 1919.

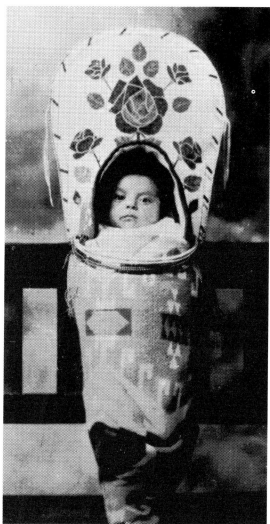

2.40. A baby in a cradle-board decorated with beadwork roses. University of Idaho, Alfred W. Bowers Laboratory of Anthropology, c. 1900.

2.39. Mary Phinney wearing a traditional Nez Perce dress, beaded leggings, and plain moccasins. Courtesy, Lorna and Douglas Marsh, c. 1905.

tangular piece of cloth with a slit made for the head in the center and triangular pieces added from the underarm to the hemline to give more width and flare to the dress. Two rectangular pieces were added across the shoulder for cape sleeves. These dresses lacked fringes and were decorated with beads, ribbons, elk teeth, trinkets, copper and brass pieces, coins, and seashells.

Women often wore leggings, depending upon their task and/or the weather; men always wore them, but there is a distinct difference between men's and women's styles. Women tied leggings on the outside, and they were not worn up the thighs nor were they supported by belts.

"Some leggings were plain and some were beaded. Some moccasins were plain and later [some were] beaded. When you put on your Indian buckskin dress or wing dress, then you can wear leggings," offered an interviewee, age eighty-four.

An eighty-two-year-old told of the change in legging styles after knitting was introduced: *"Women wore leggings for protection a lot of time in cold weather and when they were traveling. I think it was a necessary part of their dress or clothing. I have seen old ones that were just plain, everyday utility wear. At the time of the missionary era, when the yarn was introduced, women learned how to crochet, and they made these crocheted tubes like stockings without putting on the foot of them. I can remember very elderly women used to wear them. They had no feet on them. They pulled them up, put their moccasins on, and wrapped it over. One could see the red and the green stripes around and around on the leggings."*

An elderly interviewee, age eighty-six, remembered her grandmother making moccasins: *"When Grandma was living, she tanned the hides. She said never to tan the hides of an elk because the skin is thick. But deer, their skin is kind of me-*

dium, it's not too thin nor too thick. Those make the best moccasins. She would soak it for a few days before . . . She would cut the fur off of the hide, and then she would soak it after she finished. She used to make them look so beautiful, white. That was for moccasins. And she'd say that whoever wears the moccasins would have to make use of it. Their footsteps would be soft on the ground when hunting. Moccasins were something Indians made and they [ancestors] taught them [children] how to walk in them."

Before the advent of Euro-American trade, decorative items of many kinds were shaped from stone, bone, horn, elk teeth, quill, and seeds. The latter were used to form the most common beads, readily available in the immediate environment. Using natural materials, small, round "seed" beads were dyed a variety of colors such as red, orange, yellow, light blue, dark blue, green, lavender, and black, the colors preferred by the early Nez Perce. Lewis and Clark mentioned the preference for white and blue beads (Thwaites 1905, 3:78 and 5:30).

The fur trade brought not only Euro-American fabrics and blankets for clothing, but also glass beads. Glass trade beads were acquired directly through trade with fur traders, trading companies, and trading posts or indirectly through trade with other Indian groups. Most of the old trade beads were large because the small-glass bead technology did not develop until the 1830s. Even then, small trade beads did not become fashionable until the 1850s. "Pony" beads, medium in size, were actually quite large compared to the smaller seed beads of today. Pony beads were used for necklaces, dresses, cradleboards, and ornaments for horses.

The Nez Perce were most likely getting glass trade beads and some other European trade items by 1780. Brass beads were introduced by fur trad-

2.41. Georgia Ellenwood, at the Border Days Fourth of July celebration in Grangeville. The dress weighs between forty and fifty pounds. Bicentennial Historical Museum, 1953.

ers in the late 1700s, but were mostly acquired from the Hudson's Bay Company in the early 1800s and are still in popular demand. Currently, most beads originate in the Czech Republic. In addition to beads, other objects of European manufacture were used, such as trinkets, brass and copper pieces, and coins.

The common form of beading, confined mainly to dresses, was lazy stitching. This technique produced long strands of beads in parallel rows, with the strands sewed only at the ends. The Nez Perce lazy stitching was especially long. The common beadwork designs were diamonds, triangles, zigzags, wild flowers, animals, birds, and butterflies. Sometimes women would just use their hand print design. Later on, roses, the American flag, and eagles became popular. Today, beadwork remains popular among Nez Perce women and men, with a few people using the beadloom.

Echoing a concern that was shared by other interviewees, an eighty-two-year-old woman said, *"I always wonder where did all this beautiful beadwork go? Who did it go to? I just don't know. 'Collectors,' even today there are 'collectors.' Summer time, people come to buy things."*

Another woman, age eighty-four, said, *"Sometimes if a person is in need of money, it's easy to sell family things and get the money. Sometimes they sell these things to get money to buy alcohol."*

Nez Perce women embroidered with quills of the porcupine, an art form which may have been borrowed from the Plains Indians. The quills were first dyed, then flattened either with a bone tool or by the fingernails, and then sewn down on buckskin, the quill ends spliced together to add length. Nez Perce porcupine quill techniques include wrapping, sewing, and braiding. Women made narrow parallel-striped patterns on men's shirts, leggings, belts, headbands, robes, and medicine bags.

2.42. Left, Etta Moffett Davis; center, Sarah M. Jackson; and Lillie Edwards, in wing dresses with elk teeth. They are also wearing beaded belts, beaded belt-drops, beaded leggings, and plain moccasins. Etta and Lillie hold beaded and corn-husk bags. Women always carry these bags when garbed in traditional buckskin and wing dresses. Lillie has a beaded belt pouch. All three are wearing seashell jewelry. Bicentennial Historical Museum, Grangeville, Idaho. Photographer, J. W. Webster, c. 1915.

2.43. Elizabeth Penney Wilson and Effie Nesbett have on traditional styles of wing dresses with elk teeth (Effie Nesbett) or shell ornaments (Elizabeth Penney Wilson). Their panel-beaded belts, beaded belt-drops, and beaded belt pouches were also popularly worn by Nez Perce men. Aboriginal shells of abalone, haliotis, and dentalia often decorated older Nez Perce dresses. When elk teeth were not readily obtainable, bone was used. National Park Service, Nez Perce National Historical Park Collection, Stephen D. Shawley Collection. Photographer, J. W. Webster, c. 1915.

During the 1700s and up to the mid-1800s, the Nez Perce were famous throughout the continent for their horse-hair quill wrapping. Nez Perce horse-hair-wrapped quill ornaments and decorated clothing were popular items in the eastern part of the continent in intertribal trade. Upon the arrival of glass beads and after the 1877 war, quillwork as an art slowly died out. It is used by few among Nez Perce women today.

An eighty-four-year-old informant stated: *"Porcupine quillwork here [on the Nez Perce Reservation] was not as prevalent as it was with the Plains Indians. I've never seen in my life [during the twentieth century] a Nez Perce do porcupine quillwork."*

Seashells like dentalium, olivella, abalone conch, haliotis, and cowrie were obtained from the coastal tribes in intertribal trade. These items of decoration were widely dispersed as a medium of exchange by the Indians, as was wampum, which was also made from seashells.

Women as well as men used cosmetics. Some dried plants and flowers served as powdered deodorants, and certain leaves were crushed for soap. Oil was applied to skin and hair. Face paint, made by pounding various colored rocks into powder and mixing with water, was used by women, especially on eyelids and cheeks to prevent snow blindness and sunburn and, they believed, diseases brought by the Euro-Americans. Red, orange, and yellow were the favorite colors. Women made combs for their hair out of wood, sometimes with a buckskin cover for the handle.

An eighty-six-year-old woman shared her recollection of the early cosmetics: *"My grandmother used to use some kind of leaves that would turn into soap. I can't even remember the kind of leaves that she used to bring. And after that, she'd say, 'You won't ever have scars on your face if you use this,' and we did use it for awhile until I went away to school."*

2.44. Annie (left) and Katie Broncheau, "Nicodemus' children." These young girls are wearing wing dresses, beaded belts, beaded leggings, plain moccasins, and shell jewelry and holding cornhusk bags. Idaho State Historical Society, 63-221-171, Jane Gay Collection, c. 1890.

2.45. Celia Guthrie, daughter of George Guthrie, with hair parted and made into two braids wrapped with beaver fur and wearing a beaded headband. Idaho State Historical Society 77-60-11, Stephen D. Shawley Collection, c. 1930.

2.46. Delia Lowry, with her husband. Euro-American trade cloth and blankets are used for clothing. University of Idaho, Alfred W. Bowers Laboratory of Anthropology, c. 1900.

2.47. Unidentified woman wearing velveteen wing dress, lacking beading but with beaded belt-drop and wampum necklace. Cornhusk bags were carried by women even when the traditional style of clothing changed. Traditional women always cover their legs with a blanket while sitting. Bicentennial Historical Museum, Grangeville, Idaho, c. 1900.

Hairstyles were described by an eighty-two-year-old interviewee: *"Parting of hair for women was from front to clear back. Braids were made and put on the front. Women and men never threw away their hair; whatever came out after combing was collected and kept in a safe place. Then when a person died, that hair was buried with the person or was burned. Women in olden times painted their hair with red color."*

Modern innovations in hairstyle include greater decoration, said an eighty-seven-year-old interviewee. *"They wear all kinds of beaded stuff on their braids now. Fur pieces were never worn by women to decorate their hair braids; it was later added. Headbands were worn after the turn of the century. In the mid-twentieth century, single women started wearing one feather in their hair, and two feathers have been worn by the married women. Women and men did not expose their ears in olden times, they always covered their ears."*

In the majority of known cultures, clothing serves as an important indicator of status and identity for the individual and the group. Acculturation simply modified this attribute of Nez Perce clothing. When Euro-American trade cloth, blankets, and beads were introduced, the women were already skillful, productive artisans. Using the new materials, they altered their dress design and modified styles; for example, initially they blended the traditional buckskin dress with the wing dress and then, finally, completely accepted current Euro-American styles. At all periods, the women dressed modestly although they were the very ones involved in innovation.

With the adoption of the Christian faith, native garments and hair styles were discouraged and abandoned. The missionaries brought technology such as sewing machines and gave training that accelerated the adaptation of Euro-American clothing. Some Nez Perce people continued their

2.48. Elizabeth Penney Wilson, wearing a wing dress decorated with elk teeth and cowrie shells, a wampum necklace, beaded choker, shell earrings, and beaded belt, belt-drop, and belt pouch; taken at Lewiston after her return from the Carlysle, Pennsylvania Indian School. When elk teeth were not readily obtainable for decoration, facsimiles were made out of bone. University of Idaho, Alfred W. Bowers Laboratory of Anthropology, c. 1908.

2.49. Sarah Conner, wearing European dress, and son, Gilbert Conner. She was a niece of Young Chief Joseph. University of Idaho, Alfred W. Bowers Laboratory of Anthropology, c. 1895.

2.50. This group is unidentified. Notice the high heeled shoes and Mother Hubbard style of dress. The children are wearing school uniforms, white shirts and black pants. Bicentennial Historical Museum, Grangeville, Idaho, c. 1900s.

strong adherence to principle in their practice of Christianity, and so they accepted the church's ban on "heathen" customs such as ornamented traditional clothing, beaded leggings, hats, carrying bags, and the wearing of feathers in church. Customs which involved time-consuming activities were particularly discouraged.

In addition, the change in clothing was economical. Obviously, handmade articles could not compete in market price with the products of industrial and pre-industrial economies. Tremendous time was invested in the making of traditional clothing. Women artisans spent days and weeks cleaning and scraping hides to get the proper size, species, and quality for an item of clothing, to say nothing of the time spent in construction, sewing, and ornamentation. In terms of time and labor, ignoring cultural preferences, it was easier for an artisan to acquire the necessary cloth or blanket material from the trader through exchanges.

As one interviewee, age eighty-two, recalled: *"High heeled shoes, they really thought that was something. They polished them. I can remember Aunt Jeanette, who made that beaded bag. When they got ready to go to powwow, she never wore moccasins, but they wore those high top shoes. Aunt said, 'Oh yes, I wish I had high top shoes, a pair.' They polished and got them to shine and put [on] a bright muffler, and that's the way they went."*

Traditional clothing had much ceremonial meaning in the past and is now making a comeback. Articles of clothing for gift giving and the wearing of special apparel by participants were central elements in weddings, name giving ceremonies, medicine dances, war dances, and memorials. Types of clothing for these occasions were highly ornamented and precious, weighted with respect and memory. The maintenance and restoration of these traditions is continuing in spite of

2.51. Jessica Redheart wearing Indian dress. *Lewiston Morning Tribune*, c. 1975.

2.52. From left, Julia (Mrs. James) Slickpoo and Louise (nee) Slickpoo. Julia wears a traditional buckskin dress and holds a pony-beaded buffalo hide blanket. Louise's wing dress is decorated with elk teeth and she carries a cornhusk bag. Both wear shell jewelry. National Park Service, Nez Perce National Historical Park Collection 0217, c. 1910.

the early labeling of indigenous clothing as "native" or backward, particularly by the missionaries and the government, through institutions including churches, the military, and schools.

Today, traditional native clothing is a dramatic means of social and cultural identification of "Indian-ness." The integration of status and cultural identity with clothing has influenced many Nez Perce to return to the wearing of traditional dress for special occasions, particularly for dances, powwows, and parades.

An elderly woman said, *"Our elderly people really get mad when they see these young girls at the war dances, powwows, and memorials, wearing skirts, shorts, or real short dresses. I always tell my girls, 'Don't wear skirts. You've got to be formally dressed.' 'Oh, it's all right.' 'No, it is not.' You've got to learn how to be respectful to the elderly people. Then, some people think, when a rape takes place, that when these girls dress like that, that's what she gets, that's what she wants."*

Other Items of Hide and Buckskin

Besides clothing, women used animal hides for a variety of other handwork. Beaded blankets originally were of buffalo hide. It was difficult to work with buffalo hide because of its weight, so women would split it into halves in the center when it was fresh. The hide was then easier to stretch and to work in the tanning process. Later, women sewed the hide back together and hid the seam with a strip of blanket ornamented with beadwork. Women used this blanket as a shawl, or it might be used to cover their legs as they sat or traveled on horseback. It became a valuable trade item. In later times, it was replaced by Whitney blankets, followed by Hudson's Bay Company blankets, and then by Pendleton blankets, often similarly ornamented with beaded stripes.

Parfleches, popularly known as Indian suitcases, were constructed from rawhide by the women, who painted them with diamond or other geometric designs. (Nez Perce designs are very similar to those of the Plains Indians, particularly their friends, the Absoroka [Crow].) Both sexes used parfleches to carry their belongings, such as clothing. Once the bags became old, they held dry roots, meat, and berries for storage.

One elderly woman (who is currently the most skillful cornhusk weaver) stated: *"We used to make a lot of dried meat. They'd put it up in tipis and smoke it. It tasted really something different. Every family had a place to keep their meat, and they had Indian trunks—they call them* isaptakai*—made out of hide. When you'd see a kind of a greasy trunk, you knew that's where the dried meat was. But they were never without dried meat; they always had to have it because that was a very special meat to them.*

"These were also known as Indian suitcases. Isaptakai (for parfleche bag or Indian suitcase), that's an Indian name for that Indian trunk. The new ones, the clean ones, they kept their clothes in. In the old ones, they kept foods like dried meat, dried salmon, and roots of all kinds such as camas, cous, and hó-pop. They used to dig around I think. There are three kinds of roots we did and dried fruits, too, like they used to dry huckleberries, later, apples, and any kind of fruit. They used to dry and . . . fill the isaptakai with food to have in a separate room . . . but nobody does this kind of work anymore."

Cylindrical rawhide bags were used to carry roots back to camp, and they also transported meat prior to the introduction of the parfleches. Sturdy and functional, these bags lasted many seasons. Buffalo rawhide buckets, cylindrical in shape, were used for stone boiling. For this pur-

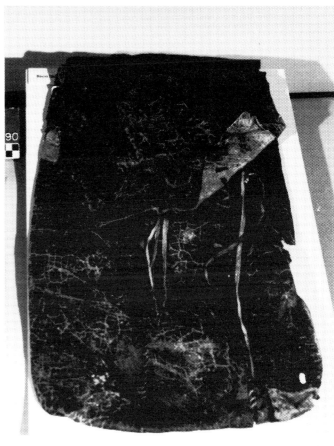

2.53. Parfleche made of buffalo rawhide. These bags were made and painted by women and were popular as wedding trade items. Worn bags were handy for carrying and storing dried meat, fish, and roots. National Park Service, Nez Perce National Historical Park Collection 2271, c. 1870.

2.54. Cylindrical buffalo rawhide bags, made by women to carry and store dried meat and roots. National Park Service, Nez Perce National Historical Park Collection, 1030, c. 1850-1880.

2.55. Mother and daughter soaking hide. In early times, women soaked their animal hides in the stream, taking care to properly weight them down with heavy rocks. Courtesy, Richard Storch, c. 1912.

pose, a circular flat stone was fastened in the bottom.

Another item which women made from animal hides was the cradleboard. Constructed of light wood and soft buckskin, cradleboards were elaborately beaded. The most ornamented and artistic part, the section above the hood, was completely covered with beadwork. The outer surface of the belt which was attached to the board was also beaded. Nez Perce children always had toys constructed by mothers, grandmothers, and aunts. Girls had babyboards and baby dolls made of buckskin stuffed with cattail down.

Cradleboard materials were described by an interviewee, age eighty-two: *"The old, old frame of the babyboard did not have a piece of wood in it. It was all rawhide or a heavy buckskin. You didn't have any flat pieces of wood a long, long time ago. . . . A lot of the old ladies would use a piece of an old parfleche. Part was cut and fitted inside. It was not wood. The modern ones are [wood] because . . . at a shop . . . they can have them made. They can drill holes too. But I remember women used old pieces of parfleche. Mine is made out of heavy buckskin."*

"The base of the cradle is a very smooth board, not rough . . . On the top at the back of the babyboard a belt . . . of buckskin is attached slightly above the center. This belt was put over the shoulders [and across the upper breasts] so . . . the weight was easy on her shoulders. Women never put this belt around their forehead while carrying the baby." Most interviewees closely agreed with this description, given by an eighty-six-year-old woman.

Responding to a photograph she was shown, a ninety-six-year-old informant said, *"Oh, that's just a doll. My mother made that, you know, and that's how they used to fix . . . dolls . . . We used to have a big doll, you know . . . for babies? That's how they used to have that . . . cradleboard . . . it was like that, and beadwork on it. But she made me that with a doll, but the doll don't show up [in the photograph]. Maybe it was a rag doll."*

Paints and Dyes

Painting, as a major decorative element, was an ancient form of art employed by the Nez Perce. Women painted on dresses, leggings, moccasins, skin, and parfleches. Paints and dyes were obtained from natural clays, minerals, or plants. Women knew which clays could be used as bleach and which kinds of flowers, leaves, fruits (berries), and plant roots could serve as dyes.

Various clays created the colors of red, orange, and yellow. A clear green came from slime on the rocks in river beds. A yellow or brown was produced when the basketry materials were soaked in a tea made from the roots of the Oregon grape. These natural dyes have now been replaced by chemical dyes that give more intense colors.

Fine, white chalk and clay were used to clean hide clothing. Later, with Euro-American clothing, soap and water were used. The cleaning of clothes was sometimes done in the river even after modern washing machines were introduced.

Said an eighty-four-year-old woman, *"I can remember how my mother used to wash her clothes, quilts, and blankets at that time down along the river because we did not have any electricity, and she had an old Maytag wringer-type machine for which we had to heat our water. I remember she could spend time washing clothes."*

Weaving

Nez Perce women extensively practiced the art of basket weaving. Besides weaving basket hats, and hoppers (mortar baskets), women wove cylindrical carrying bags for roots, winnowing baskets, watertight cooking baskets, and baskets for trans-

porting water. A small, sharp awl made of bone or horn was the only implement used in basketry. Women always carried their awl wherever they camped or traveled.

The inner bark of Indian hemp (*Apocynum cannibum*), or *kamo*, was the most widely used material in traditional Nez Perce weaving and sewing, as it formed the base material for basketry coils and the fiber for twining. In the autumn, hemp was cut and then bundled when dry at Ahsahka (Orofino) and higher up the Clearwater Valley in the direction of Lolo Pass. At home, it was buried and allowed to cure for about two weeks, then moistened, peeled, and dried again for three or four days before it was scraped and split into strands (Hunn 1990, 77; Ray 1939, 36).

Bear grass (*Xerophylum tenax*) was another important material that grew plentifully along the Lolo Trail. There it was collected after the snow had melted in August. Back at the village, its broad leaves were split and soaked for pliancy, as were other grasses gathered for false embroidery. Mud might be added to the water to create a brownish color. Women used it as a decorative element either in imbricating (folding and inserting), as part of the process of coiling, or in twining, to carry the design on the exterior side (false embroidery or overlaid twining).

Coiling, sometimes with imbricated designs, was the method used for constructing berry baskets (Fig. 2.9) and watertight cooking baskets which resembled those of the Yakima and Klickitat (Fig. 2.10 and 2.12). Hopper baskets (Fig. 2.18) and winnowing trays (Fig. 2.61) were also coiled. Berry baskets were usually constructed from cedar root and were rarely made locally but obtained in intertribal trade. Some women suggested these baskets were, only rarely, made of willow. Since birch did not grow in this area, it was not used for baskets. Women never used root bags for berries or used berry baskets to hold roots.

2.56. "Sally bags" (carrying baskets) of cornhusk were used for transporting and storing roots. National Park Service, Nez Perce National Historical Park Collection, 1952.

2.57. Top: Women's bags. The bag at the far right shows a very complicated design. Local Nez Perce women claimed that complicated designs such as butterflies originated with the Nez Perce. National Park Service, Nez Perce National Historical Park Collection 3041, c. 1870 to c. 1920.

2.58. Bottom: *Neetscow* or *leetscow*, Nez Perce woman's hat made from bear grass. Idaho State Historical Society 2681, c. 1870.

"There were two kinds of bags and baskets," said an eighty-two-year-old interviewee. *"Women used the old ones . . . for utility. Lots of them did not have fancy designs or were not ornamental. They were not made as fancy; they were mostly for practical use, and some of them were dirty. They used them and let them get dirty. They would shake them up, turn them inside out, hang them up, let them dry, and . . . use them again. Some of them might have a strip around them at intervals; they were real plain and used for utility."*

"The other kind was fancy ones for show, as used in wedding trade, later on in the parade, memorials, dances, or powwow."

Women wore basket hats woven of bear grass. All the informants had seen women's hats of this type, but bear grass was evidently never used in weaving root bags. After being dried by the sun, the bear grass became cream colored, dark brown, or yellow. Bear grass hats were all cone-shaped with a flat top and decorated with a tassel of several thin deerskin strips ending in shells. Some women embellished the center top of their hats with dentalium. A few informants said that, occasionally, women attached eagle-feather fluffs. Woven zigzag and geometric designs were prominent on most of the hats.

Mats were not woven; they were sewn of either cattail (*Typha latifolia*) or tule (*Scirpus acutus*). Tule was preferred over cattail because it was much stronger and more effective in keeping out rain. Women would often sew mats right where they had traveled and camped, in response to their immediate needs, so this skill was closely related to both their families' comfort and their actual survival (see examples of tule mat in Fig. 2.7 and 2.21.) Women not only made these mats but tended them on a daily basis.

During the prehorse period, it was very hard for women to walk the miles and miles necessary to collect many of these raw materials and to carry the heavy load home. Although traveling and packing by horse made this process much easier, the women informants often stressed that this kind of craft work was very time consuming, and today their involvement in paid employment has to be given higher priority. Traditionally, Nez Perce women did all the household work, took care of the children, and spent some time each day on handwork. In each generation, there were fine artisans. The traditional artistic handwork which many women still continue to practice is beading, the one skill now most dependent on European supplies. Sewing continues, typically with modern machines.

In general, there has been a sharp and dramatic change in the handwork of Nez Perce women over the last hundred and fifty years. Some of the speakers are sure that they could still use the older materials if these were easily accessible. These women do not believe that cornhusk is stronger than the formerly used bear grass or Indian hemp or easier to prepare and use. Others reject the old materials as rougher or more coarse than present-day synthetics.

Other Tasks

Women collected firewood for cooking and heating, a very tedious job during the winter. They usually carried the wood on their backs, sometimes for long distances through the snow. It was a woman's job also to keep the fire going, an especially important task in winter. The fire was built in the center of the tipi. Pinecones were used for kindling. The smoke hole at the top of the tipi was manipulated by moving the flap from the outside, and only the woman was experienced in determining the direction of the smoke and arranging the outlet for it. Women also obtained water for the whole household, sometimes daily, in waterproof carrying baskets they had made.

2.59. Collecting wood in winter. Women used leather straps across their shoulders to support the load on their backs. Oregon Historical Society 45972, c. 1910.

2.60. Women at well fetching water, Lapwai. Idaho State Historical Society 63-221-295, Jane Gay Collection, c. 1890.

Both wood collecting and water carrying were very heavy work essential for survival.

"Little old ladies would go to collect wood," recalled an elderly interviewee, eighty-two years old. *"They picked up light pieces of wood and took [them] home because they would not be able to get big ones. A lot of them didn't have men to help them get the big logs."*

According to an eighty-three-year-old woman, *"Some women would get together and help each other get larger sizes of wood. It was just a matter of trying to help each other. Three women or a few family women would go together, and, if it was a lot of wood, they did it for one family. The next time, they did for another, and each got their supply. Women did cutting and chopping the wood and hauled it. It was always the women that had taken care of it."*

Said one woman, age eighty-six, *"Ladies used to collect firewood. You see them packing them on their back. I know I got to do it for grandma. She sit down, and I helped her and sometimes packed little bit, not much. I would help her to put the load on her back."* (See also Fig. 5.13.)

The woman's role in tending the fire was described by an interviewee, eighty-three years old: *"Now, my father told me that, every night before they went to bed, if there was red coal, his mother, grandmother, always protected it, covered it with ashes and saved it so that they would have fire the next morning then. He said that in the morning his aunt got up early. She always built the fire, but that was the way they lived. I think it must have been the women that did it always because I cannot imagine a Nez Perce man getting up at that time. It would be a woman that did most of the work."*

"I had to fetch water because my step-grandfather was mean. I had two buckets. I had to walk down to the river, and I don't know how many trips I made. i was glad when we moved down here in Lapwai. Then, we got this house that has running water," an eighty-four-year-old grandmother of 23 grandchildren said.

"There were a lot of wells in Lapwai," according to an eighty-two-year-old woman. *"Everybody would go and get the water and haul it out. If they would miss their kid, they had to look then. Everybody would run and look into the well to see if their kids had fallen in the water. I remember Mother got scared once with my brother. She thought he had run away someplace. He'd always wander, going to school, and I can remember some of our neighbors went around to look in the well, look in the wagon. That's the way they used to hide, in wagons."*

Agriculture

The Nez Perce Indians were the first farmers in the state of Idaho. The Reverend Henry Spalding taught the Indians how to grow fruits, vegetables, and grains. Agriculture was also encouraged by the United States government to promote a sedentary lifestyle. Women and families had less time to devote to traditional activities such as root digging and spent more time on daily chores associated with farm life.

Women moved gradually from their traditional role as food gatherers to their new role as agriculturists. The work was similar, and women adapted their traditional tools to farming activities, continuing to use the *tùk'es* or digging sticks. When farming became part of Nez Perce life, the women used horses to cultivate crops, harrowing by dragging brush behind the horse. Most of the farming work—threshing, winnowing, and storing—was done by the women. Not only did the women handle work on their own farms, they also assisted white farmers in threshing and winnowing wheat and were paid in wheat instead of monetary wages.

2.61. Mrs. Lawyer (Ow-yeen) winnowing, Kamiah, Idaho. Idaho State Historical Society 63-221-4a, Jane Gay Collection, c. 1890.

Harvest was tedious, owing to the primitive mode of working. Threshing was left entirely to the women; sometimes one woman worked alone, but more often, women helped each other. If they faced a long stay in the field, they pitched an old tent and spent the night. Grain to be threshed was hauled on a skin sled to a skin-covered threshing floor. The grain was placed in such a way that two women, each on one horse and leading another, could slowly ride a circuit until the grain was separated from the straw (McBeth 1908, 138).

"They did threshing with the horses," said one eighty-year-old interviewee. *"A hide was spread in a hole. They put the sheaves of wheat in the hole and let the horses go round and round, left to right and right to left, and soon the grain would be separated from the hay."*

Describing those pictured in Fig. 2.61, an eighty-two-year old woman said, *"That's my great-grandmother, and behind that dog is my dad [Corbett Lawyer]. You see the straw hat? He said that he got a rattlesnake skin for [the] hat band. That was his dog 'Atpips,' means 'bones.' That dog was his wéyekin (spirit power). Right (standing) James Stuart. My dad's grandmother's name was 'Ow-yeen,' means 'wounded or shot.' She was shot down at the Thousand Spring near the Blackfeet [Shoshoni]. She got that name.*

"My great-grandmother, now, you look at her in this picture. There she was, up in years, when she was winnowing the wheat. She came from seed-eating country. They used that kind of winnowing tray for seeds. Those people were seed eaters and they winnow out seeds. That way, when they got through, it looked like a bunch of sand. The seeds would be small. They did not use it for cleaning the roots because roots were too large to be winnowed."

Winnowing was done by women pouring the grain and chaff from a winnowing tray held higher than the head. As the grain fell, the wind would carry the chaff away. Women also gleaned leftover wheat from the stationary threshers of white farmers.

According to one elderly woman, age eighty, winnowing was a job for two. *"Women had a square piece of canvas. They would winnow the wheat with it. Two women usually did it; one would hold the two corners at one side of the canvas with each hand and the other woman would hold the two corners at another side of the canvas with each hand and shake the wheat. If it was a windy day, then it worked out very well because the wind would blow the chaff. They would then put the wheat in the buckets."*

"Nez Perce women would do winnowing for the white farmers. In turn, they received wheat, which they would take to Lewiston and make into flour," added a second interviewee, also eighty years old.

The grain needed for familial use and for seed was put into a *we-kash*—a large dry goods box. The rest was sold. Money received from the sale of grain to people in nearby towns and mines and as supplies for miners provided the winter's supply of groceries. Various storage outbuildings were built to house the farm produce.

"There was a distinct change in the Indian attitude toward Indian land. Indians wandered from one place to another in search of their food, it depended what time of the year it was, to store food for the winter. Pretty soon, the missionary came and turned them into white farmers. They had to defend their land," observed an elderly woman of eighty-two years.

Another woman, eighty years old, told of the shift from traditional food during her grandmother's lifetime: *"My grandmother used mortar and pestle to make corn meal. Later, she would*

2.62. A Nez Perce woman, Milton George's mother, sitting with her crop covered with canvas. Women were still using their digging sticks for agriculture, gardening, and digging ditches. National Park Service, Nez Perce National Historical Park Collection 782. Photographer, A. H. Hilton, c. 1918.

67

Fig. 2.63. The Corbetts, a farm family. This photograph represents a typical reservation farm of the period, complete with the usual assortment of barns and outbuildings. The men standing near the horses and the women and children are not further identified. Idaho State Historical Society 63.221.65, Jane Gay Collection, c. 1900.

take corn to Denver, Idaho, and bring six, seven sacks of flour. They did have gardens. They did have land, cows, and they raised their horses. They had their winter supply. It was a change from their traditional supply of food, camas and kouse. It was a different food supply, but they adopted it."

Food storage methods included stocking up home-grown and home-canned foods in the cellar. Most of the women had big gardens in which they grew all kinds of vegetables and fruits, and these gardens provided much of the food for the family. The change from root digging to agriculture did little to change the work load for these women, who were highly successful in agriculture and gardening because of their experience with traditional food gathering, preserving, and storing. The *Lewiston Morning Tribune* (March 26, 1967) described how the Nez Perce women dried their corn: "[T]hey first parboiled it and placed it on white muslin. Then, they covered it with cheesecloth and let it dry in the sun. It was ground to make cornmeal. They also made hominy."

Said one eighty-six-year-old interviewee, *"My great-grandmother was always busy chopping wood, canning food. They had a cellar that they stored all kinds of canned food in. Almost all food came from the garden."*

Reflecting on her youth, a sixty-year-old woman said, *"I can remember as a young girl, during the summer time, we worked hard because my parents had a small farm there. They grew their own fruit orchard, with all kinds of fruit. They had a small garden which had all kinds of vegetables. My mother canned all of her fruits, and we had to always help. We had to pick the fruits, clean jars, peel the apples, do something to help with that canning. So we did work during the summertime."*

One woman, eighty-six, told of her own farming experiences: *"I had a hard life. I think it*

is catching up right now. I helped my mother do things. She had a big garden. I helped her do work. We lived on that—corn, potatoes, and squash—those were the main things. She always would dig a hole, put the squash away, then take it out in January. She used to dig a hole. Then she put hay around, put her squash, and covered it. She always had a opening for air for it. I guess that was needed for it. It was good in wintertime, just like [fresh]. . . . It was not spoiled in any way. That's how I learned to do lot of hard work."

"Women dug a pit, or a hole (tilapalo), *or cache,"* said an eighty-year-old interviewee. *"They would store their winter supply and cover it. My grandmother and aunts would put away onions, potatoes, and melons. At Christmas time, they'd bring all that out. It was a special treat."*

Practically every Indian family cultivated some land, ranging from garden plots to wheat farms of several hundred acres. Most commonly, however, they subsequently leased their wheat lands to white farmers. Women who were widows received rent from these leases which enabled them to pay their bills. Some of the elderly women still lease their land to farmers, while Social Security provides them with some additional income.

Initially, Indian farmers received some income from their farm products, and the opening of new railways through the reservation brought much better markets. Women learned to grow vegetables and sell their excess produce. Thus, Indians became further involved in the "money economy."

According to a BIA report (1907), by the turn of the century, a number of Indians had milk cows, and nearly all had funds from the BIA with which they could buy more cattle. The women of the household took care of the animals, milking the cows and feeding the pigs. This meant they must accept a relatively monotonous, demanding routine and not leave their homes for any extended period of time. Those engaged in dairy milking also had to learn animal husbandry. With time, the reservation adapted to the dairy industry, and as it developed among the Nez Perce, it became essential that the people not leave their homes so frequently to attend tribal dances, religious meetings, or even to visit.

As agricultural technology evolved, women and farming moved from horses to tractors. An elderly woman, age eighty, said, *"We used tractors. I even drove a Fordson tractor to help my husband out on the farm, and after that my children were there to look after."*

The Reverend Henry Spalding constructed the first sawmill and gristmill in the Idaho country in the early spring of 1840 at what is now known as Spalding. Many problems needed to be resolved; one of these was how to supply a head of water that could turn the big wooden wheel for power. Late in the fall of 1839, it became apparent that he would have to build a ditch and take water from Lapwai Creek.

In a remote country, thousands of miles from the nearest manufacturing center, with no tools to dig the ditch, Spalding turned to the Indians for help. More than one thousand Indian men, women, and children dug the ditch with their hands and with *tùk'es* sticks, using baskets to haul the dirt. Many of the laborers were elderly women and men, which was counter to the Nez Perce tradition of revering the elderly.

One cannot quite visualize the task that confronted the Nez Perce workers until one walks over the ground and traces the original location of the mill ditch. Unfortunately, in recent years, the state highway department, in its beautification and development of the memorial park of Spalding, has filled in much of the ditch course that ran through the park to the site of the sawmill and gristmill.

THREE ▲▲▲▲▲▲▲▲▲▲▲▲▲▲▲▲▲▲▲▲▲▲▲▲▲▲▲▲▲▲▲

Life Cycle
of Women

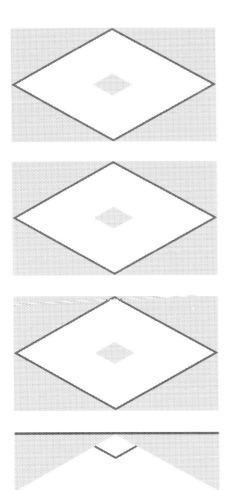

Raising Children

AN EIGHTY-TWO-YEAR-OLD woman said, *"Male children were always welcome because they provided the food like meat and fish, the sustenance for their families. They were the protectors of the families against enemies. Because from the early time on, they [their ancestors] said the Snake Indians would come, and they even would come into Kamiah and Kooskia Valley at different times and would try to steal horses, and people would catch them. And they caught a bunch of them on the other side of Cottonwood. And there is a legend of how they [the Nez Perce] chased them [the Snake Indians], and they ran into a cave, and the people piled tumbleweed in front of the cave opening, set up fire, and not one Snake Indian came out. They stayed there. So they [men] were protectors from the enemies.*

"The female children were also very important because they provided also their part of sustenance, the roots, the berries, took care of the meat and fish, dried them for the winter, provided homes—the tipis, utensils—and kept the fire going. My dad always said, while a man would ride all day, when he came home, they were going to make camp, he would get off his horse and sit under the tree and watch his wife and his women all put up the tipi, look for wood, build the fire, and get out the things to cook, and made the beds, made the fire inside the tipi to keep the beds warm

*and everything. He just sat there. He didn't have
to do anything because he took care of the horses."*

*"Women's things took precedence over men's
because they are the ones who brought life. They
are the ones who went through childbearing. They
are the ones that, when they went to dig roots,
they had control of whether they wanted a boy
child or girl child, and they took certain roots to
ensure that they had boy children. They took certain roots to increase their breast productivity and
milk. They even had medicine that they could
have miscarriages by and that's something that
not too many people know about, even nowadays:
the medicines that they used, particularly for miscarriages or for having boy children . . . ,"* said
one interviewee, age sixty, recalling her grandmother's words.

Said an eighty-six-year-old woman, *"No diet,
no rest, nothing. They did enough exercise [in
their work]. They were never told to rest or lie
down at that time. People were never allowed to
rest because there was always something to do that
they wanted to do. So they all got along because
they all had to do something."*

Some of the women gave the following description of pregnancy: *"If you are pregnant,
they put a buckskin around your stomach. It's like
protecting the life of the baby. After the baby is
born, the buckskin is buried or burnt. If you are in
a stressful situation, you are hurting your baby.
Even if your close family member died when you
are pregnant, you cannot go there to the wake.
You are not supposed to go there and see the
body."*

"I heard from my mother," said an eighty-two-
year-old interviewee, *"that many women had
miscarriages because they used to travel on horses
and did hard work. They say that a lot of women
did [have miscarriages]. A lot of them had their
babies on the way, got up, and can travel. They
never stopped to rest or anything."*

Fur traders observed that Native American attitudes toward childbirth differed profoundly
from the Euro-American or Old Testament canon
that childbirth was woman's greatest ordeal and
agony (Kirk 1983, 19). The four elderly women
who mentioned childbirth suggested that it was
not difficult for them. This is in marked contrast
to the behavior and attitudes of their daughters'
and grand-daughters' generations.

The work ethic was so strong that, according
to an eighty-year-old interviewee, *"Women
worked until they had their babies. When they
were pregnant, they were still using horses. Right
after delivery, they would get up and work some
more. There was always something to do for the
women. Women had to make a good living. Now,
they lie around or sit around."*

A seventy-nine-year-old woman, since deceased, said during her interview, *"That's what I
say now, how brave and tough the women were in
those days. They could be moving when she got in
labor. She was left there or they stopped. She had
the baby and was gone."*

A forty-four-year-old mother of two said, *"I
knew there was a big move by the physicians from
Indian Health to stop Indian women from having
many children—having their tubes tied and giving them birth control. It was in the early 1970s,
because this happened to me after my second
child was born. I was encouraged by my physician. This is the way it was at that time. I have
heard from other Nez Perce women that they
were encouraged not to have any more children.
At that time, it was a fear that the Indian population would become too great. Non-Indians were
getting fearful, losing control over our people by
numbers."*

One interviewee, age sixty, described the
traditions of which her grandmother told
her: *"Childbirth was another thing [like men-
struation] in which they were restricted into an-*

72

other tipi. The women went there when they were having their children, and their midwives went with them." The same woman stated, *"Midwives were paid in kind [actually, a gift], but most of the time they did help without expectation, and their importance was recognized by the community."*

"Nez Perce mothers usually delivered their babies in a small tipi with the help of a midwife or a female shaman and elderly female relatives. The young mother was also attended by her own mother, grandmother, and aunts when possible," said an eighty-year-old woman.

A male shaman might be called only if severe problems developed during labor. For example, as a seventy-nine-year-old interviewee related, *"There was a whipman, going for hunting, and he came upon his horse, and she was in labor. She was trying to deliver a colt. She couldn't do it. He helped her, so she gave him her spirit and gave him the power to help women, those who were in labor. He was the only man that could do that, to help women in delivery time when they had difficulty."*

Although payment was not demanded, an elderly woman of eighty said, *"[t]hey paid for such kind of work, generally like some beadwork, food, a parfleche full of some things like dried roots, berries, and meat, a pair of moccasins. They were always paid one way or the other."*

"My aunt told me that she was there when her mother was having a baby," began an eighty-two-year-old interviewee, *"and her mother-in-law was helping to deliver the baby. And, when the baby was born and after it got cleaned up, she took cold·water and just threw [the water] right on its face three times. I asked why did they do that. She said, 'Oh!, to be sure it's alive and keep it crying.'"*

Some women were pregnant and gave birth to children during wartime or when the war party was on the move from one place to another. Other women performed midwifery, using their resources to aid in a special and successful delivery during wartime.

A forty-one-year-old granddaughter narrates this story about her grandmother's birth: *"My grandmother was the only child of Hattie Hayes. She said that after the Nez Perce War was over, there was a continuity of hostility around this area. It was often dangerous for Indian people to be out, even on the reservation, and . . . Hattie and other people whom she was connected with were on horseback. They were coming back from someplace, and it was a long ride, and she was pregnant. The labor pain started, and she stopped her horse along the river, gave birth to my grandmother (Lizzy Hayes Moody), then got back on her horse and kept going. It was so dangerous. That's why she thought she wouldn't have any more children, but that was the situation when my grandmother was born."*

Breast-feeding generally continued for several years. It was believed to serve as a method of birth control, and spacing of children was valued. Sometimes this seemed to work; other times it didn't.

If a mother was unable to produce milk, she used corrective medicinal herbs, such as bitter-root. When the baby was weaned, it was given softened meats and vegetables, as well as small pieces of gristle to chew between meals, good exercise for the gums during teething. Dried roots were made into cereal, and sheep-horn spoons were used to feed the baby. If a natural mother died, the newborn was fed by another nursing mother, either related, or another wife of the husband. This was a ready-made adoption system. Until another nursing mother could be found, a type of medicinal mountain tea (Labrador tea [*Ledum gladulosum*], *pisqo*) was given to the infant, according to an elderly woman.

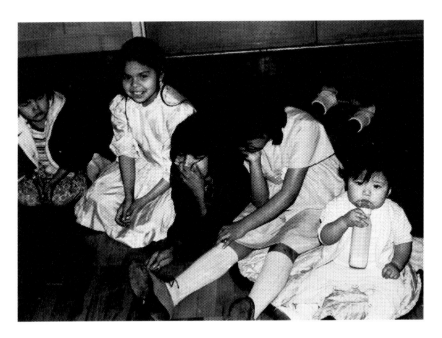

3.1 Nez Perce children in modern times. After World War II, Indian women, more likely to work outside the home, adopted bottle-feeding. This is discouraged today by the Nez Perce Tribal Child Health Care Program and the WIC program, on the basis of scientific studies. Courtesy, Mary Norie Banks, Moscow, c. 1980.

Women were very modest, and never showed any part of their bodies, even while nursing their babies. An eighty-four-year-old woman said, *"It's sure an acculturation. A long time ago, I remember when they had powwows in the old buildings. The women would put their shawls on like that [across one shoulder] and hold their breasts and hold the babies. They covered up their babies and nursed them."*

An eighty-four-year-old woman, the grandmother of nine, said, *"Babies were soon placed in cradleboards where they stayed until they were ready to walk. A mother carried the cradleboard on her back or placed it close by so she could watch the baby. These babyboards were used to secure the child during travel and at rest. The babies found the boards to be very comfortable and secure. These allowed the women more freedom of movement to perform daily chores for the family."*

"Well, she [the mother] usually didn't make the babyboard. Usually her relatives made the board for her, because she was busy doing—taking care of her home or her husband, maybe a few other children that she might have already," remembered another eighty-four-year-old woman.

"The babyboard was usually made by her husband's sister and given as a gift. Twins were considered good luck," said an eighty-year-old interviewee.

Another woman, eighty-two, said, *"Generally, a babyboard would be made by the mother or the grandmother-to-be, or it might be an aunt or . . . a best friend. My grandmother made me mine. I still got mine."*

An eighty-year-old interviewee stated, *"Ladies made the babyboard. I had to make my own. It took me all day, but a simple one, just a day. Beadwork would take awhile. Women used cedar wood and soft buckskin."*

3.2. Nez Perce baby, or *meots*, in cradleboard, or *tekash*. Beadwork on buckskin, with a hanging pouch (on right) which contains the umbilical cord. Idaho State Historical Society 714, c. 1900.

A forty-year-old woman repeated her grand-mother's words: *"The dried umbilical cord from the baby was retained within a small pouch on the cradleboard. This was done . . . in the belief that the child would maintain a close bond to its family and not become lost in older life."*

"The idea was to keep it because it was part of them. It showed they had it right there . . . covered by the buckskin. A buckskin pouch was made. They put beads on it or else just left it as it was just in the buckskin pouch," explained an eighty-two-year-old woman.

An eighty-six-year-old interviewee said, *"If the child would die, its umbilical cord, with the pouch, would go with the burial. It depended on the family."*

An elderly woman with nineteen grandchil-dren recalled, *"Some of the mothers used the board until the babies were about nine months old or a year. It was very handy having them on the babyboard; it was safer for the babies from drop-ping them or hurting them because the baby was laced in the babyboard. She used to have a belt [buckskin] attached to the back of the board. She would put the baby in the board and put the belt over her shoulders and carry the baby that way all day long. Boy! If the baby was a crybaby, she would pack her around doing household work and everything else."*

If the mother didn't have time to do beadwork on the babyboard, it went without beadwork, but usually women would find the extra time. In the summer or when the weather was hot, women used wild rose (*Rosa spp.*), or *tá·msis*, boughs to make an arch over the baby's head to shade the baby's face. It was also believed that these rose boughs kept ghosts away from the baby.

According to a woman, age eighty (also re-peated by an eighty-two-year-old woman): *"Women would use a stick of the rose bush, clean the bark, and then they'd tie it down to the board, and they would [wrap] buckskin strings [around] it, [leaving spaces] so [the stick would] dry out. They used to put it over the board just like a hood over the baby's face to protect it from sunlight without touching [the] baby's face."*

A few women saved their cradleboards and would not share them because of their sentimental attachment to them. Some women who are now close to ninety years old still have their own baby-boards, used when they were babies.

Mothers, aunts, or grandmothers always sang lullabies to put young children to sleep. Sometimes, especially in winter, a swing was built inside the tipi and the child placed in it. This kept the child occupied while the mother was busy.

Nez Perce children received the names of important ancestors who would then be expected to exert a favorable influence on the child's development. This practice continues into the present time. Girls are given their deceased grandmother's or great-grandmother's name, or that of another female relative, allowing the family name to be passed on to a new generation. At the name-giving ceremony, the family has a "give away," presenting gifts to family members or friends in the name of the deceased person. The whole family is involved in arranging, preparing, and performing these ceremonies.

"In modern days now, the name-giving ceremony has become just a giveaway," said an *eighty-two-year-old woman.* *"They just give away. You know, we are going to have a name-giving ceremony, and everybody stands up and brings their things like bundles of shawls, blankets, material for dresses, serapes and afghans, whatever they want. . . . This is the way they give away. But a long time ago, they announced [the name] when they had a General Council or a special meeting or something. They announced [for the baby], 'I am my name' or 'I am giving my aunt's name to*

this little baby because she needs a new name and that is her name.' My grandmother gave away in South Dakota. I had horses, so I gave away two horses among other things in honor of my dad. My grandmother announced that it would go to an orphan, because my father was an orphan, and she said there were two little orphan boys with their long ropes. They [the family] turned the horses loose all decorated with blankets and feathers on their tails and everything, and . . . . [e]ach of the orphan boys got a horse. She made war bonnets, and she made parfleches with things in them. And here a long time ago, they did that, and they give away a lot of buckskins. They'd make buckskin and fold it up and cut it. Then there will be enough for a pair of moccasins, for a pair of gloves. They tied it up with a bandanna handkerchief, and that was a gift you brought for a giveaway."

Childhood

A mother of six, now in her sixties, recalled her childhood: *"As a young girl, my childhood was pleasant. When I was growing up, I remember a lot of time, we were spending hours and hours swimming in the river down there. Sometimes, we took food and cooked there and spent the whole day down there.*

"I remember playing all over the hills across the river, and that was a fun time. We never had to worry about anything. We ran all over the hills and played around the fields below the house there. I never heard of any rape, or I never heard about adultery. We were sheltered over there then, until I got older, became an adult."

A sixty-year-old woman said, *"We were taught to respect animals, not to hurt them. I remember, as a child, we were trying to catch barn owls in an old vacant building, and here I stepped on a barbed wire, it came up and cut the back of my leg. I nearly believed that I was bothering* owls, that's why it happened to me. That's the way we were brought up. We were not supposed to hurt animals, and if we did, something would happen to us."

Another interviewee, age sixty, said, "A long time ago, when I was growing up, in the evening you couldn't have run around and played outside. We were not allowed to look out the window because they would tell us the spirit might see you and do something. We were never allowed to cry at night or eat outside at night. We were not allowed to do all these."

According to a Nez Perce woman, age eighty-one, "As children, we were not allowed to be [around] some who were very strong [in medicine power] or to see the things they used to do. We were strictly disciplined. Children never ran around. They were always sitting still and listening what they had to say. We were not allowed to do many things, and if you were a girl you are sure limited, too. The boys could get away with anything."

"I hope my children hang on to their traditions and understand their culture. I need to learn more myself, so I can teach them more. They seem to be pretty well adjusted. They do not understand the values of certain traditions. When we go out and do different things—dig roots, collect berries, or do hunting or fishing—we explain the value of the animal, the respect that you are supposed to carry. They seem to be very well adjusted to the non-Indian society, also. I think being able to balance that is very important, which is something I hope that they will be able to do and still hang on to their culture," said a single parent in her thirties.

Small children were rarely disciplined, but when older children misbehaved, they were whipped in groups by special whippers, elderly men and women, not necessarily related to the family but respected people in the community.

An interviewee in her eighties believed "that the children were disciplined [in the past]. The children minded the parents, and were corrected by the parents. We used to have a group whipping for the child. At that time any elderly person would whip them to discipline them. They used to do the whipping, but the discipline was in the families. There was a punishment for a female child."

Whipping was discussed by a woman in her seventies: "When I was seven, eight years old, my aunt and uncle whipped me. But there was a man—he used to live up in Kooskia, Idaho, and I used to wish that man would die now because he come down once a month, and I got a whipping from him. It was compulsory. He whipped hard. He was impartial. He did it because my family was telling him that I needed a whipping once a month. A man could whip a female child at a certain age [before puberty].

"My grandmother would always ask me when the old man finished whipping me, 'Well, are you going to do it any more?' Then, that old man would tell me right out, when he got done whipping me, and after I got done crying. He let me cry it out. And then he sat me down, and then he'd tell me why he whipped me—the reason for the whipping. My grandmother'd come and say, 'Well, you won't be doing [that] any more because now you know he is the man I can always call upon in case something happened that you did wrong, that he will correct you.'"

An eighty-two-year-old mother of five said, "A long time ago, in my mother's time, they would take their children aside and tell their kids what they expected from them—a certain behavior—and how they have to behave in the public or in some special ceremonies. In those days, children listened to their elders because "Respect your elders," was the number one guide. Even if they were not related to you, they would discipline you how to *behave. They knew they cared for you and they loved you. If a person was not related to you, it didn't matter; he or she would discipline the children. I guess, at that time, it was like everybody was a big family, and it was everybody's responsibility to mind the children. But now things are different: you cannot tell them anything."*

The discipline of children in the past encouraged cooperation. A woman in her eighties relates her memories of discipline: *"Parents and grandparents used to discipline the children, grandchildren, at least before the Christianity came. They used to get whipping. I went through [it] myself. Well, some time another man came, and he did the whipping. I was eight or nine when I got whipping. There was a group of children playing together, and if there was any problem, if one person started it, we all got whipping. Whether you were involved or not, you still got whipped. The person who whipped, he was not even related to us. It was not necessary that he was related to us, and the parents didn't mind it. It was understood in the culture that was the only discipline they had. Now, you can't do that. You would be accused of abusing the children if you done that. I think that system was good, so the children could mind and listen compared to what it is now. If you tell a child, 'Don't do that,' they do it again. I've got great-grandchildren, so I know, even if you threaten them, they won't listen."*

Interviewees also indicated that it was the aunts and uncles who did the disciplining, allowing the parents to be the agents of compassion. This seemed to reduce tension on the parents, who were themselves teenagers. Christianity at the time of the missionaries was very much supportive of corporeal punishment. If anything, Christianity encouraged more violence toward children than did the traditional Nez Perce culture.

The children acquired nearly all basic knowledge, values, and traditions from the grandparents, and grandmothers always cared for their grandchildren, even when the mother had remarried. Young girls were expected always to be in the company of elderly women or grandmothers and to learn from them. The relationship was one of mutual love and respect.

"I think that women were a very important part of the family," stated an interviewee, age sixty. *"The grandparents were, too. They took care of the children in my family. My grandmother had to do with my growing up because she was there to discipline me and to teach me when my mother was busy. She was always there for me, but she was also working all the time, either in the house or outside in the yard in the garden. But she was always there. But I think grandparents, seems to me, like, spent a lot of time with us telling stories and disciplining us."*

Recalled one woman in her forties, *"When I was growing up, my grandmother was the one that disciplined us. They never struck us with their hands, like slapping us. It was always with a switch! They would go out and get a piece of limb off a tree. We would have to lay down on the blanket. She put the blanket down on the floor, and we all laid, and she switched us. So we all got disciplined at the same time."*

"Our grandmother stressed family very strongly," a single parent in her forties said of her grandmother, explaining the older siblings cared for the younger ones. *"She would make us learn to take care of one another and not fight among each other. She would always say, 'You guys are cousins or sisters. Don't fight: you are related, you are supposed to take care of each other.' If one of us younger ones got hurt, she would line up all of the older ones and switch every single one of them. She would say, 'Now you learn to take care of each other.' So we grew up always looking out for each other, if the parents were not around, or even if we were just playing outside."*

A forty-four-year-old described her grandmother: *"My grandmother's name was Elizabeth Taltoy Samuel. She lived most of her life in Arrow Junction, at the mouth of the creek. She practiced the Catholic religion. However, for the root feast, she would prepare the food for them. She did a lot of food gathering. I spent several summers with my grandmother. I remember one time I couldn't go with my grandmother one summer. My father and mother stayed home. I cried because I couldn't be with her. She was like a second mother to me. I enjoyed spending time with her. We never communicated with her eyes. She communicated by handing me something or by moving me one direction, things like that. I would go out with her to gather moss in the trees and the mountain tea. We'd go out and get berries. I remember she gathered a lot of foods. I remember she dried a lot of meats. She had her old wood stove in the kitchen, and there was a wire line across over her stove, and she used to lay meat over that so it would dry when she had the stove going. She dried a lot of meat for us. We did go sweating together. She didn't have her own sweat lodge, so we had to go to a community sweat in Lapwai, and it was by the railroad tracks. She would take me sweating there with her. I believe every Wednesday, we'd go up there and go to the sweat lodge. That was women's night at that time. It was just a time when the women would get together and go out once and sweat together. We would have some* kouse-kouse *tied in a sock and dip it in water. My grandmother taught me to use that for cleaning, so I would take that sock and rub it on my body. It's a healing and strengthening type of a medicinal root. It's a form of medicine. If you smell it when you have a cold, it helps.*

"She was very loving. The time that I have spent with her, I feel that she had given me something, like some type of a spirit I have gotten from her. I believe that lives in me today."

Another woman, eighty years old, recalled, *"I will always remember our grandmother would tell us that 'People are the guests; we will feed them first. You children wait till they get through.' A lot of times, we'd have to sit outside, not out in the cold, but you know, wait out there till they got through, never to be noisy while the older people are there, especially the guests because you don't know who's the medicine man or medicine woman. They might think, 'Oh, they're not well behaved,' and they might have to tell you themselves, lecture you, tell you, but it's better to behave in front of people and treat them right, because it's what we're here for. Our religious training is supposed to come from these older people. They know a lot. They can tell you a lot. Our grandmother used to tell us, she'd laugh, and she'd say, 'We had our own songs; we had our own signs of speaking,' and three of them used to come together to our house, and they'd sing those old religious songs, and they'd be going like this, waving their hands.*

"One died and they felt so bad, so this other one came, and she told them that we're going to do our own religion . . . that we used to have while she was living with us. So they did their song, but we had to be quiet. We had to respect their religion, because they were old people. That's going to be gone, I'm sorry to say it, if we don't keep it up.

"What they have now is modern. Everything's modern now. Some of us tried to tell our grandchildren what we lived through and what our people came through. They made it through because they had their training from their older people. I hope that when we leave this world, we have something we have left behind for them to remember and to carry it through.

"I try to tell my grandchildren what our people were supposed to do or say. Never to mistreat elderly people, never to laugh at them. If you see them helpless, go and help them; if you see them

hungry, go feed them . . . give them your food. Your food will come back to you. Your kindness will come back to you. Never be afraid that you'll go hungry yourself because it's always the good things that will come back to you if you treat them nice, if you treat the people right. Be generous with whatever they need. Never say, never tell them to pay you back, because food can be gone. You can find some more food like that, but the people, you will never have a chance to treat them right if you mistreat them now. Now is the time for you to be good to them and be helpful. Be kind to people young and old alike.*

An eighty-four-year-old woman said, *"Nowadays, kids get into trouble. If you tell the kids to do things, they know better than their grandmothers and their mothers. They know what they are doing."*

"Grandparents were very important in those days, in extended families," said an eighty-two-year-old mother of two, *"but it is different nowadays. All want their own homes and to live as they please, not to be bothered with their grandchildren, not anymore . . . [W]e have our grandchildren growing up, but they are on their own. That's the way it is. At that time, it was different. Right now, they [grandchildren] think of money, you know, that's all . . . all we are living for is money."*

Some of the interviewees could not remember ever hearing of the puberty ceremony, even in their grandmothers' time, but a few had learned that puberty ceremonies once existed. However, menstruation was a time of isolation for girls and women.

According to an eighty-two-year-old Nez Perce woman, *"At puberty time for a girl, the Nez Perce had those menstruation lodges where women would go to have baby, or during her period . . . they go there, and they stay there. Generally, . . . the first time when the girl went there, her grandmother or mother would take her there*

and help them, explaining about it. She would stay there during that time. When I was a little girl at that age of ten to twelve, I never knew about menstruation, but nowadays kids know everything. We were just ignorant. We didn't know about anything like that. That was good too.

"My grandmother told me they used soft buffalo hide with the hair on it [for menstruation]; and then here (Nez Perce [reservation]) they used a piece of buckskin, and they'd put milkweed [on it]. . . . They disposed of it by burying it.

"They saved soft fur from the buffalo and other animals, and that's what they used. Women always tanned hides, so they always had soft fur; and they would save that and use that. They never burnt them but buried them. They had a place to go when they were menstruating—menstrual lodge. They all had to go to menstrual lodge, even when they had their babies. There is one in Kamiah. You can see [it] on the other side of the second church, that little creek over there. You can tell because it is indented. It's down deep."

An eighty-year-old woman said, *"When they had their menstruation, they had to stay in the menstruation lodge. They didn't go to funerals or any other ceremonies. They couldn't meet anybody. They cooked their own meals. They couldn't cook with or eat with anybody. They had to be by themselves."*

"In the olden days," said a woman, age eighty-two, *"when they reached a certain age, when they started menstruating, they were taken away from the general public, they weren't allowed to play with young boys at that point, or the young men, and they were set into special tipis. They were raised up and taken care of by grandmothers and aunts and were taught to be good diggers and how to make clothes, and do things like that."*

The mother and grandmother of one interviewee, age fifty, taught her that *"[w]omen are strong in our beliefs. Woman is strong when she is pregnant, woman is strong on her moon [menstruation]. She is the creator at the time of pregnancy. When woman is menstruating, they say, 'Don't have intercourse, otherwise you become pregnant.' That's why she had to keep away from everybody. Women never went to medicine dances, war dances, stick games, or funerals. They were not supposed to be anywhere if they had their menstruation. I started thinking, 'How would they know?' I would go, 'I wonder what would happen?' That's how they were separated, women and men, at childbirth and menstruation time. Woman was very sacred when she had her menstruation or whenever she was pregnant."*

Modest behavior was expected from women in the Nez Perce society, and this behavior was part of a young girl's discipline at home, taught by her grandmothers and mother from a young age. For example, a young girl would learn that a woman's clothing should cover all of her body, that as a mother she should be careful to shield her breast from view while feeding her baby, and that a woman should cover her legs with a blanket while seated. Elderly women always accompanied young girls, both for protection and for instruction.

An elderly woman, age eighty-two, talked of modesty and the women in her family: *"My dad said when he had a meeting or company, she [my grandmother] always had to light the pipe because his pipe was long, with the stem up above that high [showing about 6 inches], and it was quite a ways from him to light. She always had to fill and keep it lit. She said that she would go, keep her eyes down, not look at anybody, fix it and light it, and walk out.*

"Generally, women kept their eyes down. I can even remember that, too, when the churches in Spalding had a supper or any kind of special occasion, they see men and . . . to shake hands with them, their eyes were always down. They didn't have eye contact with men in . . . public."

Marriage and Social Relations

Historically, Nez Perce villages were comprised of interrelated, extended families. Village headmen were elected by the villagers, usually for life, but the village had no qualms about replacing them if they were not good leaders. The son, if capable, was often chosen to replace his father. A group of villages located along a tributary stream often joined in an alliance or band, with one of the notable village headmen elected chief (Marshall 1977, 143-44).

The people of the same band living in different villages were often closely related through intermarriage. A bilateral kinship system had fewer obstacles to intermarriage, and polygyny was also practiced, all of which extended kinship interaction with unrelated families. The Nez Perce form of marriage and descent thus created a wide network of kinship ties (Anastasio 1955, 174), which did much to maintain peaceful intergroup relations in the region and to encourage cooperation, hospitality, and the sharing of major resource sites. The strengthening or extension of these intergroup ties for the benefit of the whole community may have been one motive for the practice of polygyny by chiefs or headmen, in addition to the economic contribution of these wives to their husband.

Although Deward Walker and Allen Slickpoo mention three classes (Walker 1978, 136; Slickpoo 1973, 48) according to my elderly intervicwees, Nez Perce society was divided into two classes. The first class included chiefs, headmen, and warriors, who generally tended to be the wealthiest ones and were fewer in number. They were the ones who made the decisions and were also the protectors. The other group or class, more numerous, was comprised of the rest of the people: the common people.

Referring to Fig. 3.3, an eighty-two-year-old woman said, *"Dolly was his second wife. Gener-*

3.3. Left to right: the Rev. Archie B. Lawyer, holding his daughter, Rose; and his second wife, Dolly Lawyer. Bicentennial Historical Museum, Grangeville, Idaho, c. 1890.

3.4. Wedding photograph of Jackson Sundown (a former world champion rodeo rider) and Cecilia—Esther McCatty's mother's first cousin and Rose Frank's grandmother. University of Idaho, Alfred W. Bowers Laboratory of Anthropology. Photographer, J. W. Webster, c. 1920.

ally, she came from Ahsahka way. She was a descendent of a Klamath captive that was gotten down at Celilo, when everybody would go down there, and they trade and gamble. She lived there at Ahsahka. Archie Lawyer met her there at one time when he went to hold church there, and they got married.

"I don't think that the Nez Perce were as concerned about slavery because there was not enough slaves around here to consider it a 'class.' They were just taken as a wife and husband and their children treated just like anybody else. They were there, and we got them, and we took care of them. [Other elderly women interviewed made similar statements.]

"There was not even any kind of an insult for these captives. They were treated as one of us. Even poverty was nonexistent because, my father said, when they go for hunting, they killed deer. A lot of times, they all made sure that they gave to somebody who didn't have anything—that was part of the blessing, that you did that."

An eighty-three-year-old woman said, *"I never heard before that the Nez Perce kept slaves. They treated each other equally. They never made other person slave to do just like they did to the black people in the United States, that you can call them slaves. That way they [whites] have complete control that every move that they [blacks] had. I don't think they [Nez Perce] have done that here. They might have had some captives from the other tribes who came but they [Nez Perce] helped them work. As far as slaves I don't think our people had done that."*

The kinship system of the Plateau was bilateral, that is, relatives on both the mother's and father's sides were recognized as equally important or close. Marriage was barred between all known relatives by the Nez Perce and between those related to the fifth or sixth degree by some of the neighboring tribes. This comprehensive extension of the incest prohibition must have promoted intergroup marriage. By 1800, the Nez Perce Indians were increasing their marriages with the Cayuse, Walla Walla, Palus (Palouse), Umatilla, and Yakima of their own language group, as well as Salishan speakers, the "Montana Salish" (the Flathead). At the same time, bilaterality strengthened the bonds created by those marriages.

According to the interviewees, this equity may also explain why the choice of residence for the married couple was flexible, although residence with the husband's family was favored. Many of the headmen of the mid-1800s gained that position by choosing to live with their wives' families, particularly when the wife had no brother. A good example of this is Old Chief Joseph. Although place of residence was an individual decision for one's own benefit, perhaps men who were already chiefs and village headmen had particular freedom in this matter.

The practice of polygyny (plural wives) and the absence of polyandry (plural husbands) may reflect the basic economic importance of women's work in the aboriginal economy. Chiefs and headmen had a responsibility to care for their people, including giving feasts as well as food donations. Extra wives provided more food for the community and created wealth in the form of trade items and gifts. On the other hand, some interviewees believed that plural wives were an added expense.

Some polygyny was a result of the custom of marrying a brother's widow (levirate). Unmarried sisters were often chosen for additional wives (Walker 1978:138). If single, a woman ideally married her deceased sister's husband (sororate). However, neither the levirate nor the sororate marriage would be obligatory. Spouses of siblings could be sexual partners, and the approval of sexual intimacy between these potential mates (anticipatory levirate and sororate) illustrates the way the complete family—not just one couple—is united in Nez Perce traditional marriage

3.5. The family of young Chief Joseph (Hin-mah-too-yah-lat-kekht, Thunder Traveling to Loftier Heights) after the 1877 War. The woman at the left is Heyoom-yo-yikt, Chief Joseph's older wife; standing behind her is his younger wife, Springtime. The woman at the right is Heyoom-yo-yikt's sister, one of Chief Looking Glass' widows, whom Chief Joseph married while in exile. The two children are probably Chief Joseph's nephews. University of Idaho, Alfred W. Bowers Laboratory of Anthropology, Stephen D. Shawley Collection.

(Lundsgaarde 1963, 23-24). The levirate custom gave a widow and her children the chance to have less disruption in their lives following the death of a husband and father, and polygyny was practiced also because there were more women than men due to deaths in war. In times of warfare, polygyny was valued, as in the example of Chief Joseph's marriage to a widow of Chief Looking Glass, who was killed in the War of 1877.

Said one interviewee, in her eighties, *"After a sister's marriage, other unmarried younger sisters or cousins would go for visitation or to live with her. It was easy to work together with that bond or relationship; it was possible for them to care and share the same household. This process, in some cases, developed [in] a way that after [the] married sister's death, it was easy to replace her as a wife for the deceased sister's husband and . . . mother for her children, instead of another unknown woman taking the place in that household and especially for the children."*

Marriage was always an important occasion. Most first marriages were arranged between families by the parents, often when the girl was in her teens. After the first marriage, additional wives were chosen by the polygynous husband.

An eighty-three-year-old woman recalled that *"[a]rranged marriages were there, and people used to abide with it. Marriage was arranged by the parents. That was probably the good choice then; I don't think now we are picking everyone."*

Elopement was rare. Normally there was a mediator, usually an elder, respected family member who negotiated the marriage. Most often, this was a woman of the household or a family friend. There were no restraints in the choice of a mate, except the extended incest taboo, although family reputation was important. The future wife was expected to work hard. In return, the future husband was to support, respect, and protect her and the family of residence.

Up to the 1960s, successful negotiations for an important marriage might be capped by gifts to the bride's relatives, particularly if the suitor was a chief. The union, even a church marriage, was formally sanctioned by two separate ceremonial exchanges between the affined (the in-laws) over a period of a year and a half or more. Typically, at least in recent times, after the couple has lived together for a trial period of six months, the groom's family initiates the first "wedding trade." In return, after another six months has passed, the bride's relatives reciprocate with the final trade which completes the marriage.

The two occasions differ only in the type of food served at the accompanying feast. A woman in her sixties said, *"Fish, meat, and related foods are usually served at the first trade, the men's sphere. Roots, berries, and such are represented at the second, the women's, trade. Before each occasion, ten women are chosen by and from each side to conduct the trade. They kneel in two facing lines, with their goods on the floor in front of them. A leader of the host line commences, handing a first gift to the opposite guest. The guest reciprocates, and so on."*

These presents are bestowed, and the term "trade" here connotes reciprocity, with none of the narrower sense of commerce. In addition, the couple does not benefit directly from the exchange of goods. They receive nothing, although the gifts dictated by tradition for each side include items which might suggest otherwise. For example, the groom's relatives give regalia suitable for a bride, men's clothing, luggage, pots and pans, silverware, and dishes.

"Wedding trade is done from the man's side," began an eighty-two-year-old woman. *"The man's family and relatives go to the lady. They trade shawls, blankets, and materials, and mortars, that kind. From the lady's side, they give them roots like this [shown in Fig. 3.6] and bags, baskets, wampum, beaded dress, buckskin dress,*

3.6. Wedding trade. The women's family traded dried roots in root bags and dried berries in berry baskets. Alalimteeyik, grandmother of Mr. Moses Thomas. Courtesy, Rev. H. L. Sugden, Lapwai, Idaho, c. 1900.

or other kind of dress. The trading time period would differ; it depended on the family. Some waited for awhile, then they had trade. They had to get ready from both sides. From the man's side they got to get ready and buy shawls and stuff. Then they had to trade them."

A woman in her eighties said, "*The woman's side always furnishes the bags with the roots, camas, cous, or bitterroot, and the material, beads, and things like that; and the man's side would come in with the rawhide parfleche with the dry meat in it, or shawls and blankets and stuff, and the women trade.*"

Said an eighty-two-year-old elderly interviewee, "*Men didn't have anything to do with it. One old lady told me that they traded before the white men came, and what she said was that the bride party has to come along. They always sent a message ahead, and it was a young boy on a horse, and he blew a whistle [eagle bone]. He blew it and the man's side and the other side would [both] say, 'Askaya too Askaya too,' ('They are coming, they are coming'), and they'd be ready. They had dinner all laid out and everything. The dinner included meat, wild games, fish, roots, bitterroot, and dishes made out of roots.*

"*Wedding trade—the man's side went to the woman's side to trade; they brought with them blankets, shawls, and buckskin Indian suitcases. Then, they traded out the woman's side. There were root bags, maybe some dishes, whatever they had, then served dinner.*

"*They call it 'bride's bundle,' and I guess, a long time ago, they tied it up to buckskin or something. But now they use modern-type suitcases. Otherwise, it was a bundle form. You can have everything in it the woman would wear, and that was the bride's bundle. And you always have to reciprocate with that by giving extra shawls and blankets . . . The women started trading not only here [on the Nez Perce reservation] but in Pendle-*

ton, Yakima, and Washington. Everybody was trading.

"*They came in, sat down. You put down your shawl and your material. They'd take it, replace it with beaded bags or corn husk bags or something. If they want to tease you a while they throw a dress or something to you, while you have to peel off and put on this old dress. I got in, and I lost my coat and my dress, but I got a buckskin dress in return; it was pretty. Anyway, I thought it was real interesting because all the different members of the tribes were there. The women were all into this. They were real enthusiastic about it, who got married.*

"*Now we are going to trade, and what we are going to do, and pretty soon I got cheated. She didn't give me enough. I gave two bags, the roots, and I didn't get a shawl. You know, they started gambling, and I watched it, and I thought: 'This is going to be interesting.' Anyway, it [the practice] died out. But I was thinking this kind of gambling [wedding trade] might have come later on. In comparison with what was before that, they did because they wanted to give.*

"*The concept of giving is quite . . . . from an Indian point of view, is very different. In Indian culture, you got more honor by giving than by taking, and no matter who comes: give, you always give. We don't have that kind of custom [values] anymore.*"

One woman in her sixties told about giving and Indian family values: "*Indians were a really close-knit family. Everybody helped each other then. I can remember when living by the river, we never went anyplace or traveled that much, but we were in the area where people would come from Kamiah or Ahsahka or Craigmont or someplace. They would be coming by our place, and our place was in the convenient place, a stopping place, so that the older people that were coming through, sometimes they would stop overnight with us, or sometimes they would stop and visit for a while, and stop for other reasons. . . . I can* remember, summertime somebody would come, and Mom would say, 'Go out there and pick some cherries for them. Get some cantaloupes, tomatoes,'—or whatever we had—and we would give it to them. Giving was a strong part of our culture. That's the old ways. That's something I think we have lost. Our people are not given any more to help other people."

When young Nez Perce women became adults—for most girls this was when they first married—they became responsible for a very wide range of duties. While husband and wife gave each other mutual respect, emotional support, and sexual relations, it was, of course, the woman's role to bear and nurse children. This was done while continuing to be the primary forager of roots and berries, the daily carrier of firewood and water, the cook and cleaner, the crafter of utensils and clothes, and the maintainer of the living place for the entire extended family. Nez Perce women were the primary child rearers and makers of handwork, and, though mostly invisible, they were responsible for holding together the social fabric of the extended family. When the men were away hunting or on war parties for an indefinite period of time, the women were responsible for all subsistence and social activities.

When the couple lived with the groom's parents, the mother-in-law and daughter-in-law did not always have a good relationship. In extended families, the mother-in-law's sisters were considered mothers-in-law, too.

Two women describe their mothers' experiences working and living in their husbands' extended family's household: "But in her [the speaker's mother's] life as a new bride in my father's family, her mother-in-law was very good to her and kind, but her aunt (mother-in-law's sister) was rather mean and was always berating her and checking her cooking; and if she scorched something, she threw the whole pan out. And she was always saying, 'Well, how come she doesn't know how to do this, and how come she doesn't know how to do that?' And my grandmother would say 'Well, she was raised an orphan, you know; you can't really expect anybody to teach her, you know,' and so they did. My great-aunts and my grandmother taught her many things like how to tan hides and how to make buckskins and how to make moccasins and how to dig roots and how to take care of things, like. So she learned how to weave in corn husk and do all those things, and she taught me."

The second woman said, "Her mother-in-law didn't like her [the speaker's mother]. They gave her a rough time. She had really a rough time. She lost her first baby. Later, my older sister was born, and all together we were . . . thirteen . . . [and] she lost eleven. They all died. We didn't have government doctors as we have now in the clinic today.

"Her mother-in-law didn't like her. They gave her a rough time. She had to cook for the whole family. We kids used to go to school. We didn't have running water, so we brought . . . water to the house, then took some to the barn for the horse. We try to carry water by buckets and cook. Mother worked very hard. When my father had a big farm, he hired many people. Then, my mother had to cook for all these hired people, too."

Rape was a very rare thing before Western culture started intermixing with the Nez Perce culture and interfering with indigenous traditions. But there were instances of rape, and the Nez Perce punishment for this deed was very severe. An elderly Nez Perce woman, age eighty-six, was told by her father that the man who committed rape was tied to the whipping pole by his hands and legs and whipped by the whip man. A similar statement was made by a Nez Perce man in his early sixties. Another type of punishment for rape was exile from the group or band.

3.7. Nez Perce cemetery, Kamiah Presbyterian Church, Kamiah, Idaho. View of the cemetery in back of the church. University of Idaho Library, Historical Photograph Collection 5-16-3c. Photographer D. E. Warren, c. 1900.

One woman who is in her early sixties explained that, as young girls, they were told, *"Always go with someone"* when gathering roots or berry picking. If they went alone, *"men might come along and throw their clothes over their heads and rape them."* They were admonished to be alert around men, because men were *"just nasty."*

An eighty-year-old woman said, *"There was a terrible incident that happened to two sisters [early in the century], terrible! Two sisters got raped, and after they raped them, they killed them. The persons who did that never got any punishment, really sad."*

"Rape was unheard of in the old days . . . because young girls were always protected by their mothers and grandmothers. If there was a rape, that person was ostracized," related a sixty-year-old woman.

Traditional Nez Perce refer to separation, *peweeyuin*, rather than divorce. Separation was discouraged because of the strong social ties that developed between the families. Women were free to leave their husbands and go live with their parents only if the husband could not afford them or treated them poorly. Both spouses were free to remarry once the separation was accepted as final within the community.

Children always accompanied their mothers in cases of separation. Primary responsibility for the children would thus go to the mother and her family. In general, there was an interdependence between men and women that encouraged divorced or widowed women to remarry. When divorce and marriage cases were handled by state law, Nez Perce women lost their traditional freedom to separate.

Said an elderly woman, eighty-six years old: *"They never heard of divorce you know. As time went on, they began to divorce. During the First World War and the Second World War, there was a difference. They did a lot of changes from one war to another. After World War II, things changed."*

According to an interviewee, age seventy-nine, *"Divorce was not there; separation was there. The children went with the mother, mostly. The grandparents helped to take care of them after that.*

"All the belongings went with the wife. A woman always had her cooking utensils, mortar, and pestles, and her digging stick that she used—if she had a knife or knives and things like that. Her bedding, tipi, and all that she made, it belonged to her. The man always got his horses (when the horses came)."

"Whatever they had, they kept it, you know, to do with it as they wanted to," an elderly woman, age eighty-three, said. *"Basically, the women had their own choices of who they wanted to marry, even though the men thought they had this way, the influence. It was the women who, if they decided they didn't like the man, they could, you know, divorce him just by putting his things out, his moccasins outside, and he would just have to go someplace else. The women, if they didn't like him, she could just take her baby and put him in a board and put him on the saddle horn and take off. They were that independent."*

Said one eighty-year-old interviewee, *"Now, at the time of divorce, you have to go to court, but, at that time, there was no court. So we called divorce just a separation (pcweeyuin). I don't think there were too much property to be considered [at] that time. The court decides nowadays. Before that, there was no court or any system of this kind, so the man just walked out with what he had. That's about it. And the tipi belonged to the woman. I am sure it would have to. The children went with the mother. The wife went with the children to her parents' place."*

An eighty-six-year-old woman said that widows were aided by the whole family: *"Once a* woman became a widow, she was taken care of because they all began to support her. Like the men would give whatever they brought, meat for the family. They'd always give her some, help her the way they could. So I think the widowhood in the Indian tribe was good. Everybody helped her whatever she had to do. They looked after her food supply and whatever she couldn't get."

"Both sexes depended on each other for survival. Women depended on men for meat and fish, and men depended on women for roots, berries, and clothing. Therefore, it was necessary for widows to remarry; men also, because women could not survive only on roots and berries in the olden days," said one eighty-six-year-old interviewee.

The grandmother of a fifty-nine-year-old interviewee told her that "widows were the ones who, when they did remarry, sometimes they would have their eye on a certain guy, and they would go to the medicine woman and ask her to make palkth, and it's a medicine, a love medicine."

Death

Burial traditions were described by an eighty-six-year-old woman: "They used to wrap the body in a buckskin and a tule mat. They kept the belongings and gave them to the friends and relatives. If a female died, her clothes, corn husk bags, beaded bags, pestles, digging stick, wampum, and dentalium shells were given to her relatives and friends."

In the past, it was the custom to have burial services only in the religion which one observed in one's lifetime. Today, when a person dies, they can request more than one religion to handle burial services. Traditional burial ceremonies were elaborate, and the Nez Perce people used rock-chamber burial grounds on east-facing slopes before the arrival of Christianity. After the adoption of Christian beliefs, many tribal people preferred the Christian form of burial. Some of the informants mentioned that men and women both cut their hair in the mourning period, and when the hair would grow down to the shoulder (about one year), they were able to remarry.

An elderly woman, age eighty-four, said, "After the funeral they serve luncheon. A lot of people don't live here; they come from long ways. That is a chance for them to see other people before they go back to their hometown. A lot of them are working in different places, and they come for the funeral. A long time ago they used to give a dinner immediately following the burial. In those days it was hard to get around with horses. Those days they used to put [up] teepees for these breakfasts, luncheons, and dinners. That was kind of a part of their religion to feed the people. In the beginning the whites could not understand this. But I have gone to a white woman's funeral; she used to work here at the school. I went to Lewiston, and they did the same, they gave us a luncheon. Indians always gave a memorial for people. . . ."

One interviewee, age eighty-four, gave the following description of burial traditions: "Memorials were performed . . . to honor deceased persons. They ate first, the dinner, and afterwards they distributed what they wanted to give away. Just like we have done up here [on the Nez Perce reservation], that was like an old custom. Then, they would have a memorial. . . . and the things they left behind, whatever the [deceased] husband had given, it was given away [by the wife and the husband's family]. After a year they can remarry again or find another person to live with."

An elderly woman, age eighty, said, "Black clothing for mourning came with the Western or Euro-American culture. We didn't have the black *color . . . so in the mourning period, they would stay away from all the celebrations for a year. Stay at home, I guess that's how they observed that mourning period—about a year. When black color came, after a year, they had to change the clothing from black color to brighter colors. I don't believe the Nez Perce cut their hair in that mourning period; it may be Euro-American culture or came from a different tribe. I don't think they did. Women collect their hair after combing in a pouch; don't throw it away. They bury it, or when they die it went with them."*

FOUR ▲▲▲▲▲▲▲▲▲▲▲▲▲▲▲▲▲▲▲▲▲▲▲▲▲▲▲▲▲▲▲

Travel and Trade

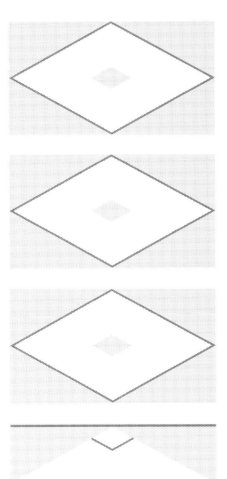

Introduction of Horses

In aboriginal times, the Nez Perce conducted their seasonal round on foot or by dugout canoe, covering great distances to harvest roots and berries, to hunt, fish, trade, and socialize. They used pack dogs to transport their goods. Starting in the 1730s, the acquisition of horses revolutionized their way of life, bringing new ease and productivity to their basic tasks and a valuable currency for prestige and trade (Haines 1938, 435; Ray 1939, 14). The lifestyle and role of Nez Perce women was permanently altered.

An eighty-two-year-old woman described travel by foot as told to her by her grandmother: *"My father's grandmother, she came from Rocky Canyon when they used to go to the buffalo country. The trail was worn so deep that it [the sides] came to her knees. The dogs were in front of her and the dogs were behind her. That is the way they protected their young girls. They stayed in the buffalo country for a year or two. Pack dogs were used. It must have been before the horses. They must have packed the dogs. They never mentioned horses."*

The most significant effect of the horse was to raise the standard of living considerably. Wealth itself began to be measured in terms of numbers of horses or size of herds, although the Nez Perce were not motivated by profit in the Euro-American sense. Horses served women in their daily

95

4.1. Mrs. Pa-ka-la-pykt, identified as "Old Joshua's wife carrying wood." Women soon adopted horses to carry out daily tasks, such as the packing of firewood. Idaho State Historical Society 63-221-121. Jane Gay Collection, c. 1890.

4.2. Women with horse and travois used for carrying children and old people and hauling wood and heavy loads. Idaho State Historical Society 3793-6, c. 1915.

activities, carrying them back and forth to the root-digging grounds and berry-picking places. The whole family moved to the camas grounds each summer, the pack horses carrying mats, robes, hides, and tools. Many loads of dried camas came back on the return trip. The most dramatic change was increased access to buffalo. The horses enabled whole families to travel to distant hunting grounds, taking extra mounts to transport the meat. Women dried the meat so that larger quantities were easier to transport.

The Nez Perce developed special gear, such as horse packs, and techniques for transporting goods over mountainous and timbered terrain. The women used trade blankets under and on the saddle to make travel more comfortable for both horse and rider. They employed the travois with horses on suitable open ground to haul firewood, to carry loads, and to safely, more easily move children and the old or sick. A travois could be made from tipi poles in emergencies, such as carrying the wounded and dead in the 1877 War.

An elderly woman, age ninety-seven, said, *"I used to see my mother, when my dad would be gone, you know, to the woods. And my mother would take the horse down and get wood, you know, and load it on the horse, bring it home."*

"And when we had horses," said an eighty-four-year-old woman, *"and when we'd be going up to the mountains, we used to use horses, wagon, take the food up with wagon, and we'd be riding saddle horses all the way up, us older ones that knew how to ride. And then we'd just follow the wagon with Dad and Mom leading in the wagon. And there was no roads up in the mountains to go huckleberrying, like it is now. Now, we've got roads all over, logging roads and all that. Now you can get up there with a four-wheel drive or a car to go huckleberrying. A long time ago, we used to just . . . get so far with the wagon,*

leave our wagon there, and then all ride the horses and pack up our stuff on the pack horses, and then we'd go up in the hills. That used to be a lot of fun."

A few days each year, horses carried women to the camas meadows and home again with their harvest. Women also rode horses to Lolo Pass to collect fibers such as bear grass for their hats and other types of grass for their bags. When mounted women traveled, their dogs always accompanied them, even just into the woods to collect firewood, for the Nez Perce recognized the importance of dogs' special sense of smell. The dogs, which were never eaten, could detect an enemy, or any predatory animal, and warn their owner. Dogs were still used occasionally for transporting small packs.

Women had plain rawhide saddle skirts but beaded rawhide saddle blankets. Horn drinking cups, awl cases, and other essentials were hung by thongs from the womens' high-horn saddle. Many women were skilled in raising and handling horses, and the possession of horses brought great respect to them, just as it did to men.

According to an interviewee, age eighty-six, *"Women work on the top of that horn; they sew gloves and other things. This shows that women occupied their time very wisely."*

A Nez Perce woman in her early forties said, *"My grandmother was an excellent horse rider. She raised her own horses. . . . I heard this story about [her from] a man who said, 'Oh, that's your grandmother,' and he told my older sister a story about how, when they were kids, they were playing with her horses out past her house in a field. They were trying to ride it, and it didn't have a saddle or anything. My grandmother even at that time was an older lady. She was probably in her sixties or so, and she was tiny. She was real small. And she came running out and cursing them out in Indian and telling them to keep away from her horses and don't even bother them any-*

4.3. Saddle made by Penahwenonmi (Helping Another) while a fugitive in Montana during the War of 1877. She used this saddle on her return to Idaho from Sitting Bull's camp in Canada. Collected by L. V. McWhorter, July 1926, from the maker's daughter, Mrs. Susie White. Washington State University Libraries 82-033, Historical Photograph Collection, McWhorter Collection.

4.4. Women's saddle, decorated for a parade. Annie Montieth, aunt of Rachel Frank. The women began to make decorative items such as saddle blankets, horse collars, and martingales for their horses, expressing their particular esteem for the vital role of the horse in Nez Perce life. This photo shows a horn cup being tied to the saddle. Idaho State Historical Society 63-221-128, Jane Gay Collection, c. 1890.

4.5. When traveling great distances, women loaded all their belongings onto the horses. Occasionally, the cradleboard with baby included was hung from the saddle horn to provide a natural rocking motion while the family traveled, familiarizing the child with horses from infancy. National Park Service, Nez Perce National Historical Park Collection, c. 1910.

4.6. Jeanette Wilson (E-we-tahnt-my), great-granddaughter of Tiskoup, who was a sister of Rabbit Skin Leggings. Idaho State Historical Society 686, c. 1902.

more. *He said she grabbed the mane of the horse, and she leaped onto the horse and rode it as fast as she could back up to the house and tied it to the pole in front of the house, still swearing and telling them to stay away from her property. He was just shocked because she was so old, and we were just amazed that this little old lady came running out, jumped on the horse's bare back, without a saddle, and rode it up to the house as fast as she could."*

A Nez Perce woman in her early seventies said, *"Women who were widows had a horse. . . . They commanded a lot of property and a great deal of respect because of it. They were head of their own household, and they managed fairly well . . . Many women became widows because of wars they . . . survived. . . . Many of them were elderly ladies who controlled their allotted land and whatever they had.*

"My mother owned Penney Ranch," said a woman in her eighties. *"She always had owned eight or ten head of horses. She was a very independent woman. . . . [I]t doesn't seem like we ever wanted for anything, even when just mother and I were living up there."*

An elderly woman, age eighty-two, reminisced, *"I remember when they had Lewiston Roundup. I can remember Lottie Spencer. She was sixteen years old. They had Indian women's race. Oh boy! She could run. She won bareback. She had a whip in her hand, she was whipping her horse, and she won it."*

Railroads

Railroads were introduced to the Northwest by the 1880s, and Spalding, Idaho, became a railroad boomtown. The Nez Perce began to travel more frequently to areas off the reservation. Women enjoyed riding the trains and did so to attend boarding schools or to visit relatives and family.

Trade

The individual accumulation of material goods was not valued in traditional Nez Perce society. Instead, wealth was shared within the tribe. Before the white man appeared, Nez Perce trade was not for profit; it was largely the exchange of essentials for survival, closely dependent on cooperation and sharing with other tribes. Nez Perce women would bring dried roots such as camas, kouse, bitterroot, wild carrot, berries, meat, fish, and medicine roots like kouse-kouse. They would exchange hides, hide clothing, gloves, moccasins, cornhusk bags, elk teeth for ornaments, earth paints, and Indian hemp. Women also traded for goods like hard baskets, cedar root, dried buffalo meat, seashells (dentalium and abalone), salmon oil, and parfleche bags. In later times, beaded and more decorative items were traded.

When the fur trade came (1780-1840), women obtained items like trade blankets, shawls, trade cloth, cotton cloth, colored beads, trinkets, brass pieces, needles, thread, and ribbon. Through trade, the Nez Perce women spread widely their handwork of flat wallets of Indian hemp, and, later, cornhusk root bags, basketry, and parfleches. After white settlement, the Nez Perce began to trade food, clothing, and garden products to the newcomers, precipitating communication and friendship.

"My grandmother traded a lot of roots," said an eighty-year-old Nez Perce woman. *"She used to dig a lot, dried them, baked them, and traded them—dried salmon and berries, too."*

"All the food we had was dried. Five or six fires were in the center of the longhouse. We dried food inside the longhouse or tipi. [After drying] [w]e hung them in hides or bags. We did not sell them—there was no money—but exchanged for things," said an elderly woman, age eighty-six.

4.7. Women on horses. Left, unidentified; center, Mrs. Johnson Hoyt, sister of Jeanette Wilson; right, E-we-tahnt-my. Idaho State Historical Society 694, c. 1902.

4.8. Nez Perce Indian women in a parade. Note they are carrying European-style parasols; canvas tipis are seen in the background. Idaho State Historical Society 659, c. 1920.

4.9. Railroad station, Lapwai, Idaho. National Park Service, Nez Perce National Historical Park Collection 396, c. 1909.

4.10. Girls traveling to boarding school, waiting for a train at the railroad station. Courtesy, Richard Storch, c. 1912.

4.11. Whites trading with Indians around the tents above the road. In the foreground is a burial ground where people are attending a funeral. University of Idaho, Alfred W. Bowers Laboratory of Anthropology, c. 1900.

Another interviewee, age eighty-two, stated that "[c]amas-digging season was a time when many tribes and bands would come together to trade, gamble, race horses, and look for matches; and that's how intermarrying with other tribes became possible."

"Grandmothers and other women went to dig edible roots. They stayed maybe two or three weeks and dug the roots. They would dry them. By the time they went home on horseback—pack horses—they had quite a few roots for their winter supply, and they also used them for . . . trading with other people," a seventy-nine-year-old Nez Perce woman said.

"They got bitterroot in trade from the Yakima Indians," according to an eighty-two-year-old interviewee. "They traded dry salmon. In order to save it, they had to dry it. The women went to Celilo Falls. That's where they made dry, finely pounded salmon, called ton-nut. Not many women do it any more. Women did trade the food items."

Nez Perce women also traded with the Chinese miners who mined along the Snake River. Agnes Moses, who was born in 1868, the daughter of Tolo, spoke of the Chinese miners in an article in the Lewiston Morning Tribune of January 17, 1960. She said that when she was a child, "[w]e loved to watch the Chinese miners as they worked along the river and talked to each other. We were often invited to eat with them. Their Chinese New Year was a big celebration with a big feast of roasted pigs with the snouts pointing eastward. We would often play games and pretend that we were Chinese, too!"

Many traditional as well as modern trade items such as quilts, shawls, beaded items, pots and pans, and fabric are donated today for church

4.12. Indian women trading with white women in Burgdorf, Idaho. Courtesy, Richard Storch, c. 1909.

4.13. Three Indian women on horseback with a white woman in Burgdorf, Idaho. Courtesy: Richard Storch, c. 1909.

sales, bazaars, and the funding of root feasts, dances, and memorials.

Said an eighty-year-old Nez Perce woman, *"My great-great-grandma and grandfather would all go up to White Bird, and we had a lot of cattle right there, and then we had a lot of horses to travel with, pack horses. We'd take a wagon. We had a wagon. We'd go up there with it, up to White Bird, and then clear up to New Meadows. We'd travel up there, and then we had a camp up at New Meadows.*

"My grandmother used to make buckskin gloves and always trade them in for a hide for her to make some more gloves that white people used to [use] up there. And they'd go and trade all that, and then grandmother would tan all of the hides right there where we camped. . . . She'd tan it and smoke it, and then make gloves. That's where I learned a lot of my trade for things, that Indians used to do."

"I think it [trade] formed in the early times," said a woman in her early seventies. *"The women used to make gloves. I used to see my mother and aunts, and some of them grandaunts and grandmothers, they made moccasins, and they made gloves, and they used this as an exchange . . . for their food staples. I mean, it made them very independent. They were able to do what they wanted to do because they had a talent of their own. And I know there was a town toward Grangeville called Fenn, and a gentleman (white man) lived there. A lot of the elderly women took their work up there, and a gentleman bought them all the time. He was one of the traders. There used to be buying places in town, in Lewiston, that also bought Indian gloves and moccasins for sale, too."*

A forty-seven-year-old woman said, *"The memory I have with my grandmother is that she, all winter long, would bead, and she would cornhusk. We had wood stove, and there was quite a*

few of them there. She never made me feel I was an outsider. I remember seeing her cornhusk or beadwork. She had a rocking chair where she would sit, and she'd do her work all the fall and winter. And, by the time summer came, she would take all her traditional crafts she had made then. She headed down to Arizona, and she traded for comparables."

A seventy-year-old woman spoke of the value of trade to Nez Perce women, *"And it was a form of cash for those women, and it made them responsible persons. I mean, they were somebody that you had to contend with, because they did have their own money, and they weren't dependent on anyone."*

Social Activities

Aboriginally, the Nez Perce traveled to distant places by walking or canoeing. The whole family would travel great distances to hunt, fish, trade, and socialize. Many bands of the Nez Perce and other tribes met at the Celilo Falls fishing grounds on the Columbia River near what is now The Dalles, Oregon. This provided opportunities to socialize, exchange news, and arrange social and economic pacts essential to tribal cooperation and enterprise.

With the advent of horses, the Nez Perce traveled longer distances and did more trading. Trade with other tribes was not only an economic activity but it was social, too, and included gambling, dances, and conducting and participating in ceremonies such as powwows and root feasts.

A forty-seven-year-old woman said, *"My mother raised horses. She used them for hunting. She trapped beavers and sold the pelts to make money for her school clothes. She used to trap beavers over in the Pendleton area. They lived up Squaw Creek and near Umatilla River. That was the common thing that the Indians did. My*

4.14. Dogs often accompanied Indians on trips such as canoeing from Spotted Eagle's place to Pete Nicodemus' (present-day bridge crossing into Kooskia). Left to right, unidentified woman, Jeanette Jackson looking through her mother's bag, Maggie Jackson, and son Enoch Jackson. Idaho State Historical Society 3793.12, c. 1900.

mother never mentioned any other game, just beavers. The Indians had access to whoever was a trader, and they could take it to him. There was a trading store at Pendleton—Grave's Trading Store maybe. That was the really old standing store where they took the pelts. That might have been the place where she took them. She also used a twenty-two and hunted. She lost her mother and her father taught her how to hunt. She used to go out and hunt small game, so she picked up a lot of traits from her father."

The stick game was an indigenous form of gambling common among the Plateau tribes in which both women and men participated (Anastasio 1955, 62). It was a contest of spirit power as well as a guessing game of much skill, often involving high stakes that might include dressed hides, blankets, clothing, bags, baskets, and beaded items.

Success in gambling was believed to be dependent on the individual's supernatural power (Mandelbaum 1938, 186-92), thought to help one hide and guess well. In the 1920s, the stick game was abolished by Idaho state laws. Today, it is still played on reservations in the surrounding states.

Songs were part of the stick game. Like riddles that had to be solved, these songs were sung by one party for the other party to guess. Occasionally songs were extemporized on the spot.

In the old days, Nez Perce women did not participate in the war dance, even the slow war dance. They did perform the circle dance, however, in which the dancers, both elderly and young women, moved sideways in a circle. Women as well as men performed the owl dance also. The drum beat sets the pace for the tribal dances; when the drums stop, the dancers stop.

4.15. Gambling at a Nez Perce Tribal powwow. Idaho State Historical Society 1875-L, c. 1905.

4.16. Stick game. University of Idaho, Alfred W. Bowers Laboratory of Anthropology, c. 1940.

4.17. Listening to gramophone music. Traditional social activities were altered by the introduction of Western material culture. Courtesy, Richard Storch, c. 1909.

"I went to the war dance when I was about, maybe, twenty-three years old," said one elderly woman, now age eighty-four. "One evening . . . I dressed up. I used Aunt Lily's dress that had roses on it. She let me use that. So, I went up to the war dance with Lily Linsley and Sherilyn Reynolds, my aunt, but those days they never used to call it powwow . . . it was war dance, and I went up there and watched. The ladies were never dancing; it was just men only. The only thing we did was circle dance and some other little dances they had."

An eighty-year-old woman reminisced: "This circle dance is for anybody to go out there and dance. That's about the only time they have where the ladies and the men go out. A long time ago, there used to be just men war dancing. Nowadays, you see ladies and children, everybody war dancing. That's how they break their feathers, you know, because of the kids or others. They always said that they broke their feather or something like that, and blame the kids for running against them. They used to have just men in the war dance, would-be men and the boys dancing. Ladies used to only dance like the owl dance, circle dance, rabbit dance, . . . just the three of them there. . . . I know that's all they used to dance."

"There are a lot of dances that we don't do anymore," said one eighty-year-old woman. "They used to call it eel dance. They'd all get in between one another like that [eel motion] and just go around like that, and that was the eel dance. And that's the way they used to have that other dance, only they'd go around in a circle . . . hanging on to one another's hips and dance, all going round and round. It used to be a lot of fun. I used to always end up on the tail end, with people swinging them around, you know, when they go around like that. I used to have a lot a fun when I was little. And there's other dances."

A whip woman, age eighty, who inherited the position, said, "I was going to say about being a whip woman, you know, when the circle dance used to start, I used to watch my grandmother. She was one of the whip women. She'd be there, and as soon as they'd say, 'Well, it's circle dance,' she'd get up, and she'd go around . . . , you know, going around, having that whip to go like that, just touch them like that [softly], and if they don't listen to you, the third time you just go and switch them. That is supposed to make them get out there and not sit there and watch. After all, they got the Indian costume on, they're supposed to be dancing out there, instead of sitting around. That's why I feel so funny going around now. I can't go run out there and dance or do anything else.

"Us older people ought to teach the kids not to do this and that, so I got up there, and I told the kids, 'You girls, all the girls, . . . when they quit drumming, you're supposed to stand still and wait for the second drum to go on. Then, you can dance.' And they'd twist themselves around, kick one another, or push one another around. That ain't the way it's supposed to be. You're supposed to stand still, it's a religious part, instead of to go in there and play.

"I watched this little tiny girl: her grandma or ma would grab her by the dress, 'Sit down, behave yourself,' or the same thing, too, 'Better go to the restroom, you know, then you wouldn't have to run in and out in front of people.' That's the way they used to tell me or a bunch of us kids, that's a long time ago. And then nowadays, first thing they get here, they come to the restroom, and when they're in there, they run in and out, find some excuse to run in and out. That ain't the way it's supposed to be."

The tradition of whip woman and whip man originated years ago when war dances were held in villages and when the semi-nomadic bands of Nez Perce moved camp. The whip women and men kept order. There are two ways to become a whip woman. This honored position can either be

4.18. Dance, Lapwai, Idaho. Samuel Jackson, in hat, was the head drummer. Courtesy, *The Spokesman Review/ Spokane Chronicle*, c. 1955.

4.19. Powwow. From left, Susie Penney, Darryl Broncheau, and Ellen Wood. A Nez Perce dance in the mid-twentieth-century. Courtesy, Mary Norie Banks, Moscow, Idaho, c. 1960.

passed down from parent to child or be earned by election. In the latter case, when the whip woman retires she will pass her whip on to a young woman of her own choosing.

On the dance floor, the whip man closely monitors the male dancers and male children, and the whip woman is responsible for the females. Both the whip woman and whip man have to signal the start of the dance, knowing from the sound of the drums when it is time to begin. They supervise the children especially closely, teaching them to respect this and other aspects of their culture. Similarly, before the turn of the century, the whip man and whip woman traveled through communities and disciplined the children at their parents' request. The fear and respect which the children felt for the whip man and whip woman encouraged good behavior.

But in this century, the authority of the whip woman and man is confined to the powwow dance floor. Their responsibilities include making sure that traditions are closely followed. If an eagle feather is dropped on the floor, no one but a veteran of war or a whip man can handle it, and it is returned only after a giveaway by the owner. If this is impossible, the whip man and whip woman will provide the payment.

During the owl dance, which is a woman's choice dance, a man may not refuse to dance. If he makes this mistake, the whip woman will impose a fine. She is also in charge of the circle dance, making sure that the proper male/female order is followed. These are only a few of the duties of these very important persons.

The eighty-year-old whip woman also said, *"If you're going to pick a guy to dance with you and he refuses you . . . two, three times you try to get him to dance . . . you have that reported to me or to the guy that's announcer on the announcing stand. You go and tell him, 'That guy didn't even go out and dance with me. He refused.' Then they*

have to charge him five dollars, ten dollars, whatever they want. They have to make him pay a fine.

"That's the way it was all the time. And I brought this whip; that's why they were giving me it, 'Why don't you go check on them?' You know, but you can't go out there and chase them into the war dance. What if they're just having a contest? You can't have everybody in that, you know, mixed up in the contest. That's the way it used to be, but now everything has changed . . . the money. It's money crazy nowadays. They have to be paid in order to do something.

"I've been the, what do you call it, floor manager, for the powwows here for I don't know how many years now. . . . I've seen a lot of things go on. See, my grandmother was a whip woman, too, before anybody else. Then, they put me in that position because my grandmother's relations were supposed to be, you know, taking over all the time. . . .

"Nowadays, everything is so different. . . . I never used to see them that way. . . . I don't know if I believe in it the way they do it now or the way I used to see it. . . . Like nowadays they have to pay the drummers, they have to pay the war dancers, and everything else.

"And I went and caught heck from one lady that I remember. Since I am a whip woman, she comes over and tells me, 'You're supposed to be telling them that, you're supposed to be doing all that.' You can't go out there and disturb the contest. Nowadays, that's all they do is have a contest; just once in a great while they'll say, 'Well.' . . .

"And that is, you know, the difference between nowadays and the old days. Then, they maintained order on the floor and they maintained order off the floor, and they had the responsibility of all the dances, to protect the dance floor. But now everybody war dances. If I stand in one place and dance like the old people did, they look at me real strange. And of course, they bounce around too

4.20. Chloe Halfmoon Calfrobe and Roy White dancing in "ladies' choice." University of Idaho Library, Historical Photograph Collection 6-24-2e. Photographer, D. E. Warren, c. 1963.

4.21. Nez Perce from Lapwai, Washington State University music program. From left, Jeannie Compo, Mike Harrison, Julia Davis, and Marcus Arthur. Courtesy, *The Spokesman Review/Spokane Chronicle*, c. 1960.

much, they're making, you know, all the dances just a little too pan-Indian, in the respect that they're all trying to copy each other and not do their own traditional dances. And the whip woman should know the difference between all the dances, whether they're from the Plains, or if they're Plateau, or from the Basin, or from the Southwest, you know, or Southeast, to know the difference between all these dances, so that she can inform the judges as to what these differences are. But they don't do those things nowadays."

Another whip woman, now in her eighties, said, "I think the dances have . . . changed a lot. Years ago, the dances were war dances; today they're powwows. Years ago, they weren't as elaborate as they are today. I mean, today there are beautiful feathers, beautiful outfits, and hours and hours of work went into them. . . . A variety of materials go into everything that they do these days. Fast dancing is the modern version; traditional dances were very slow."

Today, Christian Indians still hesitate to participate in the powwow. Said a Christian woman in her late sixties: "I go sometimes to watch. But we weren't raised in it, and it just hasn't been something that I've . . . been a part of. There are two sets of Nez Perce. . . . [W]e were brought up in the church, you know, in the Christian way of living. And a long time ago . . . when we had the missionaries come . . . they told our Indians that it was heathenistic, you know, heathens, to be that way, so they kind of more or less . . . made them choose one or the other. And that's the way we were brought up in the church. So I just never was brought up in it, so I just never have been interested in it. My little girl, when she was little, she used to love to dance a lot, so I was going to . . . start her out or let her do whatever . . . if she wanted to. I wasn't going to hold her back from it. . . . I got her outfits and let her go out and dance when she was just tiny. My hus-

band, when he was alive, he took pictures of her. She really loved it, but after she got to be, oh, nineteen years old, then she just all of a sudden quit. I didn't tell her yes or no or anything, I just let her choose whatever she wanted . . . and she just quit dancing; I don't know what made her quit."

A part of the ancient war dance was the farewell song of the warriors. On the night before a mission, the men paused before each lodge, singing and beating time on a buffalo-rawhide blanket. The farewell song had many different verses. Women followed behind and joined in the chorus (Spinden 1908, 265).

One interviewee, age eighty-four and a member of the Wallowa band, said of the serenade described by Spinden, "Ki-neem-aama *is the name of the song. They would sing when they went from one tipi to another tipi. They used to go around the tipis. They used to drum [on a hide] and sing. They would go from one tipi to another, clear around. The song they used to sing most of the time. Men did that, and a lot of the time ladies joined them. They had to stand behind the men."*

The *Kihl-lo-wow-ya* serenade was also a farewell to warriors preparing to raid a rival group. This circular dance was performed with the singers in the center, the women behind the men and all singing together. Women presented gifts to the warriors. According to Slickpoo, these gifts were highly prized (1973, 23). Some interviewees said that examples of such gifts would be moccasins and dried foods.

The Nez Perce traditionally had annual encampment gatherings honoring roots, fish, and fruits. These gatherings are now called powwows and root feasts and are held at the tribal community activity center, *Pi-nee-waus,* in Lapwai, Idaho. At the time of this writing, root feasts and powwows were being organized in Kamiah, also. People travel long distances to these celebrations, which are a time for sharing food and shelter, visiting and exchanging information, reestablishing kinship ties, and making new friends.

Powwow celebrations take place when roots are harvested or when the salmon arrive from the sea and include feasts, dances, and rodeos. A typical powwow begins on Thursday at noon with the arrival of guests. Tents and tipis are erected. Activity picks up on Friday afternoon with the visiting of friends and relatives. Saturday night marks the time for exhibition and competitive war dancing, the competition not being completed until Sunday afternoon.

Root feasts occur on Sunday at noon. The Nez Perce women spend the morning cooking the food and preparing the dining area. A ceremony in which the participants face east and move rhythmically and sing songs starts the event. Swaying motions of the right hand, sometimes holding a feather across the breast, also accompany the songs. A series of bell ringings ends the songs and signals the beginning of the meal. Several aboriginal foods along with American fare are served, and a small drink of water is ritually taken at the beginning and end of the meal. Speechmaking by local dignitaries and visitors is common. The largest of these powwows, the Four Nations Powwow, occurs in the fall (mid-to late October). Tribes from all over the U.S. and Canada are invited.

A young, single mother of two children said, *"I see that our traditions are getting strong again. I see a lot of families that I never used to see at celebration. I see their kids are participating in the powwows, celebrations, and dinners—kids helping out with dinners. Especially [helping out] with our elderly people; there are certainly more . . . elders [needing help]. I have never seen so many women come together that make a dinner. That's always my favorite."*

FIVE ▲▲▲

Women in History

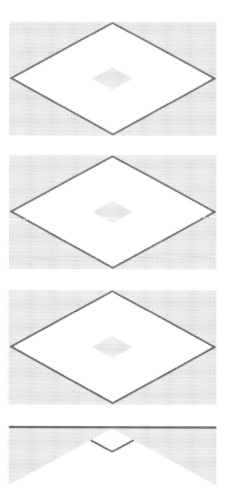

Women's Involvement in Council

THERE HAS BEEN little documentation of the role of women in tribal government matters because in Nez Perce culture women were not publicly involved in political decision making, although a woman's attendance at council meetings was important. Tribal decisions were taken by consensus, not majority rule, and unanimity was wisely considered essential to insure the active cooperation of the whole village, band, or tribe. Women were always in the background, however, supporting men.

Women gave feedback to men in many ways. For instance, although Chief Joseph had the respect of his followers, he did not always have the final say in his own household, judging by this remark attributed to him: "When you can get the last word with an echo you may have the last word with your wife." (Howard 1969, 83). And at councils, women voted by their presence; if they did not support the decision, they left. Evidently, Nez Perce women always participated in this way in historical and political events. Prior to 1877, and later in the village councils, women were thus indirectly involved in decision making.

An elderly Nez Perce woman, eighty years old, explained, *"Women were involved side-by-side with men in all walks of their lives. In the Nez Perce culture, indirect involvement of women or*

119

5.1. Tribal council around 1900. James McConville, on horse. Standing, John Moses, on left; Clayton Dixon, fourth from left; Alex Williams' father, fifth from left. Thunder Eyes, on right; all others unidentified. Idaho State Historical Society 77-60-31. Courtesy, Stephen D. Shawley, c. 1900.

their presence with men was sufficient to influence political discussions."

A woman in her late eighties said, *"Women were not chiefs, but, in a way, they did have leadership and power: leadership among women. There were women that the position may be like teachings that they gave about survival and other things. Maybe that spirit they gave, and they were kind of looked to as counselors. These women were from chieftain families as well as from the common families. It was quite an accomplishment; they could be someone."*

In traditional society, the aged were given tremendous respect. It was assumed that they spoke from a great wealth of knowledge gained by experience, and, in fact, age may have overridden gender in the evaluation of counsel. Certainly, as women grew older, they were even more highly regarded by men, by other women, and by the tribe as a whole.

Women and War

When the warriors returned to their villages after a battle, the wives and mothers of those who had been killed or who had participated with great valor were venerated in a special ceremony. One manifestation of this honor was the privilege of wearing a war bonnet in the ceremony. (This information was offered independently by two eighty-five-year-old women.) A tremendous distinction for women who were thus honored, this ceremonial recognition must have given significant emotional and psychological support to the families of warriors.

Family stories of battle were recollected by an eighty-two-year-old interviewee: *"A lot of them had been in the battle, or they showed any kind of bravery like my great-grandmother. . . . [W]hen they had this big battle of the Thousand Springs, and his [great-grandfather's] horse was playing*

5.2. Mrs. Moise, a member of the Flathead Tribe. A few women could wear men's war bonnets during special recognition ceremonies relating to war honors. The same ceremony was performed by the Nez Perce. National Park Service, Nez Perce National Historical Park Collection 2463, c. 1900.

5.3. Nontreaty Indians, prior to the War of 1877, who would not live on the reservation but held on to their traditional life. From left, 1. unidentified, 2. Istipi Takmallim—Shell (with hat on), 3. Wilakaikt, 4. Tainsas—Briar, 5. Tainsas' daughter, 6. Shéewiai—Without Paint, 7. Waílakanit—Sunshine, 8. Itsayáiya Ilpilp—Red Coyote, 9. Red Coyote's daughter, 10. Wátass Tsitslainin—Broken Earth, 11. Timpusmin, 12. Ishamaya. Idaho State Historical Society 2715, c. 1870.

out [exhausted] because they fought, she went through the battle line and took him an extra horse and took the other horse out, so that night, well, they gave her a feather. A feather was a symbol of honor. It was kind of an honor and an award for a deed of courage or bravery. It was mostly an eagle feather they used for a war bonnet or for fans. It was an honor; they generally used the feather plume.

"When their husband, father, or grandfather and a son took part in a war, and he did something brave and courageous—killed a lot of enemies—and he was killed in the war, they honored his family. That would be his mother and his wife that would accept the honor on that, generally, as I said, an eagle feather plume."

The impositions of the United States government, missionaries, and settlers left the Nez Perce uprooted from their land, while they were also suffering acculturation, loss of their language and religion, and loss of lives. As a result, the Nez Perce

5.4. Nontreaty Nez Perce Indians, with BIA employees. Washington State University, Historical Photograph Collections, c. 1877.

had no choice but to take a stand to recover their land and their tribal identity. In 1877, the Nez Perce Tribe fought the United States government to try to reclaim some of the Nez Perce territory lost in the treaties of 1855 and 1863 (see Fig. 1.3).

The Nez Perce war with the United States government was, indeed, devastating. The Nez Perce lost not only many lives, but much territory—their very subsistence base, the source of food, shelter, and clothing. These were great changes with few gains and many losses, and the Nez Perce were forced to learn a new way of life. At the time of the War of 1877, women and children accompanied the warriors. Women's survival skills were crucial when the tribe camped for any length of time for, as explained previously, they performed all the essential jobs, such as arranging the lodge, providing fresh horses in the field, cooking, and gathering wood, while the men were protecting them.

All the hardships, atrocities, and ragged conditions suffered by the warriors and chiefs were felt as severely by the women of the tribe. Generally, history has remained silent about the effects of war on women. This particular war is no different. Although tribal women were a forceful part of the war, their experiences have not been given importance by historians.

In the battle of Big Hole, Pe-nah-we-non-mi describes how she and others were attacked: *"The only time we put up teepees was the place where buffalo calves used to be found. We camped on the prairie by the river. The next day we digged camas and baked it in the ground. That is the old Indian way of cooking it. To be good, camas must remain in the hot earth overnight. It was still in the pits the next morning when the soldiers charged our camp. We were sleeping when they came. Many women who had camas were killed. Their camas was left where they had baked it when we had to leave. Lost grub, and some*

5.5. Ayatootonmi and Jasper, the wife and younger son of Yellow Wolf, a warrior in the War of 1877. Washington State University Libraries 82-056, Historical Photograph Collection, c. 1908.

teepees. We escaped almost naked" (McWhorter Papers 1926).

Mounted women assisted by warning others of danger. Some women, after their husbands were shot, took a gun and shot the enemy. They told children and old people where to hide or how to leave the place of attack quickly. Women stayed back, facing death. In this way, they saved many but sacrificed their own lives. They brought fresh horses, food, and water to the men on the battle field, caring for the wounded ones with ingenuity in the absence of stretchers or medical supplies.

During combat, women cooked and fed the children, the old, and the warriors. Believing their men to be involved in a war to protect them and their land from the United States government, they did their job without complaint, displaying a keen sense of responsibility and independence of judgment in every challenging situation. They did not need the counsel of men to understand their crucial role.

Children who were part of the War of 1877 remembered it vividly in adulthood and told stories about it to their families to insure that history would not be forgotten. Some of those women's stories, as recorded by L. V. McWhorter in *Yellow Wolf: His Own Story* (1983), give us insight into their thinking and the character of their participation.

Chief PeoPeo Tholekt, a warrior of the Chief Looking Glass band before the War of 1877 and afterward a member of the Wallawa band, says of this woman: "The wife of Peter Pliater, with her baby wrapped to her back, tried to escape across the Clearwater north of the village. . . . The strong current drew her horse under and all drowned. Her body was found near Kamiah. The baby was never recovered" (McWhorter 1952, 269). This was the first woman and child killed as a direct result of the war. Many more died in later battles.

A story of this same event was told by Martha Morris of Clear Creek to her son, Gene Ellenwood, who recorded it on June 1, 1966: *"We were at the site on the Clearwater above Clear Creek . . . [H]ere is that place where the woman and the baby swam across. She was one of the members [of the Looking Glass band] who lived under the white flag, and yet the soldiers gave them a surprise attack. This is where she swam across, just about to the other side, when the soldiers shot at her."* Here, Gene's mother corrected him, and he changed his story as follows: *"On that, where I said a woman got shot crossing the river, . . . that's the way I hear it in my time. But then she, [his mother, Martha Morris] said the woman got drowned with the baby, and later on they found the woman without the baby, so I'll have to take that off [the] record."*

PeoPeo Tholekt described to McWhorter the story of the 1877 attack on the Looking Glass band's camp at Clear Creek near present day Kooskia. PeoPeo Tholekt had been shot in the right leg and was trying to control his horse as he fled from the soldiers. He picked up a man on foot. "As we continued on the one horse, trying to escape from the cavalry, we saw a woman riding toward us. I do not know what she intended, but believe she was ready to fight the soldiers. She had around her shoulders a hide of wolf. We met and she attended to my wound, wrapping it up. Her name was Etemiere (Arrowhead). She was a brave woman" (McWhorter 1952, 269).

One interviewee, age eighty, heard a story about the War of 1877. She said: *"My husband's grandmother had a half-sister by the name of Eunice. She was Salish. She said at the Big Hole*

125

battle she hid herself among the tall grasses grow-ing in the river along the banks. She watched the soldiers kill everyone: men, women, old people, and children. They didn't care who they took, they just mowed them down."

A seventy-eight-year-old woman described an event as told to her by the late Sam Watters: *"People were going over Lolo Pass, and this woman had a little baby. It kept on crying, and men told her, 'You know that the soldiers are right behind us; they will know just where we are. If you let this baby cry, they will catch us. They are not very far away from us. We don't want the soldiers to know where we are.' The little baby kept crying, and, finally, the men told her, 'You better kill that baby,' and they came to agree. She had to throw it against the tree and kill that little baby to keep it from crying. This woman saved many lives while sacrificing her one and only child. It was hard on the mother, but she did it for the sake of others. This happened when they were heading for Montana running away from the U.S. Army in 1877.*"

Outstanding Nez Perce warrior, Yellow Wolf, gives this account of his mother's resourcefulness and bravery:

My mother was with them. She was with Look-ing Glass' family when soldiers attacked his village. His tipi was burned, but my mother escaped with the others. She remembered to save my rifle, took it apart and hid it in her pack from being seen by whites. I was glad to see my rifle. My parents had bought it for me with one good horse. I now had my own sixteen-shot rifle for the rest of the war.

My mother could use the gun against sol-diers if they bothered her. She could ride any wild horse and shoot straight. She could shoot the buffalo, and was not afraid of the grizzly bear (McWhorter 1983, 77-78).

Yellow Wolf also narrates the story of a woman called Ah-tims in "The Last Battle." In the midst of battle, some warriors were fighting from a lo-cation with little cover, and they began to run out of bullets.

Ah-tims was a fine-looking girl of about eight-een snows. From her shelter-pit, she saw and understood. Ah-tims had a strong Power: a Power to protect her in dangerous undertak-ings. She told the people of her Power, and said: 'I will go bring the cartridges!' The distance was about four hundred steps. Ah-tims ran, but not swiftly. Shots came about her, but she was not hit. Gathering up the cartridges, she ran for the rifle pit. Bullets struck about her, throwing up snow and dirt. She reached the rifle pit in safety. Her Power had protected her. Bullet holes were in her clothing, in her red shawl. But she had no wounds. The warriors now had ammuni-tion for their rifles. They were no longer use-less. Everybody recognized Ah-tims as a brave woman, and so respected her" (McWhorter Papers 1926).

We-ya-yo-yikt (Martha Minthorn), daughter of Chief Looking Glass, was with Chief Joseph's band on its historic retreat in 1877. She remained with the band during the summer of 1877 when the battles at Cottonwood, Whitebird, Mount Idaho, and Kamiah were fought and was with the band as it fought its way through the Bitterroots and along the Lolo Trail to Bear's Paw Mountain in Montana, only a few miles from the Canadian border. On this mountain, her father was killed in the final battle, and Chief Joseph surrendered on October 5, 1877.

On the night of the surrender, Mrs. Minthorn joined Chief White Bird and forty other Nez Perce

5.6. Yiyik Wasmwah, Geese-Lighting (from flight), Yellow Wolf's mother and sister of Chief Joseph. This photo was taken after her exile in Indian territory. Washington State University Libraries, Historical Photograph Collection, McWhorter Collection, c. 1905.

5.7. Martha Minthorn (We-ya-yo-yikt), at age ninety-three, the daughter of Chief Looking Glass. She was born at Sweetwater, near Lapwai, on November 20, 1856, and witnessed the surrender of Chief Joseph in the War of 1877. She remembered vividly the gruesome scenes of war, the casualties, and the valiant fighting of the outnumbered Nez Perce people. Courtesy, *Lewiston Morning Tribune*, Feb. 9, 1949.

5.8. Penahwenonmi (Helping Another), wife of Wounded Head, at Spalding, Idaho, in 1928. Women always covered their legs with a blanket when sitting; also notice that the traditional hat is replaced by a bandanna. Washington State University Libraries 91-142, Historical Photograph Collection, McWhorter Collection.

men, women, and children who stole away from the encampment and headed toward Canada, crossing the border under the protection of the British government. After living in Canada for nine years in the special reserve set aside for the Nez Perce fugitives, she returned to reside in Sweetwater, on the Nez Perce Reservation in Idaho. She died on February 9, 1949 at the age of ninety-three.

In *Yellow Wolf: His Own Story*, L. V. Mc-Whorter gives many accounts of women's suffering and heroism during the battle of Big Hole. Penahwenonmi (Helping Another), wife of Husis'owyeen (Wounded Head), related how the wife of Wahlitits died in the Big Hole Battle. Her husband, who was beside her, was shot and fell. She grabbed his gun and shot and killed the soldier, then tried to flee as several other soldiers fired at her. She died on the spot. She was in an advanced stage of pregnancy at the time (McWhorter 1983, 136) and was the only woman known to have killed a soldier. She is still revered.

Penahwenonmi spoke of her own experience during the battle:

I hid under some willow brush, lying like this [flat on side]. A little girl lay close, my arm over her. Bullets cut twigs down on us like rain. The little girl was killed. Killed under my arm . . . many little children were killed. Out in the open, a baby lay on its dead mother's breast, crying. [The baby] was swinging one arm shattered by a bullet. The hand, all bloody, hanging by a string of flesh and skin, dropped back and forth with the moving arm.

I saw two women lying in a small tepee, dead. Both had been shot there in their blankets. A newborn baby was in its mother's arms. The baby's head had been crushed. (McWhorter 1983, 136-37)

5.9. Wetatonmi, wife of Ollokot. Subsequent to Ollokot's death, his widow remarried, becoming Mrs. Susie McConville. She is shown with a child from her second marriage on her lap. Wetatonmi was almost blind from trachoma, and she died in May of 1934. Washington State University Libraries 82-051, Historical Photograph Collection, McWhorter Collection, c. 1879.

Wetatonmi, the wife of Ollokot, gave a description of the Big Hole battle as she saw it: "Some wounded died on the trail and were buried. Two women died of wounds. We had travois for worst wounded, but no stretchers. I do not know how many suns we traveled when we had to leave one old man who could go no farther" (McWhorter 1983, 137-38).

Chief White Bird, the younger, was ten years old at the Big Hole battle. He described bullets hitting the tipi, and then

[m]y mother jumped up. She caught my hand, pulling me from the blankets. She took me out the doorway with her. My mother said to me, 'Go that way! Get away as fast as you can!'

I did as my mother told me. Horses hitched overnight, ready to go . . . were all killed. I ran only a little ways and saw a low place in the ground. I stopped and lay down. Several women were there, and my mother came fast after me. I heard the voice of a man speaking very loud. He came where we were lying and called, 'Soldiers are right on us! They are now in our camp! Get away somewhere or you will be killed or captured!'

My mother picked me up, saying, 'Come, son, let us run from here.' She took my right hand in her left and we ran. A bullet took off her middle finger and tip of her thumb, and my thumb, as you see. The same bullet did it all. My mother pointed to the creek and said, 'Get down to the water. There we may escape away!'

I started. She told me to go up the creek to some bushes to get out into the stream. I noticed one woman digging in the bank where she could hide (Chief White Bird's sister).

One soldier was shooting at everybody. We reached the bushes and my mother sat down, her head only above water. I stood up, the water almost to my shoulders. While there was a little brush, we could be seen. Five of us were there, and two more came, all women and children.

One little girl was shot through the underpart of her upper arm. She held her arm up from the cold water, it hurt so. I could see through that bullet hole. It was not full day when we ran to the creek. But it grew light as the sun came up. . . .

The woman I saw digging in the bank was shot in the left breast. She pitched in the water, and I saw her struggling. She floated by us, and my mother caught her and drew her to her side. She placed the dying woman's head on a gravel bar just out of the water. She was soon dead—a fine-looking woman, and I remember the blood coloring the water.

Some soldiers leveled their guns at us. My mother threw up her hand and called, 'Only woman! Only woman!' as she jerked me entirely under water. An officer spoke to the soldier, who let down their guns and went away. (McWhorter 1983, 139-40)

Kowtoliks (Charley Kowtoliks) was fifteen years old at the time of the Big Hole battle. When he heard the firing of guns, he ran out from his tipi: "[A]n old woman, Patsikonmi, came out from the tipi and did the same thing—bent down on knees and hands. She was to my left and was shot in the breast. I heard the bullet strike. She said to me, 'You better not stay here. Be going, I'm shot.' Then she died" (McWhorter 1983, 144).

An elderly women in her seventies narrated this story: "*I come from Whitebird Lum-ta-ma [band], from Whitebird. At the time of [the] war, I was told, . . . there was an old lady sitting in her tipi, and they [United States soldiers] were taking the young boys, whether they were killing them or what they were doing to them. This little boy (he*

5.10. White Feather, In-who-lise, a Nez Perce woman seventeen or eighteen years old. She was badly wounded by soldiers in 1877 in the battle of Big Hole. She later married Andrew Garcia, a white pioneer, and died at the hands of the Blackfeet in the summer of 1879. Washington State University Libraries 82-068, Historical Photograph Collection, McWhorter Collection, c. 1878.

5.11. Tolo (Alab-lernot) rode from Slate Creek to the Florence mining camp to get help during Indian trouble on the Salmon River in 1877. Idaho State Historical Society 61-102-1, c. 1890.

5.12. Elizabeth Wilson, Lillian Moses, and Agnes Moses, daughter of Tolo. Courtesy, *Lewiston Morning Tribune*, c. 1960.

Lewis and Clark party, and the Nez Perce would shoot them.

"Wet-khoo-weis was . . . kind of elderly at that time when Lewis and Clark came. She was laying in her tent. It was summer time and the tent [sides] folded up for a cool wind to come in. They came running there and said, 'These people have come. We have never seen these people before. There is a black man with them, black face, and there is an Indian woman with them.' She said, 'Don't kill them because they are the same kind of people who helped me.' She had to help these people [with whom she had lived]. They called them 'So-yap-po.' That's not a Nez Perce word; it pertains to their hats, so she called them So-yap-po, 'the crowned ones.' She told these people, 'Don't kill them; they are not going to hurt you; they are your friends. They will give you gifts." And they did give them gifts. They gave them bars of soap. The Nez Perce did not know what the soap was, so they thought it was to eat. They took a bite, and the taste was weird.

"A woman like Wet-khoo-weis helped and saved the whole crew of Lewis and Clark because she did not forget white people's kindness. She was the one who built the bridge of friendship between the whites and the Nez Perce. She was the binding force behind Lewis and Clark's successful expedition in this area."

This famous episode has been interpreted along these lines by the missionary, Kate C. McBeth (1908, 25-26), and the historian, Francis Haines (1955, 26-27), as well as the Nez Perce historian Allen Slickpoo. Slickpoo goes on to suggest that the threat to the explorers originated from the sense of vulnerability of a small number of men left behind to protect camas gatherers after a large war party had moved on. "The question, even today, has been asked, 'Would the Lewis and Clark Expedition have survived the meeting of the Nez Perces, if they had met the whole band,

rather than a handful of warriors?'" (Slickpoo 1973, 68).

A woman in her seventies related the story of Tolo: *"When the Mexicans came up there from the south, they [the Nez Perce] used to show them how to play card games and gambling. Tolo apparently used to gamble. She gambled her shawls and everything (by that time we had shawls). Suddenly, she became a different person. She got a vision, and she became a member of ?ipnú·cililpt an Indian religion. As soon as she became a member of it, she quit all her gambling. The spirit told her not to do wrong things. Then, she helped her white friends when the war [of 1877] started. She got on a stallion and went way up towards Florence [26 miles] [and] warned them that the war has started: 'The whites and Indians are at war, and they are shooting at each other. You better get out of the way'. When she got to their camps, the horse fell dead because she was going so fast. She became kind of a heroine, and she has a big tombstone on her grave. They gave her a big remembrance because that was her way, and she wanted to say to these people that they were her friends. Tolo kept her loyalty with her [white] friends by saving their lives."*

Tolo was an excellent poker player. Her friends called her Tulekals Chikchamit (Placing Money on Betting Cards). Her name was shortened to Tule, and then to Tolo by the whites (McWhorter 1983, 52). After the war, Tolo worked for the Ben Large family as she had previously worked for other white settlers, doing washing, housework, and nursing the sick.

Her later years were spent near Winona with Chief Yellow Bull and his wife. Tolo died there in 1898. She is buried at Red Rock, near Winona, close to the scene of her historic ride. A monument erected by the American Legion in the Winona cemetery marks her grave. The whites named Tolo Lake to honor her courageous act. In

5.13. Toko-ma-po, an old woman carrying a bundle of firewood. Note the Hudson's Bay Company knife tied to her wrist. University of Oregon Library M4040, Moorehouse Collection, c. 1910.

5.14. Mrs. Lilly (Pittsteen) Lindsley. Courtesy, *Lewiston Morning Tribune*, July 1965.

5.15. The last survivor of the War of 1877, I-o-tu-ton-my, stands beside her grand-daughter, Hazel Jane Agapitt, who holds a pestle which was traditionally passed down from mother to daughter. She is wearing a traditional buckskin dress inherited from her mother (*Seattle Post Intelligencer*, May 15, 1950). Courtesy, MONAC Museum, Spokane, Washington.

5.16. Hattie Enos and great-grandchildren on her ninetieth birthday. Hattie, who died May 28, 1977, at 103 years of age, had 16 grandchildren, 53 great-grand-children, and six great-great-grandchildren. University of Idaho Library, Historical Photograph Collection 6-24-1e. Photographer, D. E. Warren, 1964.

Allen Slickpoo's words, "For her deed her reward was small" (1973, 186).

Agnes Moses was Tolo's daughter, born at Weippe, according to the *Lewiston Morning Tribune* of January 17, 1960. She was nine years old when Tolo made her historic ride to Florence. Agnes Moses recalled: "My mother rode a black horse on this twenty-five-mile trip. The horse was so tired that it dropped dead after the long trip, and my mother never received the payment promised her by the white settlers." Regarding the causes of the war, Agnes believed, "The young warriors were the ones who wanted to cause trouble. Both the white and Nez Perce were at fault. There were good Indians and bad ones. There were good whites and bad ones."

The oldest member of the Nez Perce tribe, Chic-ma-po, or Toko-ma-po as the Indians called her, lived on the Colville Reservation near Nespelem, Washington, early in the century. An aunt of Chief Joseph, she had accompanied his band on its historic retreat in 1877 (her personal narrative is summarized by Gidley [1979, 83-91]). Mayor Lee Moorehouse of Pendleton visited the Colville Reservation and obtained the picture of her carrying a huge load of sticks to her tipi for her fire (Fig. 5.13). She lived to be a very old woman, but instead of being known as a survivor of the Nez Perce retreat and a participant in the battle of Big Hole, she was famous because a widely circulated and reproduced photograph showed her as an old woman with an enormous load of branches on her bowed back. It was simply titled *Stick Woman*.

An anecdote from her later years was described in the *Spokesman-Review* of April 16, 1905: "Several years ago when living on the Colville Reservation, Toko-ma-po mounted her cayuse and started for the Yakima Valley to pick hops. She was thrown and suffered a fracture of her left wrist.

Recovered somewhat from this accident, the following year, she again started for the hop fields and was again thrown from her horse and her right wrist fractured. Neither fracture entirely healed."

An article in the *Lewiston Morning Tribune* in July of 1965 told the story of Mrs. Lilly (Pittsteen) Lindsley, who was born in 1874 at Alpowa. She was three years old when she was taken on the long retreat of the Nez Perce War of 1877. Her father, E-luute-Pah-Awh-Yene, died in the conflict from a bullet wound in the stomach.

After the retreat ended in surrender in October 1877 on Bear's Paw Mountain in Montana, Mrs. Lindsley was taken as a prisoner of war to Oklahoma by the United States cavalry. She was held on the Ponca Reservation and completed her schooling there. From 1898 on, she lived in Nespelem, Washington, until she returned to Lapwai. There, she taught cornhusk weaving and beadwork to many of the participants in this study. She died of infirmities at the age of ninety-one.

An elderly woman, eighty-four, said, *"Lilly Lindsley was a beautiful bead worker and cornhusk worker. Some of the women got a lot of good beadwork and cornhusk work from her in a trade."*

I-o-tu-ton-my was the last survivor of the great retreat of Chief Joseph's band. As a child of seven or eight, she was among the women and children fired at in the battle of Big Hole.

Mrs. Hattie Enos, the daughter of Felix and Deborah Corbett, was born June 1, 1873, about five miles east of Kamiah on the Woodland grade. As reported in the *Lewiston Morning Tribune* of May 29, 1977, when the Nez Perce Indian War broke out in 1877, Mrs. Enos was four years old. She remembers hiding in a grain field and watching General O. O. Howard and his troops ride down Doty Ridge south of Kamiah toward the Clearwater River.

She traveled by steamboat from Lewiston to Portland at the age of seven to attend the Forest Grove Government School for Indians near that city. The school burned a few years later, and she was transferred to Chemawa School near Salem.

Her soprano voice attracted talent scouts while she was still a student, and she was offered a scholarship to study opera in Boston. She turned it down, however, because she feared leaving her family. Instead, she married Henry Enos and settled in the Kamiah area. Mrs. Enos lived with her daughter since 1966, and returned to the Clearwater Valley often, including a visit to the Talmaks encampment each summer. She went up in the Space Needle at the World's Fair in Seattle at the age of 90 and flew on an airplane for the first time at the age of 99. According to her daughter, she was delighted with these experiences. Mrs. Enos had never been hospitalized until her final illness. She died at the age of 103.

An eighty-two-year-old woman said, *"There are so many things, like the War of 1877, that people are finding out about each family, what they know. But a lot of people are thinking this way: they went through so much, why say anything about it now? That's the way a lot of people think."*

Religion

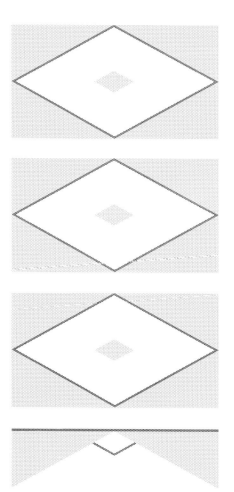

Native Religion

ALL NEZ PERCE CEREMONIES included a time to recognize the Creator and to express thankfulness for blessings that had been given. When an individual deserved special recognition, a ceremony would be held in honor of the occasion. These ceremonial activities included people of all ages. Ceremonies were performed for a woman after the delivery of a newborn, for children at the time of name giving (see p. 76), for a girl when she reached puberty, for a couple at the time of marriage (wedding trade [see p. 86-88]), and for the deceased (see p. 92). Special ceremonies were also performed for a boy at the time of his first game killing and for a girl at the time of her first root digging and berry picking. Singing and dancing were part of many ceremonial activities.

According to several interviewees, girls from the ages of nine to fourteen were sent to the mountains to seek their *wéyekin*, or supernatural spirit. Boys between the ages of five and ten years would seek their *wéyekin* in the same way ....er 1985, 18). Medicine men and women were helpful guides, providing advice and support. These young girls and boys spent six or seven days in lonely isolation without food or water. Only if they had received their *wéyekin* could they come home earlier. The child often left behind an object given earlier to prove that she or he had been there.

A vision, believed to become the child's guardian spirit, came as a dream or while the child was in a semidelirious state and gave the individual a song. The individual was then identified with the spirit and was thus reborn as a new being. The spirit might be an ancestor or other human being, an animal, a bird, an inanimate object, or a natural feature like the sun or moon, thunder, mountains, or light. (These accounts by the interviewees are in accord with Deward Walker's description of the wéyekin [1967, 70].)

"Wéyekin *is something you search for; you go to the mountains, fast for days, and pray until your power comes.* Wéyekin *spirit is like a medicine man and woman's spirit, [but] stronger than anything they had,"* explained one interviewee, a woman in her eighties.

A woman, age seventy, who grew up in a medicine woman's family, said, *"Songs were within the families. They were passed on from one generation to another. Sometimes your own songs came from your power. We believed that we had a special song and spirit and dance. It was individual. Sometimes it could be handed down from parent to parent, or from relative to relative. It just depends. Like, if my mom would sing a song, they would say, 'That's a very old song. That comes from so-and-so,' and a lot of that's been lost now because they don't remember."*

One interviewee, now deceased, who was in her early sixties at the time of the interview, said, *"I think other songs are just as important as some of the drumming songs that they do. They have medicine songs or holy songs that were part of the traditional Nez Perce old religion. They also have songs that honor water (Salmon River songs), the sun, animals, plants, and the earth. These things gave them life. They have healing songs, mourning songs, courtship songs, and stick game songs. Some of the songs sung in the coyote stories, some of the older people know them. But*

from my generation, I don't think they do know. I think now some of them sing it and don't know what they're singing. Someone has to be around to know what those things are for. Songs were owned by an individual in them days and also sold by an individual just like a name was owned and sold by an individual."

An eighty-year-old interviewee said, *"There was a religious ceremony involving medicine men and medicine women who were very successful and strong in their* wéyekin *spirit. They would participate in their* wéyik wecit, *or guardian spirit dance. These dances always took place in the winter season in the longhouses. These dances were arranged by the medicine people to honor their spirits. These dances were part of the traditional old religion of the Nez Perce. Gift giving was a part of this religious ceremony by the medicine people who host this ceremony. A feast would be given. In the evening, they dressed in their ceremonial, colorful, and decorated clothing. They would start dancing and they danced the whole night. During the dances, the medicine people would make symbols like a feather or fur and wave them. These symbols were related to their spirits. While dancing, they revealed their identified spirits, and they sang their sacred songs that had been given or taught by their* wéyekin *spirits.*

"Sometimes an individual would be recognized as more powerful than the rest of the medicine people. If there was one more powerful than that person, then while dancing, they would touch others. And, all of a sudden, [the person touched] would fall on the floor or go into a trance. Then, that most powerful would touch them and kind of make them straight. It was a sort of contest, maintaining supremacy over other medicine people. The most powerful person stands over them, and they called this 'wé·yes;' they called their power 'wé·yes.' Wé·yes meant . . . all these medicine people . . . must dance [and] sing their songs to

*strengthen themselves. Medicine women partici-
pated in these medicine dances, and some of the
medicine women were more powerful than medicine men."*

A woman in her sixties explained how the floor
was purified for the medicine dance: *"My aunt
and uncle were involved in medicine dances. My
uncle, Mr. Moore, was especially involved; then
my aunt got involved in it. She was kind of nowadays like a rookie [reiki?], new, the ones who had
to go through so many rituals to gain power. . . .
But one thing I can tell you, that them days the
only time that you knew that they were medicine
people was when you got out there, when you
went to the medicine dances. You would see all
these people standing in a line on the sides [of
the room]. The center floor was clear for either
the man or the medicine lady that was
head—in that he or she would be the main one to
clean [purify] that floor, nobody else, . . . so that
these medicine people could come in to get more
and more better power. Cleaning of the floor
means she stands and walks up and down that
floor. She didn't take no fan to clean the floor.
She just would sing and would go from one end
to another. These songs were very old and related
to their own powers. These songs were given to
them by their* wéyekin. *My aunt told me how she
got her* wéyekin *song. We used to have an old
spring below . . . Culdesac. My aunt was just a
young girl, and she would go down there. Her
grandmother would give her a little bucket to go
down there and get some water for her. She would
play down there. According to my aunt, one day
she ended up falling asleep, so her* wéyekin *was a
species of the water.*

*"When the main person would open the floor,
it was either a male or a female who would decide
to get up and would stand in front of her. They
would sing a slow song to build themselves back
up spiritually. This is the power that nobody can
ever describe. It is hard to describe. People nowadays think it is easy, but it is not."*

An eighty-two-year-old Nez Perce woman
spoke of the wéyekin *spirits of Ow-yeen, Chief
Lawyer's wife: "In 1868, Chief Lawyer went to
Washington, D.C., with two other Nez Perce Indians. The other two died on the way. Chief Lawyer
was coming home alone, and the word came
through the agency here to Monteith that he
would be returning, so his band from Kamiah
went to Wallula because that was as far as the
train came. There his band camped and waited
for the train. When he got out, they decided they
would have a big celebration. They had a big
medicine dance to welcome him. They said that
his wife [see Fig. 2.61] went, and she was glad to
see him. She did her medicine dance. Her medicine power was a grizzly bear. She held her hands
up just like they were paws, and she danced
around there. The grizzly bear was considered one
of the strongest powers of all the animals. She had
two guardian spirits: the grizzly bear and the
other, the wolf. She met and talked to the wolf at
one time, at Weippe, and the wolf gave her his
power. The grizzly bear and the wolf are both considered the strongest of all guardian spirits. That's
why Miss McBeth [a Presbyterian missionary]
was scared of her."*

A woman in her sixties said, *"I was a very
young child. At that time, we lived in Chiwikta,
tse-week-te. A medicine man's house used to be
across the creek from us. They were having a medicine dance that time there. I was sitting there listening and watching the old ladies. They would
get up and dance. These ladies were pretty heavy,
but they were very light on their feet. This one
time, this elderly lady was singing and her name
was Sustina. She was singing her song, and she
was going along, and all of a sudden she fell backward. To me, she hit the floor so hard, but it did
not even hurt her. What she was feeling was the*

spirit or the power. That's the way these dancers were, a lot of power in them. I couldn't get over that. I got a little bit afraid of the power that goes through them because you never know what they can do.

"At that time, there was a medicine man. He had power. I went up to Sweetwater [near Lapwai, Idaho], where his son lives right now. His mother used to have medicine dances. I can't remember her Indian name. She used to have medicine dances. I remember being up there. I must have been a teenager then. I can also remember them having dances here in Lapwai. I really enjoyed those dances.

"The older people who used to do those medicine dances, they all passed away. The younger people have not carried out these dances. For some reason, I don't know why. I guess we lost that power. Now, I don't know anybody that has that kind of power."

Medicine women, or *tiwe'ts*, acquired a special ability to heal by practicing their *wéyekin*. Medicine women and men were very powerful within the tribal bands because of their healing ability. According to a number of interviewees, a specific spirit was believed to give an individual woman the power to fulfill her needs, for example, to become a powerful medicine woman (female shaman) or to dig roots successfully. Medicine women were regarded as more powerful than men in areas of healing and curing certain illnesses.

Female shamans were thought to be more able than male shamans because of the potency of menstruation. They prophesied, led ceremonies like medicine dances, healed by removing disease-causing malevolent spirits, and interpreted dreams.

Said an elderly woman, eighty years old: "Indians had to worry . . . I mean, the women had to worry about health problems. When this was done, well, there were certain woman that had to

be a medicine woman. She would be there to help. Like if the woman was sick, well, this lady would come in, put their hand on this lady who was ill, and sing a song. But this woman that was supposed to be a medicine woman had to be really careful what, and how she spoke to people, how she treated people. She wasn't supposed to get angry at anyone. She had to keep her mind clean, keep her home clean, keep her family . . . with strict rules what to live by so that her children also knew that she was supposed to be that way. She kept herself clean, kind to people, willing to help when they needed help. It was kind of a hard life for her to live, but then she helped a lot of these people that became ill, and they would get well. She had to be generous. She had to be kind to people. She had to be able to share what she had, to show the younger generation what they should be like. And so many things they did, these people, that our generation and generations to come [would be all right] . . . I am sorry if we have to lose all of that."

One woman, now in her sixties, who grew up with her grandparents, said, "Medicine women and medicine men in those days were respected. They were held in esteem because some of them really did heal. So they just thought it was done by that power. I think they did. But today it is different. They pretend like they have power, but they did not have enough power because they used to go way up in the mountains and go up there and seek their power. This power they searched for, and it came to them. It taught them a lot, like what kinds of plants to use for medicine, what things to take so they won't poison anybody. They received it through their power, spirit, and their dreams."

"My grandmother was a medicine woman," said one interviewee, age sixty. "My mother used to have seizures—which today is diagnosed as epilepsy. [My grandmother] used to try and help her

6.1. Henry Spencer and Delia Lowry. According to an elderly woman, age eighty-two, "*She [Delia] was a very powerful medicine woman who was capable of handling rattlesnakes. She was also a very good coyote storyteller.*" This photograph was taken at Kooskia, Idaho. Idaho State Historical Society 77-60-22, c. 1910–15.

with her songs and medicines. She used to sing and put her hands over her head and over her body and sing these medicine songs. That was her way of trying to help her."

An eighty-year-old interviewee said, "*A man told me his grandmother had great powers. When people would get sick, or something happened to them, she would already know they were coming after her. She would say, 'So and so is coming to get me. I have to go with them to use my medicine.' That time, this man who told me was a little boy. He said that when they come, they get their horse ready and then bridle it, saddle it, and keep riding about with his grandmother. They watched her, whatever she did. Healing and whatever happened, she would be there to help, and he would*

be with her. He got to learn all the methods. . . . [A] lot of the medicine they got was from their power that they had. Sometimes it came to them at night, and then probably they had a vision of the plants, whatever was good to fit this and that. It sort of taught them."

"*She, my grandmother, I remember her as a medicine woman,*" an eighty-one-year-old interviewee reminisced. "*I heard stories about her from lots of people. I myself knew that people used to come to her house many times to get help. She told me one morning, 'Hurry up and eat. Finish getting cleaned up because people are coming.' How did she know this? She said, 'They stay here for a day or so and may eat.' Every day at a certain time, she made us go out of the house. We*

6.2. Standing, from left: Nellie Moody (Horace Axtell's mother), Mary Phinney (Archie Phinney's mother), Annie Moody. Sitting, Lydia Wilkinson (Horace Axtell's grand-aunt), a very strong medicine woman whose Indian name was Táklá Sunmy and whose maiden name was Maggie Williams. She is wearing the traditional pony-beaded skin dress. The other women are in different styles of decorated wing dresses. University of Idaho, Alfred W. Bowers Laboratory of Anthropology, Stephen D. Shawley Collection. Photographer, J. W. Webster, c. 1915.

didn't watch her or peep through the window; we just left. We relied on her."

Horace Axtell told this story about his grandmother:

Not long ago, maybe two years ago [1990], I was talking to a man over in the Pendleton area. It's called Mission, Oregon. I knew this man for quite a while. His name is Alex Johnson. When I was talking to him, he was telling me about his old house, and there they used to have medicine dances. Finally, I said my granddad . . . was Taklasha. He paused for a moment. He said that when he was twelve, thirteen years old, he became blind. They took him several different places. Finally, one day they took him to her [Horace Axtell's grandmother]. [Johnson said,] "She went around and around, and with her hand, she came back to my head. . . . Next morning, she started again, went to the top of my head and went down. She got to that spot, and she said, 'Get ready.' She started pushing from my back and pushed all the way to my feet and said, 'It's gone. I took it out of you.' That evening everybody went to bed, and I could feel the difference. Next morning, I woke up, and I could see."

She cured his eyes, that's the story he was telling. He said, "My eyes are still very good. I can see clearly." I did not know this about my grandmother, what he told me. He is still alive. He lives in Oregon. He is now ninety-five years old.

An eighty-year-old interviewee remembered, *"My great-great-grandma was . . . where I was born . . . with her around. I used to be very curious all the time. That's the way I know a lot of things. When I was little, up at Red Rock there . . . every time that I was just really curious, when I'd see her getting up, and then if she made [a] funny*

noise, then I'd run over to her bedside. And she always says 'Aahhh,' like that. She must have had a dream or something. Boy, I'd run right over there and sit by her. Well, nowadays, nobody can understand them that talk Indian. I used to. I'd sit right by her, and then she'd tell us what she was dreaming about.

"I know for one that she got up, and she says, 'They're going to be after me.' Then we asked her why. Then she says, 'Oh, there's a lady going to be here to see me today. She's going to come after me. There's a man pretty low at Kooskia there, and that lady's going to be here with her horseback. She's going to come up from Kooskia clear over to Red Rock.' And she said, 'If you don't believe me, you watch that gate.' She told me, you know, because I was the one that was curious. And I . . . just got up and put my shoes and things on, and I went out on the porch and sat there, and if the old lady was telling the truth, I'd tell myself, you know. And surely enough, she says, 'She's going to have a white horse, that lady. She's going to get off and open that gate, and she'll come through.' And that's why I was sitting outside, to see if she was telling the truth, you know. And sure enough, I seen the white horse, and the lady opened the gate. So I run in there and told grandma, 'There she comes. That's what you said she was going to have, a white horse . . .' Of course, in those days we talked Indian all the time.

"She got there, and then I was just curious what that lady was going to tell my great-great-grandma. And I'd sit there and listen because she told us . . . all the things that she was going to . . . promise [Grandma] to go doctor this man. And she just sat there and listened to her. . . . And sure enough, she had all that. And then great-great-grandma just kept sitting there. Then, that lady was real worried about the patient that she was coming after her for, you know. And then she said, that lady said, 'Well, you going to come down

147

with me?' 'Well, I'll wait just a little bit longer before I come down there.' And here this lady was pretty worried because he was pretty low.

"And here, that lady left; she said, 'Well, I think I better go, because I'm worried that something might happen to him.' So she left, and then we were sitting there. Then, Grandma started laughing. She said, 'I bet that lady . . . thought I was stubborn, you know. I won't go with her, and here my spirit is already watching that patient over there. He won't die.' She told us that. She already knew. She got ready and told Dad, 'Well, you can drive me down in the wagon.' You know, we had no car. And they had to what you call harness the horses up and fix the wagon up and told her, 'Well, I'll take you down.' So they went down, and they got there, and that man was already sitting up. Heck, he was alright. Her spirit was the one that worked on that guy. That's how powerful that she was. Anything that she'd tell us, that would happen.

"And then, she'd dream about the whole valley here, up towards Kamiah, up here in Lapwai, or getting pneumonia and really sick down this way. Then, she'd put paint over my face like that on each side . . . red. She'd put paint right here, and she'd tell me, 'You go outside to the porch and face the porch, like.' It was like this: we used to have a big porch out there. 'Then, stand out there for a while,' so I'd stand out there. And then I'd come back in, and she'd tell me, 'Well, that sickness is going to go around us. It won't come near to us.' And that's how she used to stop . . . whatever was happening other places. Anyway, that's how much I know of the Indian power."

It was believed that female shamans, like their male counterparts, could also send evil to others. However, the misuse or abuse of power for selfish or unethical goals could cause its weakening or loss. This power was given to them to heal people and not to do harm. While some medicine women used their power to harm people, others used their power to save people from bad medicine power.

An elderly interviewee in her eighties said, "Dad told me a story that happened in Kamiah. Sometime these medicine people are no good. This depends on their own thinking and heart. This one medicine woman—apparently sometimes they control you, but the spirit controls them. A lot of young boys began to die, and they wanted to know what was killing them. So this medicine man came there, and they were in a big tent in Kamiah. They met and he sang his songs, and then he went to this boy and worked under the boy's foot, and a woodworm came out. He held it in his hand, and he sat there. 'What shall I do with it, kill it? Shall I burn it or just throw it away?' They said, 'Burn it; this is what is killing them. It has been going on because of this one medicine woman. She is old now, but she is over there in another camp where they are digging and preparing to bake their camas. She is there.' One man said, 'Throw it in the fire.' The minute he threw it in the fire—she was sleeping on the edge where they were digging . . . they had a big fire going [to heat the rocks]—and the old lady jumped up and ran and ran and [committed] suicide in the fire. The minute the worm dropped in, she went in. So that's how she was killed.

"This medicine man knew about her because he said, 'She is over there in the camp where they are cooking camas, and they built their fire. It is burning up now. She ran and jumped in the fire.'

"I had a sister who died. She rubbed her eyes. And when she was doing that, the people around her usually asked, 'Who did this to you?' Sometimes they would tell the name. But this old lady used to live near the creek. She was part blind. Two ladies were living there. When we went to pump our water, we'd go and visit them. These two old ladies, one would ask if we could thread up the needle for her. We would thread up a bunch of needles for her. That way she could pull out needles. We took so much thread and broke it. Then, she would pull out another needle, and she had quite a few needles to thread them. She used them to sew. . . .

"She was a powerful medicine woman. This cousin of mine went [with her] to the mountain past Salt Creek. They went over the hill, and then she stopped. And they went down the hill quite a ways, and they found plants. She told her to help her pick the plants. It was for the medicine. You can use it as a love potion, and she sold it to people who buy from her so that they could use it to catch a man or to keep him. They can sense in their dreams. They picked certain plants. Then, she did not like that kids would run back and forth, and they have eyes to see, because she regretted that she was blind. My little, younger sister was running around when she was dying; she was rubbing her eyes. They said she [the medicine woman] must have got stirred and killed her because of her sister's vision. Because my sister died rubbing her eyes. They said because the lady was blind, she thought these kids were running around with eyes."

According to a woman in her late sixties, "They used medicine power on me, and my husbands were taken away from me. I was married four times." Her daughter said, "There was an Indian lady crazy about my father, and this lady knew a medicine woman who fixed her some kind of medicine. Rattlesnake. My mother would hang up her undergarments on the line after washing. This woman would come and put that on, and she would have sores. She did so her husband (my father) would not care for her no more."

The mother continued, "My father's grandmother, she used to bring wild roses, boiled them in water, and bathed me; she fixed me up. Every day in a sweat house, morning and evening, for two weeks straight. Then, after I got that, and

then she got some kind of medicine put over me. After I got well, my husband started coming back to me. She told me, 'Get even! Don't take him back!' That's why I never took him back."

Said one fifty-year-old interviewee: "My grandmother would come all the way from Montana, and she wanted her mom, our great-grandmother, to fix her a potion so she could take it back to get rid of her daughter-in-law."

Knowledge of medicinal plants has been handed down from one generation to another. Unfortunately, in the early days it was believed that the more you exposed the medicine, the more its power weakened, and so many medicine women died without passing on their knowledge. The present generations, more inclined toward modern medicine, have not taken an interest in learning of these plants and their medicinal value, and even those with an interest cannot collect plants in the traditional areas because these areas are now private property.

"My grandfather told me a story about my grandmother," said a woman in her forties, recalling her grandmother's medicine power. "When they were young, they had gone to go huckleberry picking, and they rode their horses there. They were surprised by a snow blizzard that came. It was in the middle of summer and was unexpected. Some man rode into their camp, and he was very, very sick through the stomach. My grandmother at that time went out and got these leaves that were growing in the mountain. Like they are kind of wild strawberries or raspberries, he said raspberry leaves. She took, she boiled, and she made tea out of it and gave it to him. That cured him, whatever was bothering him."

A sixty-year-old woman described some of the medicine of her childhood, "We have kouse-kouse, which is the medicinal root. You can use it either for sweating or use it as tea. My grandmother used to use cockleburr [Xanthium strumarium] *on me whenever I had a sore throat. I al-ways had a sore throat. She used to pound the leaves of the cockleburr and dampened it with warm water. Then, she would pack that on my neck and wrap that with a bandanna. I would keep that on over night or however long it took for my throat to get better. As I grew up, I have done that by myself after a while whenever my throat bothered me; I still do the same.*"

A woman nearly forty years old said, "*My father said that he knew medicine women and other medicine men that knew so much about the land and about the plants that they would have special kinds of medicines that they would put on them that would heal almost instantaneously. But they lost that. They don't have that any more. He'd tell stories like that where Indian people knew about medicines and about the plants and herbs and things that would help them be well. They've lost a lot of that.*"

Sweat house baths offered both physical and spiritual cleansing and strengthening through rigorous training which alternated heat with a cold bath. Women used the sweat house separately from and after the men. Women went there for purification after their menstrual period ended and before and after childbirth. Following the death of a family member, a sweat bath was essential for the spiritual cleansing and purification of either men or women after handling the body of the deceased.

Medicine women used the sweat lodge for meditation to seek their powers, singing their special songs. The meditations and sweating cleansed impure minds and gave wisdom. The extremes of hot and cold also disciplined children to endure mental and physical pain and hardship.

According to Guy Marden, some Plateau mythology relevant to sweat bathing directly involved female characters. The fact that these myths were related and/or recorded by women may have influenced their content. Although both grandparents were respected among Plateau peoples, mythologically, the grandmother's advice carried more weight than the grandfather's (Marden 1983, 24-25). In one Nez Perce myth, an older woman advised a young male to sweat bathe in order to resolve a problem (Clark 1966, 33-36).

A woman almost eighty years old said, "*The sweat house was both spiritual and physical. The old people used to believe in spirits; sometimes, they sang their medicine songs there, and then they cleaned themselves and their spirit, also. They did not want to be ugly. They wanted to be good people by their spirit. That's why they cleaned themselves inside and out. They always called it 'kheeln,' like an old man, and they called the sweat house 'kheeln' because they say they pray to him.*

"*Now, the sweat houses are just a common thing . . . it isn't a place like our people had, where they would talk to the spirit . . . they'd call it the old man. . . .*"

"*In the sweat house, they have a song,*" said an eighty-six-year-old woman. "*And [through] that song, they would request whatever they wished for, or whatever they wanted their health to be . . . to be in good health. And, after you came out of there, you had to use real cold water to rinse out all that sweat and all that dirt.*"

According to an eighty-eight-year-old interviewee, "*Sometimes they would have a party. They'd call it a sweat-bath party, be a group of women who would take turns crawling in there and taking a sweat bath. And it was something that we all looked forward to. Of course, they'd let us young ones go in after they came out, but they wouldn't let us put any water on the rocks because they told us we didn't know how. We kinda knew how, but then they still wouldn't let us because it took a certain woman [medicine woman] to sprinkle that water on the rocks that was in there. You*

*couldn't just go in and sprinkle any old way. You
had to be, I suppose, a leader [medicine woman]
of the group. And we miss that a lot."*

Christianity

Native Americans believed in the power of the
elements of nature, ancestors, spirits, animals,
and often a supreme power. In the aboriginal
culture, the natural and supernatural were thor-
oughly intertwined. The missionaries who came
to spread Christianity and bring religious change
found the soil prepared by their hosts who saw
supernatural forces everywhere. Euro-Americans,
on the other hand, often place religion in a separate compartment. Native Americans adopted
Christianity not only because they were com-
pelled to but because they heard something familiar. Christianity touched upon social and natural
elements they knew well.

An elderly woman, eighty-six, said, *"Well,
[now it is] Christianity. They had their belief in
their own Indian religion. But it was beautiful . . .
[O]ur grandmother used to talk to us. . . . Before
the sunrise, people were up, cleaned up their tipis
where they lived, or wherever they lived. They had
it all cleaned up. Everything was in place, even their
own personal appearance. They would have to be
clean and neatly dressed. Grandmother used to
say they'd have to comb their hair, wash up before
sunrise. I had to be up . . . we were naturally . . .
used to getting up early. It was a daily habit. . . .
Grandmother was a very strong religious person.
She taught us to thank the creator for everything.
For all the new food and before eating our meals,
she would give thanks to the creator. Before going
to bed she would give thanks to the creator."*

"According to Indian religion," said one
woman, almost eighty years old, *"they told us it
is not right to fish and hunt or do anything on
Sunday because old people believe in Indian relig-*
*ion and never took game on Sunday. Even before
Christianity came in, they had that* housipawal,
*in Indian language. But they had a day already.
They did have the knowledge. When grandparents
take their grandchildren and sing those old songs,
they say they were [talking] about the Bible. It
was before the white man came. So when the
white missionaries came and they called us pa-
gans, they didn't believe in their own religion.*

*"[My grandparents] never joined, so they be-
came a part of Indian religion apart from the
Christian church. But, if you think, a lot of the
teachings are like the scripture. They all taught
those things in their Indian religion.*

*"According to my husband, he had to worship
with his grandfather. He said that they'd go to this
longhouse, all come in. They were like Quakers:
they'd sit there awhile, a long time in silence.
They'd meditate, then all of a sudden one would
get up and speak and break the silence. It would
open the door, and others would get in. They'd ex-
pound what the teaching was in the Indian religion. Just sort of like preaching. My grandmother
used to say some of the things they have put into
their scripture.*

*"My grandmother's name was Piviyatnaha
Pavit. When she used to go to the river, a family,
they were from miles away, now living there. She
went over there. She had friends called the
Howards. She would go over the swing bridge, and
when they saw her they would say, 'Hello Sunday.
We . . . [get] to see you on Sunday,' because* pavit
*means Sunday in the Indian language. It was
there before the whites came."*

*A woman in her early sixties said, "In the old,
old religion, not the Seven Drum but the Tulian,
their concept of life . . . they prophesied. They had
prophesy songs that told of the coming of the white
man. They had prophesy songs that told of the
coming of one who would teach them how to live.
In his hand, he would hold a book, you know, and*

they prophesied that they had a heaven, and they had deities like angels, spirits, who watched over people. This is before the coming of white men, according to my father, you know. And even though the anthropologists say that this was after the coming of white men to the area, my dad says that this was long before that. The only way you could get into this heaven was by how good you lived, and by your good works, and this is why it was so readily acceptable for Nez Perce to accept the Judeo-Christian faith. They had the whole concept before. . . ."

Before the coming of traders, military forces, and the missionaries, the Nez Perce were wholly self-sufficient. From a time beyond memory, they had managed to feed, clothe, and shelter themselves; their family system (to some extent polygamous) worked well, providing for children, widows, the poor, and those at risk. It had ways of taking care of and respecting elders and of utilizing elders to help the children learn various skills, discipline, and their cultural heritage. Their society had a high level of handwork and ceremonies—helping individuals to find their inner spirit and self-esteem and supporting traditions which strengthened tribal social cohesion.

The intervention of Christian missionaries into Nez Perce culture caused deep turbulence and great and abiding changes. This was the initiation of their acculturation: learning to read and write, with access not just to the Bible but to a vast Euro-American literature translated into English. Formal schooling, Western medicine and hospitals, and the introduction of technologically advanced agriculture, sewing, and other mechanization soon followed. The Nez Perce suffered great losses at the hands of even the most well intentioned and able missionaries. The Christian missionaries who came were of strong commitment: they were authoritarian and rigid. They considered the entire lifestyle of the Nez Perce to be dangerously heathen and were willing to go to any length to remove these traditional beliefs and practices.

There is considerable controversy within the Nez Perce Nation regarding the impact of Christian missionaries. Some Nez Perce, especially among church members, think that the introduction of Christianity was the best thing that ever happened to the tribe. Other Nez Perce take the opposite view and see it as the worst thing that could have happened to their culture. Many stand somewhere in between.

The introduction of Christianity thus divided the Nez Perce Nation and destroyed the traditional unity within the tribal system. Missionaries brought conflict and created splits by their proselytizing. Converted Christians were regarded as civilized and progressive; non-Christian Nez Perce were thought heathen and uncivilized. The repercussions of this division continue on the reservation to this day.

An eighty-two-year-old elderly woman said, *"The understanding according to the old religion was given to us by our elderly people that, before the sun went down, you have to go and tell that lady, 'I am sorry I told you like that,' or 'I thought about you like that.' Nowadays, they come and tell you awful things, and they never say they are sorry. That's the difference now. They think they are right and they can go on."*

"As far as religion was concerned, she let us go to any religion that we wanted to," said a thirty-five-year-old single mother of two, whose own mother comes from the Lemhi tribe and her father from the Nez Perce. *"She became a Catholic because my dad was a Catholic, and there was a big missionary push at that time back when they were put into the reservation. The . . . big thing, all the Catholics came in and baptized and all of that. So a lot of the Native Americans were Catholic if they were anything at all, unless they prac-*

ticed . . . the religion on the reservation called the Seven Drums religion, where they do have their own language and their own ceremonies and their own thing."

Said an eighty-year-old woman, "My dad gave me an eagle feather [symbol of my wéyekin spirit]. He told me that when you become thirty years old, your song will come, and you will have power. I got saved when I was twenty-eight years old. I threw away my feather in a fire. Although I loved my dad, I said I have nothing to do with this power, spirit of the world, because the Holy Spirit is pure and holy. You can have them [eagle feathers] to kill and you can have them [for healing], but the Holy Spirit, it is over everything. It is a big blessing and a big help. It destroys the enemy power by your prayer. That's the way I believe, you know."

Nez Perce families who became Christian went on horseback from outlying allotment areas to attend worship services. One seventy-eight-year-old interviewee described these outings: "Grandma and her children . . . would go to church every Sunday on horseback . . . [T]hat would be about nineteen or twenty miles round trip. Grandma and her family would go to First Church on horseback. The older children . . . my mother was the oldest of the four . . . and she would either have one of the children ride with her, and Grandmother would hold the younger one . . . that would be Rachel . . . and then Uncle Ben would ride his horse. And they traveled . . . [T]here were no roads then; there were just trails. They would go to First Church every Sunday, take their picnic lunch, and leave after church back up the rivers."

An elderly woman, eighty-six, said, "So I had two girls, and I was married to a man who was the grandson of a minister. I tried to teach my children the way of a Christian life. It comes natural if your people were Christian. Their belief was

6.3. The first Presbyterian Church was built on the Nez Perce Reservation near Kamiah in December 1871. This old church has been remodeled and is still in use. University of Idaho Library, Historical Photograph Collection 5-16-3b. Photographer, D. E. Warren, 1871.

153

6.4. Unidentified woman, after embracing Christianity, wearing a cross as a symbol. *The Spokesman Review*, c. 1911.

6.5. Chief Joseph's sister and niece, at Lapwai, Idaho. This photo was taken when they accepted Christianity. University of Idaho Library, Historical Photograph Collection PG-32, B. Laney Collection, c. 1890.

that way, that even the children knew that they had to have something to believe in, so God was first. They learned that from their Sunday School teachers, that religion came first and that they should live as they grow up so that they would be Christian people."

Another interviewee, eighty years old, said, *"So many times our people were having services . . . [T]hey used to have it for a week; they called it evangelistic. They were people that would come to church and hear the word from the ministers, and they would become Christians. That's what they called it—evangelistic. There were people that traveled on trains to get to these church services. Now there's no train, and . . . after that they traveled with horses. Of course, after that horses became something else, so they travel with cars to get to these services."*

In keeping with their own beliefs, many Nez Perce assumed that the power of the new religion would give them the advantages of Euro-American material goods. This factor may have encouraged some to change their native beliefs and strengthened the influence of Euro-American religions, particularly the Presbyterian, Methodist, and Catholic churches (Walker 1985, 40-41).

The Nez Perce were taught that native customs and dress were socially undesirable, and missionaries enforced their convictions by the use of force—physical beatings of women as well as men, other forms of social ridicule, or economic deprivation. To gain the Natives' cooperation, missionaries would withhold goods, withhold the sacrament, or accuse the miscreants of being heathens and heading to hell (Drury 1958, 172; Walker 1958, 41).

"My mother used to say she went to the Presbyterian church in Spalding," said one woman in her eighties. *"She used to watch everybody. Even older people could not even look at anybody coming into the entrance door. If you would have en-*

tered first and sat in the church, you could not look back [to see] who has entered through the door. If you looked at them, you'd get whipped for it. That's how the Presbyterian missionaries were. You can't go to a show. You can't go to war dances. Now it is different. All are gathering and participating in these powwows."

A seventy-seven-year-old woman, now deceased, said, *"My grandfather, I don't know of him going to church, but my grandmother always went to church. . . . I remember when I was a little girl, and after that my mother and my aunts would tell me about what a cruel person Reverend Spalding was, how he used to whip the elderly women. He'd tell them to pack in their winter wood. I won't talk about Reverend Spalding anymore because I get too emotional."*

"A lot of people don't like Christianity, but that's only way they could survive. Missionaries treated them so badly, too. They wanted them to come to church. Sometimes, the people were not around to come to church. When, they'd go over there, they hit them around. The people they were beating could not understand English. They did not know what they were saying," said an elderly widow, eighty-two years old.

Another eighty-two-year-old woman and mother of five commented, *"When missionaries got here, they told us that we couldn't have any other regalias—those were things that were beaded, pretty bags they made with buckskins. My grandmother had a small bag, and it had buckskin on top and had a draw string. It had a pretty design on one side with real small beads. They came from France, and they were real pretty. The other side of the bag had some kind of flower. She had that, and she took it to church. She thought everybody would be using [things like] it. They told her that things that were shiny were not allowed in the church, so she went back and got real light-colored material, took the buckskin off and put the material up there and also made a draw string out of it and took the bag again to the church. They told her that it did not make any difference because still the beads were shiny, so she just put it away. You couldn't wear your necklace and buckskin dress. They barely let them wear the shawls, I think because at that time it was the style of the people to wear the kerchiefs that replace their hats. Nowadays, everything has changed; now, you can wear your traditional things and use them. I still wonder how they made them believe that [Christianity], how they made them understand that."*

A forty-year-old woman was told the following experience by her grandmother, who grew up in Kamiah and had known the missionary McBeth sisters: *"When they [the Nez Perce] converted to Christianity from their Indian beliefs, then the missionaries would have a ceremony, and they would dig a hole in the ground. And then, in the ground, they have to put their Indian things like buckskins, their beadwork, and things that missionaries said were heathen, and then buried that. And, when they buried that, covered up, it was as if it was dead; that part of their life was dead. She said you could tell it had a real devastating effect on everybody. . . .*

"[I]t was many years later after she died—I got hit by the sadness of it, because, when she would tell it to me, she was so strong. She would not show any emotions. She told me that story a lot of times. She told it to me enough times—it's something she wanted people to know, that kind of trauma. If you think about what happened to that generation, and then you look to the next generation, you see the alcohol start to come in. There is a relationship between that oppression of the spirit, the oppression of your own identity and self-worth, [and] the onset of using alcohol as a medication. I think you can trace it through the families and see it."

An eighty-two-year-old woman said, *"This is just my opinion, but I always thought that white people thought that their religion was superior. They believed in one God, but so did the Indians. They believed in our creator. One time, we had an old man come to ask Dad advice about his land, and we fed him. Dad asked him to say grace, and he started in, and he went on and on, and he was naming everybody. After he left I asked my dad what was he talking about; he said, 'That's an old pre-Christian prayer.' I said, 'Write it down for me,' and he began it: 'Thou Creator, our Creator, bless the things on earth, bless those things that live under the earth, bless those that are in the air, bless all living things on this earth, bless us—Nee me poo, . . .' So, he began with our ancestors of seven generations back, and he was naming down to my dad. That was an old, old religious belief. White people that weren't of their color didn't believe them, that Indians did have any kind of religion.*

"When Reverend Spalding came here, he was going to force them to all become like white people, like, 'You have to all become farmers!' He brought them locust trees; the seeds came from Spalding. He had an orchard, and he was going to make everybody farmers. Well, the Indians were not used to that. They had no conception of being a farmer or raising anything. They depended upon their Creator to provide for them, and he did.

"Then, when the McBeth women came, they tended to call Indians heathens. I think that all Protestant religions all over the country called them heathens because they didn't have the same type of religion as the white man. They looked down upon them, and then they destroyed all of their clothing. Their clothing was wrong, their food was wrong, the way they raised their children was wrong, and their attitude towards women was wrong, and everything was wrong. They said they

156

6.6. Josiah Redwolf and his wife, Frances Raboin, in Euro-American dress. He was five years old at the time of the War of 1877. National Park Service, Nez Perce National Historical Park Collection, c. 1910.

6.7. Two girls and a boy (unidentified) following baptism. Bicentennial Historical Museum, c. 1905.

6.8. Church group picnicking at Kamiah. Idaho State Historical Society 2792, c. 1890.

6.9. Talmaks Choir, 1910. Front row, from left: Nellie Axtell, unidentified, Pauline Corbett, unidentified, unidentified, Ruth Corbett Jackson, Susie Spencer, unidentified, Josephine Corbett Dixon, Lillian Corbett, Frank Corbett. Back row, from left: Elizabeth Crawford, David McFarland, Kathryn Lowrey, Mary Crawford, Jo Black Eagle, unidentified, Richard Moffett, Elizabeth Penney Wilson (in back row, next to Richard Moffett). Francis McFarland with horn. (Others unidentified.) Idaho State Historical Society 63-221-212, Jane Gay Collection, c. 1910.

6.10. Nancy Halfmoon, playing the piano in church; Bob Burns; Esther McAtty; Ida Black Eagle; and Viola Morris. National Park Service, Nez Perce National Historical Park Collection, c. 1967.

6.11. Father Emil Ball, standing in the back row, fourth from the left, and a group of Nez Perce at St. Joseph Mission, Jacquespur, Idaho. Father Ball was assigned to the Sacred Heart Church at Lapwai. He spoke the Nez Perce language fluently and performed mass in that language so the Indian congregation could participate. Courtesy, Alta Guzman, c. 1930.

6.12. Spalding Presbyterian Church, Spalding, Idaho. Bill Parsons and Lydia Corbett standing by a plaque showing the names of missionaries that served the church from 1836 to 1936. University of Idaho Library, Historical Photograph Collection 3-16-3f. Photographer, D. E. Warren, c. 1970.

are going to civilize them, because people are heathen. They didn't want them to talk their own language; they couldn't talk their own language. They said that when they sent policemen up to Kamiah after all other kids in the fall to start school. My dad said he did not know what school was.

"They brought them down here, and first thing they did was cut their hair, for both sexes, and take all their clothes off. For women, they put these real tight Mother Hubbard type dresses on them. They burned their native clothes. Up there in Kamiah, there is a story about how they burned their fancy clothing, like their feathers and stuff . . . like furs that they used to dress up when they war dance or were going to have to go to a ceremony. They made them burn them up. That is not right. That's what they did, and they attempted to destroy it. It's funny how they did that, and now in modern America . . . 'Oh! Save your culture! This is important!' They switched around and changed it. 'Now look what has happened to the young Indian people!'"

The missionaries opposed *te-wats* (medicine people), and medicine women found their power and their ability to heal challenged. Often, they had to hide the practice of their craft, while Euro-American medicine gradually usurped many traditional healing methods. Indigenous healing and its social influence was fading away along with its emotional and psychological contribution.

Missionaries blamed medicine women and medicine men for the high death rate from smallpox and tuberculosis. They believed that many did not recover because of *te-wat* medicine and sweat house treatments. Definitely, the medicine people challenged Christianity and the missionaries' authority.

An elderly woman, eighty years old, said, "They called the Indian religion heathen. They called us heathen people because, according to them, we believe in devil worship like the medicine dances that were held at night and got through in the morning. They started labeling because they didn't want Indians to carry out their culture. They were strong. They had medicine. They had a way to take care of themselves, also curing. There was a medicine woman who used to take care of our family. She used to come and pray for us and give different medicines from her own, and she used to sing for us old songs."

Missionaries started converting Nez Perce couples who were already married according to the traditional Nez Perce marriage system. These marriages were condemned, and the couples were remarried and introduced to the Christian dogma of their particular denomination. Children of non-Christian couples were considered illegitimate until they received Christian baptism and names. Only then, from the missionary standpoint, did they become legitimate. All marriages were registered, and all baptisms were recorded. Monogamy was promoted. The missionaries brought Euro-American culture into the life of the family as church weddings and the baptism of children and adults were widely adopted and honored.

In the Nez Perce culture, women had an important and respected place, even in a polygamous household, but the missionaries viewed polygamous marriage within the successful Nez Perce family system as adultery, which they considered a sin. They insisted that polygamy was the cause of the decrease in population among the Nez Perce. They also believed that women miscarried often because they were subjected to every kind of hardship: digging all the roots, cutting all the firewood and carrying it on their backs, packing all the effects when the family traveled, and traveling on horseback (Drury 1958, 137-38).

One woman, nearly eighty years old, said, "The missionaries told men that they must marry

163

one, and they must marry her legally. About the time when my sister was born and was a little girl, my dad married my mother. So most everybody had to get married, according to the McBeth sisters. Becoming a member of a church, you must be married. When you baptized the children, you had to have a legal mother and a legal father."

Missionaries also introduced summer camp meetings. The various Indian Presbyterian churches on reservations organized the Talmaks Camp Association, held every summer during the Fourth of July at Craig Mountain. At these camps, the Nez Perce formed choirs that sang Christian hymns and prayers in the Nez Perce language.

Through their churches, the Presbyterian missionaries started training men, especially chiefs, for clergy positions and many Indian men became ministers (see Fig. 2.31). The Presbyterian church gave a kind of authority to ministers that the chiefs in traditional society never possessed. Chiefs were counselors, mediators, and protectors, while the church governed all aspects of life. This produced a special and higher class among the Nez Perce. Indian women, like their white counterparts, were barred from clergy work but encouraged in subordinate roles within the church.

A woman who was almost ninety-six years old and who has since passed away said, *"I went to the Catholic school at the St. Joseph convent. I learned music; I learned music from the missionaries. They taught me how to play the piano. I played for the church. I was in the choir."*

SEVEN ▲▲▲▲▲▲▲▲▲▲▲▲▲▲▲▲▲▲▲▲▲▲▲▲▲▲▲▲▲▲▲▲▲▲▲▲▲

Education

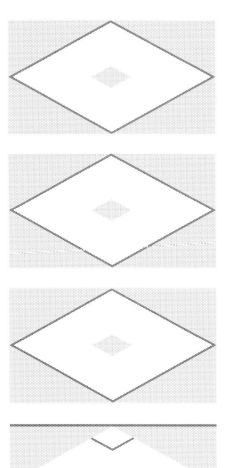

Nez Perce Traditional Education

AN EIGHTY-YEAR-OLD interviewee said, *"My mother always stressed, 'Give them a good education so they'll know how to take care of themselves.'"*

Education, including instruction in practical skills, was closely interwoven with religion in Nez Perce culture. The children were taught by observation, through lectures, and, most importantly, through myths and legends designed to inculcate knowledge and fundamental values. These stories were usually relayed by grandparents, often during the long, sedentary winter. A Nez Perce man recalled long evenings during the winter: "In wintertime a lot of teaching happened, like history and storytelling, because of the weather—you're confined inside. These were thoughts to carry on in their lives during that time: legends, myths, and stories. There are no experts left as our ancestors. You can watch TV, radio, movies, and learn different ideas."

The elderly were the initial teachers who built the spiritual, moral, and social character of the young. On the reservation today, elderly men continue to credit grandmothers for providing their traditional values and knowledge, although it has been widely believed that grandfathers were the mainstay in the education of boys. A Nez Perce man in his fifties said,

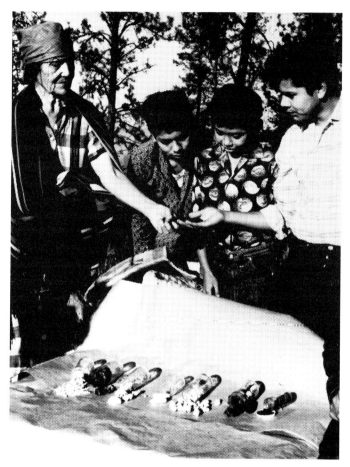

7.1. Elizabeth Penney Wilson, teaching her grandson, Ike. University of Idaho, Alfred W. Bowers Laboratory of Anthropology, Steve Shawley Collection, c. 1970.

7.2. Elizabeth Penney Wilson teaching the Ellenwood brothers and Lester Moses about roots and medicinal herbs. University of Idaho Library, Historical Photograph Collection 6-24-15. Photographer, D. E. Warren, c. 1970.

Family groups, just by telling stories every night while they cooked or during meals or after the meals or when people were sitting down together closing the day, those were story times. There are many stories. That was our education system. Grandmothers knew all coyote stories. That is how the grandmothers hold together the traditions and customs. Today, we are losing a lot of our grandmothers, and the present generation never carried on those stories. The reasons why things were the way they were, that's why the coyote stories—that's what the purpose was. It is true to all cultures: If you lose your grandmother, you lose your tradition.

Said a woman in her forties, *"I feel education is important. I think today, in this time, in this day and age, it is very important. It's going to be one of the things that helps our people, and yet, at the same time, education and learning can be more than just pen and paper, a grade, or something that shows you've learnt something through a piece of paper. There are numerous leaders within Native American people that were not formally in an education system. But they were wise people. They were strong spiritual leaders for our people, so it depends on what kind of education you are talking about. There are numerous ways of being educated. There have been numerous chiefs that were self-educated, but they did a lot of things that helped our people.*

"So like I say, a lot of our [old] educational processes worked . . . even though I'm saying that they were not educated, [I mean] they were not educated in the white man's world. But they had a specific way that things were done, and they taught us continually just by talking, and doing, and by example. That was pretty common. That's the way the knowledge was passed from generation to generation. They always taught."

The Euro-American Education System

The Nez Perce traditional educational system changed radically as missionaries undermined the authority of grandparents and elderly adults who had played a key role in the transmission of knowledge. The role of grandmothers, who had been regarded as teachers, was taken over by Euro-American educators.

Women as well as men moved from traditional education to Euro-American education due to efforts to "civilize" the Indians by conversion to Christianity. As a part of federal policy, missionaries were encouraged to live among the Indians and to set up schools and churches. Some denominations moved into Nez Perce territory and established mission schools to educate the Indians. Mrs. Spalding opened a school for Indians on January 27, 1837, at Spalding, Idaho. There were approximately one hundred Indian students at the school, primarily women and children.

The missionaries wanted the women to become literate in the Nez Perce language so that they could read the Bible. They gave the women Bibles and hymnals and taught them reading, writing, and phonics. An elementary primer in Nez Perce was introduced somewhere between 1842 and 1850. The pupils were expected to memorize their lessons, sitting on the floor of the schoolroom with their infants propped up in cradleboards.

The missionaries made a sincere effort to educate but in a fashion that would encourage the women to forget the old life and ways. Their emphasis was on moral values, even in the teaching of household arts, and if a woman was living in adultery, the missionaries would not place a Bible in her hands.

The traditional Euro-American concept of the woman's domestic role was presented to the Nez Perce women along with much training in household skills. Women were to learn to care for their

7.3. The missionary Miss Sue McBeth's first schoolroom and home in Kamiah, Idaho. This was the first school to educate Nez Perce women and is still standing today. University of Idaho Library, Historical Photograph Collection 5-16-1a, c. 1890.

7.4. First missionary society in Idaho. Kate McBeth, back row, second from right, and Nez Perce women and children. Idaho State Historical Society 63-221-264, Jane Gay Collection, January 8, 1891.

7.5. Kate McBeth and a group of women at First Church, Kamiah. Idaho State Historical Society 63-221-205a, Jane Gay Collection, c. 1890.

families as if for the first time: to keep a house, to cook, and to make Western clothes. Each one had a recipe book for detailed, careful instruction in how to make dry yeast, yeast bread, cakes, and snacks. There were lessons in knitting, darning, laundering, routine sanitation, and the manufacture of soap. The most eagerly accepted novelty must have been the sewing machine, which was introduced to facilitate the construction of the new style of clothes for all members of the family. Often, a sewing machine was the first thing a woman bought when she received government payment from the sale of surplus land. Traditionally cooperative, women helped each other with their sewing.

The English language was soon introduced through literacy education. Later on, it was forced as a medium of instruction in the schools, and pupils who conversed in the Nez Perce language were beaten and made to feel ashamed of their culture.

There was no room for bilingual education in those years, and today only older generations can converse in the Nez Perce language. As a consequence, its structure, vocabulary, and richness are being lost. Recently, there has been an effort to teach the language, but with unknown success. As the language has declined, so have many elements of the culture for which it was the vehicle.

With the passage of time, the focus of education shifted from women to young children, still under the auspices of the United States government, the Bureau of Indian Affairs agent, and the missionaries. Increasingly, this education had to be combined with efforts to deal with terrible epidemics of European-introduced diseases.

The Bureau of Indian Affairs opened the first school in Lapwai, Idaho, in the fall of 1868. A

7.6. An unidentified woman working on a sewing machine. Note the baby buggy and other Western cultural material. National Park Service, Nez Perce National Historical Park Collection 2291, c. 1910.

smallpox scare in Lewiston, Idaho, ten miles away, caused the parents to withdraw their children in January 1869, but the school was reopened in April with some success.

Tuberculosis first made its appearance among the Nez Perce Indians in the winter of 1871. The BIA agent, in his report of February of that year, stated that tuberculosis had caused an unusually large number of deaths and was one of the causes of the high death rate among Indians. Subsequently, tuberculosis hospitals and schools were established in tandem on the Nez Perce Reservation.

The Ft. Lapwai Sanitorium was the first institution of its kind, established by the Bureau of Indian Affairs in 1879 for the treatment of tuberculosis. The buildings of Fort Lapwai, an army post, were taken over in 1886 by the BIA, and the boarding school, which was then at Spalding, was moved to Lapwai and became a school for tubercular children.

The school physician, Dr. J. N. Alley, the physician in charge in Lapwai, thought that at least 75 percent of the Nez Perce Indians had tuberculosis in some form. There was not a family on the reservation free from the disease, and some families had lost from two to twelve children to it. Tuberculosis patients, with their weakened immune systems, showed a marked tendency to contract other illnesses as well.

"I had two daughters," said a ninety-six-year-old woman, who has now passed away. "Both of my daughters died with pneumonia and tuberculosis. I don't know where we got that sickness. Till today, if you go to Ahsahka cemetery, you will see how many children died due to this sickness."

The curriculum of the sanitorium school was modified to fit students' special needs. Most of the patients attended school—always in outdoor rooms except in very bad weather—for two hours daily. A smaller number required more rest, and

these would attend for only one hour. Occasionally, a patient passed the eighth grade and was given special studies, including shorthand, if the student so desired. Those who were cured were discharged.

Many of these students had to repeat the same grade for a couple of years, having missed school because of their lack of resistance. Some interviewees who were in this sanitorium school still feel educationally disadvantaged. They were left behind in their classes while other students progressed. Out of embarrassment, they never returned to school after they left the sanitorium.

An eighty-year-old woman shared her story: "I started going to school here in Kamiah. I remember I still lived . . . where we grew up. I remember coming to school, and the mud would be so thick, and we'd have our galoshes on, and we'd step, and our boots would get stuck in the mud. . . . I went to school until, it must have been about fourth grade. I was in fourth grade when my dad died; he died of tuberculosis. Then, my brother died the following month, and then we all got tuberculosis, my sister and I. So I was in the sanitorium at Lapwai until I was about twelve. We had strict bed rest and a strict diet. I was twelve years old when I came home. By that time, the kids had gone on in school, and I was behind, so I went to Chemawa. I went to school there one year, seventh grade. Then, I came back and started eighth grade here, and I was older than the rest of the kids, so then I never did finish going on to high school because they thought I was too old for my classmates."

Another woman, eighty-four years old, offered her own memories: "While we were in the sanitorium, I used to feel sorry for my mom. She'd come driving down to see us. She'd try to get there often. But, after my dad died, I think she just kind of fell apart. So when we got out of the sanitorium, we just, I don't know, we just went every

7.7. From left, John Alley Jr.; Ralph Alley; Dr. John Alley; Virginia Alley, on Dr. Alley's lap; Mrs. Alley. Courtesy, Rev. H. L. Sugden, Lapwai, Idaho, c. 1890.

7.8. Children on the porch of the BIA school, Spalding. Idaho State Historical Society 63-221-241, c. 1890.

7.9. A group of Indian children at Spalding, Idaho, probably on school steps. Idaho State Historical Society 61-159-7, c. 1890.

7.10. The old hospital, replaced in 1880. Courtesy, Rev. H. L. Sugden, Lapwai, Idaho, c. 1890.

7.11. Women and children suffering from tuberculosis. The woman on the left is Fanny Samuels, mother of Milton George; the woman on the right is Mrs. Moos-Moos Jonathan, half-sister of Mrs. Felix Corbett. Idaho State Historical Society 63-221-70, Jane Gay Collection, c. 1890.

7.12. Fort Lapwai Indian Sanitorium, which has since burned down. Notice the open walls on the second story, the sleeping quarters for the patients. Many complained of the drafty conditions, especially in winter, although fresh air and low temperatures were specifically prescribed for tuberculosis patients at the time. University of Idaho Library, Historical Photograph Collection 5-13-7d. Photographer, Wilson, Lewiston, Idaho, c. 1910.

7.13. A classroom at Fort Lapwai Indian Sanitorium. Idaho State Historical Society 80-37-8, c. 1910.

7.14. Vaccination time at Fort Lapwai Indian Sanitorium. Foreground, Dr. J. N. Alley, physician in charge at Lapwai. Idaho State Historical Society 80-37-7, c. 1910.

which way. I wish we'd have kept our culture up. But later on, my mother got married again, settled down. She went to Coates Christian Training School, and we all moved down there; at that time I was married."

"I think where I really lost out," said an elderly woman, eighty-six, "is where I was in the TB sanitorium. I would have learned more of my Indian language and more about digging roots, medicines, and these sort of things. But I was in there from eight years old to twelve. And I was almost a teenager, and when I got out I didn't want to, like when you're a teenager you want to go out and do different things, and that's when I was out. And I'm sorry because I wish I could have done it."

A woman nearly eighty years old said, "In 1928, when my cousin went to high school, then the doctor came around from the sanitorium here in Lapwai. He examined everybody. I started school in sixth grade that fall in October. My mother got a letter that my sister and I were supposed to go to the sanitorium to be checked over and to get our tonsils out. So we left home, and we came down. That was a sad occasion for me. I cried. I hated to be away from home. I was there from 1928 to 1932. We stayed there, and our tonsils were not out until the fall of 1928. They waited till springtime, and they took us to the hospital. That was the Agency, that was our hospital; the east wing was the boys' building, which burnt down (see Fig. 7.12). The girls' school was still in use. They have the Head Start [program] in there now. A new dining hall came into being before I left, and we had a big dining hall. This was an army base, where the army lived before they fought with us in 1877. After that, the government gave it to the Nez Perce tribe. We had all different tribes' children from different reservations. There were Spokane Indians, Umatilla, Montana, Oklahoma, Dakotas, and Alaska natives. There were lots of kids all over when I was there."

According to another woman, age eighty: "We used to have, what they call, every morning, a half-day school which put me behind because I never got to go to school. We all had to be detailed for a job like cleaning a certain area of the building, maybe the dressing room or the bedrooms. We had several bedrooms, long dormitories. Each girl was assigned what to do. I was twelve when I got there, and I left when I was sixteen. I had something to do, and some of the girls were assigned to go to the kitchen across the campus. . . . [T]he hospital has its own kitchen, and they were assigned there. . . . In the hospital . . . [t]here was a boys' side and a girls' side. . . . [Y]ears later I tried to look for some of the friends I knew. I went to Browning, Montana, but nobody knew them. There were people from Arlee, Flathead tribe. They would come over, and the Crow Indians. So it seems like all the kids were sent there to get rid of the TB."

A woman, age eighty-four, recalled her experience at the sanitorium: "I had tuberculosis. I had to go to the sanitorium. I was worried about my brother, because he also got it. My mother had to support both of us. That was the depression time, so when we went to the sanitorium, at least my mother didn't have to worry about our treatment. When I was there, my first night at the sanitorium, two girls tried to beat me up. One straddled me. I could not get my arm out because she was sitting on it. Then, the other girl ran for me, and I kicked her over on the next bed. We had part-time school. We had two hours' school, then rest period, then two hours of school. I was a teacher's aide, first to fourth grade. When the teacher used to leave for Christmas, then I taught religion classes. They had a record of a marching band; the teacher told me, 'When you can't control them, play that and make them march.' That's what I used to do until they'd say, 'We are tired; we'll be good.'"

Another elderly Nez Perce woman, age eighty-two, reluctantly accepted life at the sanitorium: *"I finally got used to the life in the sanitorium. I enjoyed it because we had to march like soldiers. We got to know all the steps, go like squads. We practiced and marched. We watched boys practicing their march; we were just like soldiers. Some of the kids went from there to Chemawa. Chemawa was just as bad. They marched them. They were really kept so they could not run away. They had several buildings for boys and girls. I was there in 1935. I didn't stay for too long; I just asked to come home."*

"On Sundays, we had to put on uniforms and march to church. School days, we wore our own clothes, blue skirts, white top, and a jacket."

"The Catholic children would go with the matron," an eighty-year-old woman remembered. *"The matron would come early in the morning to go to mass. Our church was gone; it was an auditorium. There we went to see the movies on Thursdays, and we had our Christmas plays. Protestants would go there and even on Sundays for Christians. We went in the morning for our Sunday School, and we had some Presbyterians at the McBeth Mission, had some missionaries [who] liked to go over and teach us. The Catholics would get up real early. We marched to the dining hall, and they would come later. But we had to pray at every table and a certain prayer every group. I wish[ed] I was Catholic. I admired them, the way they had to get up and go for the mass, a kind of mystical thing. Then, I went to upstairs where we had to have our church. I went to their church upstairs, those beautiful pictures all around and purple curtains, and ours was so dry. The Catholics said that if I don't join them I might go to hell."*

Said an eighty-two-year-old Nez Perce woman: *"A lot of people died due to tuberculosis. They had a graveyard this side of the sanitorium, up there on the hill some place. Quite a few kids died. They did not send them [the bodies] home. That's where they buried them."*

"There was one winter where everybody got sick," an eighty-year-old interviewee remembered, *"and even the girls working in the kitchen were sick. There were a few who were able to get back and forth. I don't think I got sick. We had to go to the dining hall and bring the meals to the sick ones. It was kind of a flu. There was one young girl who died; I think her name was Ernestine. I remember that she was so sick. The next day I heard that she passed away. We never saw her being taken or anything. They just told us she died. I felt very bad. There was another girl real sick in the hospital, and they locked the room. They wouldn't let anybody into that room, just the nurses. She died, too. Her father was a Nez Perce, and her mother was from Poplar, Montana. They met at Chemawa, got married, and came to this area."*

As recollected by an eighty-six-year-old interviewee: *"I did not finish my education. I had problems with my eyes. I was in the sanitorium (I did not have TB) for my eye treatment. Sanitorium hospital took care of other ailments too, besides TB. I took care of my sister who had tuberculosis. Once we went up in the mountains, and she got tired. She said, 'I cannot walk back.' I had to pack her, and she told me not to tell mother because she would worry. So my life was always busy.*

"I felt very bad when my sister died due to tuberculosis because we were very close. When she had money, that was just like my money. When I had money, I gave it to her."

Said an eighty-year-old woman, *"When I went to school, I did not have very good schooling because, in between my schooling, I got tuberculosis. I did not finish high school. As far as I went was ninth grade then. I got tuberculosis again. I didn't finish my ninth grade. I got tuberculosis, so*

I had to spend my time in sanitorium till I was thirteen years old. I finally got well. I almost died from tuberculosis. I had been to sanitorium so many times; that's why I am not so well educated. I never finished schooling. I never went back to school.

"They made us take a lot of rest, good food, milk, and medicine. When I was there, they just made us rest, mostly. We were not allowed to visit home, but my parents could visit me. I thought it was a prison. Parents could come in, but you couldn't go out.

"When I was thirteen years old, I started becoming better. I used to go home on weekends. When we were young, we had to stay in the hospital, inside the buildings. And, once in awhile, they let us exercise outside and play around. Otherwise, you'd get punished.

"There were all kinds of people there from different reservations, like Montana, Dakota, and Alaska; all were Indians, no whites. Sometimes, it was terrible when some children died. When your sister or cousin died, it was terrible. When my niece was dying, she was suffering very bad. She was screaming; we could not go to comfort her. I was so glad that I got out of it.

"Some nurses treated us like mean, and some were nice. Some of the kids used to run away from the hospital. Then, they would get them back and punish them. They would make us sit in a room or stay in bed and not talk to anyone. You had to stay in your room. Sometimes, they would lock the kids in a basement for a week or two. The food and blankets were shoved [at you]. When you get better, they would send you to the boarding dormitory. The girls' and boys' dormitories were separated.

"We had half-day school. Afternoons, we used to sleep till 3 p.m., then get up, play around, and go to bed at seven. In half-day school, we did not learn much. Sometimes, they taught us how to make

things like crochet and knitting in the hospital. They would come to see you and then teach you.

"I got married when I was sixteen. I was not in a sanitorium. I left the sanitorium when I was fourteen. When I was seventeen, my first child was born, and I got tuberculosis again so my parents took care of my daughter, and I went back to sanitorium again."

Former women patients, twenty-five to thirty years of age and in sound physical and mental health, were accepted as housekeepers at the sanitorium, undertaking this work with the understanding that the first three years were to be regarded as training in child care and preparation for a position as a nurse in an Indian sanitorium. Women also were trained as dietitians and as cooks for the patients. (A few of my elderly interviewees had been cooks in the sanitorium.) Women received classroom instruction to become seamstresses as well and made all the uniforms for the children at the sanitorium.

Later, the BIA ruled that cases no longer contagious could be returned to their homes as no further treatment was necessary. Tuberculosis remained a serious health problem for the Nez Perce well into the twentieth century. BIA records showed an excess of deaths over births through the five-year period from 1923 to 1927. The population of the tribe continued to decrease. The sanitorium school at Lapwai was finally closed on June 30, 1942.

A woman in her early fifties said, *"I was born premature; I was three pounds. When I got older, they found out that my mother had tuberculosis. When I was born, I had to have x-rays every year. Before the x-rays, they gave shots, then tested me; it came out positive. Still I had to have x-rays every year, and so did my family. They put me on tuberculosis medicine. I was following through, and I let them know. Finally, when . . . I was fifteen years old, I really learned that my mom had*

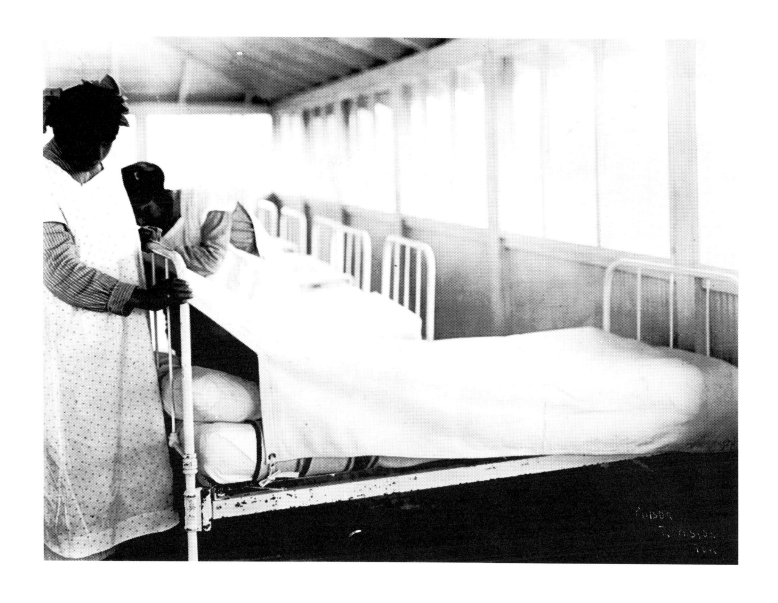

7.15. Fort Lapwai Indian Sanitorium. Nurses caring for patients on the sleeping porch. University of Idaho Library, Historical Photograph Collection 5-13-7p. Photographer, Wilson, Lewiston, Idaho, c. 1910.

7.16. A group of nurses at Fort Lapwai Indian Sanitorium. University of Idaho Library, Historical Photograph Collection 5-13-7e. Photographer, Wilson, Lewiston, Idaho.

7.17. A seamstress giving instruction to girls in sewing class at Fort Lapwai Indian Sanitorium. University of Idaho Library, Historical Photograph Collection 5-13-7k. Photographer, Wilson, Lewiston, Idaho, c. 1910.

tuberculosis when she had me. Then, I fully under-
stood why my grandparents took care of me, be-
cause she was sick, and then I always had to
take pills. We did not have a good health system
then . . . [or] now. They made me take pills for
two years. Another doctor came in and checked
me. Then, he would check my medication, and
he said, 'Why are you taking those pills?' I was in
my twenties that time. This second doctor told
me, 'You don't have to take pills. You just have
to have tuberculosis x-rays taken. Make sure
that your lungs stay healthy, that's all.' So that
was straightened out. He threw away all my
medicine."

The Bureau of Indian Affairs determined that the attendance of children at public school in Lapwai was unsatisfactory. Seven or eight fall fairs (Indian powwows) were held on the reservation and in towns nearby, and many parents took their whole family and spent several weeks going from place to place attending these fairs. Many also went on hunting and fishing expeditions for several weeks at a time. On these trips, children missed school. Superintendents seemed powerless to prevent this truancy, for while state law made school attendance compulsory, there was no mechanism for enforcement. Lawmakers found it a slow process convincing parents of the importance of education.

Recurring absences frustrated the teachers who worked for weeks with a child only to have the child leave on a trip of three or four months. The details and routine of schoolwork had to be relearned after this length of time. Even the children in regular attendance did not progress as rapidly as the teachers desired, for they always spoke their own language on the playground and away from school.

An eighty-two-year-old woman said, *"I went to school, and I didn't know English. The school was here in Kamiah. I hated going to school. I didn't want to go because I didn't understand one word of English."*

In its 1907 report, the Bureau of Indian Affairs concluded that regional boarding schools offered the best solution to the attendance problem, actually a justification for what the BIA and the missionaries had already done. A boarding school had been established at Fort Lapwai for the local reservation students in the latter nineteenth century. Children removed far from the distractions of home life could be supervised fully, with strict standards of conduct enforced through a system of penalties.

The anguish to the children was ignored. Due to the emotional shock and the loneliness of being separated from their extended families, most of these children lapsed into depression; they did not eat or sleep in these strange places. Others became malnourished and suffered from infections and related diseases. Some of them died. Illnesses arose from the radical change of diet, the shift from a free, outdoor life to close confinement, and the loneliness caused by removal from the extended family. All of these influences had a depressive and physically depleting effect which made the pupils easy prey to tuberculosis and other diseases.

A sixty-year-old woman said, *"My mother went to Mission School Jasper on Mission Creek. I don't know how old she was. She was the youngest and shorter than most of the children. My mother said that Irene Allen used to comb her hair. She had long hair. But then she had to have her hair cut. That was her first hair cut. They [teachers/nuns] were very strict there. When she left the school, I don't know when did she leave, but after that, she had very long and thick hair as an adult. People always noticed her for her long, black, and thick hair."*

Another interviewee, in her early seventies, said, *"I went to St. Joseph Catholic Mission*

7.18. Lapwai school children. From left, Elizabeth Wilson, Jane Pankin, and Jane Swan. Idaho State Historical Society 63-221-22, Jane Gay Collection c. 1892.

School. I went in when I was seven years old and stayed there eight years. It was a boarding school, too. I came home only at Christmas and summer time. When I saw other little girls, I stayed there with them. I never thought of home. I did like the boarding school for the first three to four years, until I got little bit older. The religion itself we had before we could receive First Communion. We had to go to catechism, and that took months to prepare, maybe more than a year. Finally, we received our First Holy Communion. Still, we had a lot of religious lessons to go through to prepare for our confirmation. That took all the time plus my playing time. There were English books, arithmetic books, history books; we had two history books. We had a regular world history, and then we had a Bible history. It had to be combined in a catechism that had to be memorized all the way through. [The book] was thick. I was in the mission up to seventh grade. Then, I moved to the public school. That was a whole lot different. I got too much freedom. If I wanted to go to school, I would go. If I didn't, I would not."

A woman in her forties recalled, "When I was in mission school, we were very poor. Our parents couldn't take care of us, so we lived with nuns and priests, and we wore a little uniform, boys on one side of the court and girls on the other side. There was a flag pole in the middle of the court. We lived there, day and night. And the nuns took care of us, and . . . there was really a tight group of children that lived in the school. It was very strict. We got up every morning. We lined up and went to classes with the nuns. Our basic needs were met. We had sponsoring foster parents that would write letters to us, and would . . . send little gifts for being able to experience that mission. And so we had foster parents that sponsored us there. Loneliness, being away from home, I didn't think I was learning enough from that boarding school so I went home."

According to an elderly woman of eighty: "Lapwai School was based on vocational work. Some would come on the train to the boarding school, and a buggy was waiting there to pick them up. My grandmother used to hate those

184

7.19. Girls at boarding school. Clockwise from left, Mary Broncheau (Lawyer), Sophia Broncheau (Henry), Mary Ann Broncheau (Whitefield), unidentified, Matilda Maxwell Taylor. Idaho State Historical Society 63-221-317, c. 1890.

dresses with long sleeves and buttons in front, but they were forced to wear them. They had to make forced transition [from the way] they were living. It was an unnatural way for them."

Said an eighty-nine-year-old interviewee, *"The boys had to wear soldiers' outfits. It was based on a military way of conducting school. They had to salute, march, wear caps, and wear uniforms. They weren't allowed to talk Indian. They had to wear name tags. They had to give up their traditions and culture. If they did practice them, they got beaten on their heads. The boys and the girls had to be there on the parade ground. All Indian schools were patterned the same way."*

A forty-seven-year-old woman said, *"In boarding schools, you did not learn. You did not have your parents there to give you the examples. All you saw was the regimentation of boarding schools, rather than a happy face giving you love and companionship . . . early morning when you went to breakfast, somebody to encourage you to go to school."*

"Boarding school was a lot of hard work for me," said a young woman, age forty-four. *"When I got up in the morning, I had a job working in the kitchen. They would assign an area for each student, either doing the dishes or serving the food. They would assign you a job, so my job was to get up at five o'clock in the morning and go to the kitchen and work there until breakfast finished, and then go to class from 8 A.M. to 4 P.M. Then, I had a job working at the student's bank as a teller. The bank closed at 5 P.M. Then, I had a job working for the teacher, correcting papers and bookkeeping. It was hard work. We had to keep our rooms clean; we had to keep ourselves clean. We had room inspections. We had several people telling us what to do, rather than a set of parents. We could walk around with an opposite sex, but we could not do anything more than hold hands,* or we would be in trouble. If there was any kissing, we would be in trouble, or any other type of sexual activity. They would get in trouble, be restricted to the [dormitory], be restricted to the room or base, lose some privileges like going to the movies. We had a movie house on campus, and there were movies on Friday night, or maybe a dance to attend, regular modern dance, and if you lost those privileges, you cannot attend. If you did something wrong, you cannot attend. If your room was not clean, you cannot attend. If you violated one of those rules and regulations, then you cannot attend. You had to keep your room clean; you had to keep yourself clean; clothes were all clean. We had to wear dresses—we could not wear pants. The boys had to have short hair. They could not have long hair.*

"They tried to direct us towards vocation rather than four-year degrees at that time; it was in the late '60s. They felt that we were capable of getting the vocational degree but not the four-year degree or anything above that. When I was going to school, they felt that I should be going to the dry-cleaning business, so I went through dry cleaning for a year and a half. And then they finally discovered that I was excelling quite well in dry cleaning. My grade showed that I was [doing] quite well. They wanted me to take a job in Rochester, New York. I was seventeen at that time. I felt that it was too much for me to go to Rochester, New York, so did not go. Then, my mother had asked me to return home—the Grand Coulie Dam area—and finish school. That's what I did. I went home for the last half of my school year, but I spent a year and a half in the board school.

"The thing I think that probably was best in the boarding school was being able to meet kids from another tribe, to know people from other reservations, getting to know a little bit about their culture and traditions, things that they had when they were growing up. I think that was one of the

things I liked about it. Other than that, it was a difficult time for me. It was hard, hard work! I remember before I had gone home I had a bloody nose for three days, and they couldn't make it stop right away. They figured it was due to work pressure, that I was trying to do too much work. I was assigned too much work at one time for my body."

Teachers in the boarding schools emphasized a moral code and strict discipline. The Bureau of Indian Affairs reported in 1929,

> Six Indian girls have been returned expelled from boarding schools . . . [because] they had broken out of the dormitory and were out all night. . . . to seek the companionship of boys . . . [L]ectured for the first offense, . . . for the second offense the only means of maintaining discipline in the school was to send them back to the reservation, where none of the three have homes worthy of the name, with no one capable of or responsible for their discipline until their offenses become sufficient to require the intervention of the law. Society may be in a measure thus protected, but the girls will doubtless be a total loss.

The BIA concluded that boarding school did not completely solve the attendance problem. Occasionally, a pupil was permitted to visit her or his family for a short time. Teachers objected to such visits because those short visits at home could make students forget all that the school had taught them. They suggested to the administration that the children be removed from the families for an indefinite number of years without any visitation or holidays. It was evidently believed that if children were to be educated, they must be confined for years in boarding schools and must be removed as far as possible from their parents.

The entire social structure of the tribe had to change. United States government assimilation policy mandated that children be taken away from home to schools to receive non-Indian education. This experience was often extremely difficult for the Indian children who were raised in extended families. Women had traditionally taken care of the children, and this role was taken away from them. After schooling, children no longer displayed Indian cultural behavior or spoke their language or wore their native clothing.

Orphaned children, instead of returning to the tribe for the summer, were sent to work as servants in the households of white families. Many students who came back to the reservation used their education to "civilize" the rest of the tribe. For example, the girls would teach their families how to keep the house in order, how to dress properly, to use correct table manners, and to speak in English.

An eighty-four-year-old elderly woman said, *"I went to a Riverside, California, boarding school. Students came from different tribes. I was there for seven years. I liked it because I had no home to come to. So I just stayed there. We had to work."*

A forty-one-year-old woman said, *"My grandmother was among the first groups that went back to Carlisle, Pennsylvania. She was with Elizabeth Penney Wilson and, I think it was, Nancy George, three of them on the train, and they went back to Carlisle. I think she was thirteen or fourteen when she went back, and she stayed there until she was a young woman, maybe twenty or so. A lot of what they did was learning domestic help sort of jobs that they would go to school. And there were Indian people from all over, and then she would work during vacations and all through summer. They would assign [them to] some of the rich families in that area to be their domestic help. She said that that's where she learned how to cook and do lot of the cooking and food preparation and preserving foods, things*

7.20. Nez Perce Indian students at the Indian School, Carlisle, Pennsylvania. Standing, fourth from left, Lizzie Hayes. Courtesy, JoAnn Kauffman, c. 1903.

7.21. Classrooms, Indian School, Carlisle, Pennsylvania. Courtesy, JoAnn Kauffman, c. 1903.

like that, by being sent out to do domestic help. She said that she was there when Young Chief Joseph visited the school; that was in 1903. We went back there a year before he died. That time Nez Perce kids were out there. She said that there were a lot of good athletes besides Jim Thorpe. He was one."

In 1879, the first non-reservation Indian boarding school was established at Carlisle, Pennsylvania, and other schools were established elsewhere. Many Nez Perce students attended the school at Carlisle. Of these off reservation schools, many offered domestic science degrees: the study of the art of Euro-American living and training for occupations such as seamstress, cook, nutritionist, or child care provider. Another vocation for trainees was clerk/typist. Some graduates returned with basic office skills and were employed by the Bureau of Indian Affairs in Lapwai. The various Indian schools taught different skills to the students. As well as typing, printing was taught as a component of vocational training.

Teachers found their students to be very musical and promoted choirs and hymn singing in the churches. Both sexes received music lessons, including instrumental music. This was contrary to traditional practice, since drums and flutes had been strictly in the province of men, and it was culturally unacceptable for females to play musical instruments. A few women interviewees mentioned that their mothers and/or grandmothers had received degrees in music from the Carlisle Institute. Some of my interviewees felt that "if women would have been given a chance [in traditional culture], they would have played a musical instrument."

A forty-one-year-old interviewee said, *"My grandmother had a great influence on my life because she really demanded responsibility. One of the things she did that probably had the biggest impact on me was not things she did to me or*

7.22. Nora McFarland, taken at Carlisle, Pennsylvania. Nora was the daughter of Janet Lawyer and Phillip McFarland of Wallowa Bend. She was married to Louis Harrison, and some of their children are buried in Wallowa. Her mother, Janet Lawyer, was the daughter of John Lawyer, the niece of Archie Lawyer, and the granddaughter of Chief Lawyer. Courtesy, JoAnn Kauffman, c. 1903.

7.23. Elizabeth Penney Wilson, employed at Lewiston, Idaho, after her return from the Carlisle, Pennsylvania, Indian School. University of Idaho, Alfred W. Bowers Laboratory of Anthropology, Steve Shawley Collection, c. 1890.

with me [but] things that she let me see. When I was thinking about her, she was a real orator. She would always be asked, wherever we went—whether to church, or a dinner, or a meeting—she would be asked to say some words. So without blinking an eye, she would stand up, and she would talk for twenty minutes or thirty minutes, something, and give this great speech. I figured that it was a great speech because I looked around and people would say, 'Encore, encore . . .' She was really a powerful speaker. Whenever I had to get up and do something, and I always get nervous about it, give a talk or give a speech or get in front of a group, that's the person I reach back [to] in my memory and pull her memory out, because she was a real powerful person. She went to Carlisle."

A forty-year-old woman recalled "the boarding schools, the places they would send them after they were moved onto the reservations. How we learned as Native Americans through our education, our education was practice. We were told stories, and we were taught, and we applied. For example, for these big huge dinners, these big huge gatherings, we were taught how to do those things by practice. We were sent out [to do it]. . . My mom would say, 'Now listen . . . you do this, this, and this, and you do it now.' And so, through continual practice, we learned what was expected of us as Native Americans. We learned how to dance by practice . . . [T]hey would just dress us and then push us out there and say, 'Go dance.'"

Said an eighty-year-old interviewee, "Western education was not important. Indian parents didn't want female children to go to school. It became important later."

"On my father's side, my grandmother only knew the Nez Perce language," said a woman, age

190

7.24. Lapwai women. Left, Harriet Stewart, who survived the War of 1877 as a child; right, Annie Parnell Little. Both sisters attended the Carlisle, Pennsylvania, Indian School. Idaho State Historical Society 63-221-83d, Jane Gay Collection.

forty. "[S]he didn't know English. She only knew a very few English words, and my aunt and my dad would translate for her. When we were young, they would teach us how to pray in Nez Perce, some Nez Perce words, but they never really actively taught us Nez Perce. We didn't grow up learning the language. My uncle, the medicine man, told me that they both knew that when they went to boarding schools when they were first being culturalized, supposedly, that they were forced to speak their [the English] language, and, if they did speak their [own] language, they were punished for it. And my dad was a firm believer in letting us adapt, so that we wouldn't suffer the things that they suffered. Because, if they spoke their language, they were beaten for it. . . . They couldn't practice their culture, wear their native clothing, because they were beaten for it."

Another woman, who is in her early forties, remarked, "My father didn't put emphasis on it [the Nez Perce culture] because they had suffered so much by trying to carry it forth. Back in the days when the government took over the Indian reservations, they would place them in boarding schools. My dad and my uncle would tell stories about how, if they talked their own language, they would be beaten across the hands with a ruler until it was bloody. They would suffer. They would punish them if they continued to speak their own language and keep their own culture. So my father felt that if we could get in at a young age and adapt to the world as it is now, then it would be all that much better for us; we wouldn't suffer as he did. He emphasized education, felt that it was important, and he felt that adapting was very important. So he would integrate us into the mainstream system, and we weren't in his side. We weren't allowed to participate in the Indian dances and things like that because he felt that it may harm us more than do us any good."

"The world was changing," said an elderly woman, who at eighty has seen many changes in her lifetime. "It has changed tremendously even in the past ten years . . . the computer age has come in . . . things like this my father could see. The world was changing so fast that he felt there might not be much value in teaching us what he knew [traditional knowledge], when in essence he knew a lot."

Another elderly woman, age eighty, said, "My grandmother was converted to Christianity at a very early age, so a lot of things were not shared. They were raised at the time when it was not far removed from the Nez Perce War of 1877. There was a lot of repression from the greater society. If you want to get along in this world, you have to give up those things and adopt this other way of living. So things that were important for them to pass on to their kids, looking generations down, I think that's what kept them from passing."

According to a BIA report (1910), the Fort Lapwai School was integrated in 1910 to allow white children from the area to attend: "The Indian children from our boarding school enter the classrooms with the white children. . . . No distinction is made between Indians and whites in the school." This integrated school had departments of music, agriculture, domestic science, and manual training, in addition to the regular curriculum. Some of the narrators in this text graduated from that school.

Women and Modern Education

A young woman who has graduated from the University of Idaho spoke of her memories of grade school. "We had so much discrimination in school that we wouldn't go out of school when we were in grade school without fighting at least once. Teachers would sit us in the back room and let us

7.25. Fort Lapwai Indian School. Idaho State Historical Society 80-37-9, c. 1910.

7.26. Fort Lapwai Indian School. An eighty-four-year-old elderly woman said, *"Notice the transitional stage: the school shoes did not fit them, but they took them and they had to suffer."* National Park Service, Nez Perce National Historical Park Collection 394, c. 1908.

L-R top row: Lapwai Indian School (1908)

Ella Lawrence, Nancy Edwards, Nancy Lowry. Susie Corbett, Elizabeth Williams; 2 Row. Annie Moody, Susie McConville, Etta Moffett, Amelia John, Martha Nesbitt: 3 Row, Lillie Hoyt, Hattie James, Edna Hayes, Iva Lawrence & Katie Smith: 4th Row; Irene Wilkenson, Lucy Moody, Viola Spencer, Elizabeth Miles, Augusta Hill, and Agnes Hill

3051

7.27. From left, Agnes Moody, Lah-tso-sah, and baby, Willie Moody. Lah-tso-sah was the first wife of George Moody, who was instrumental in establishing the first tribal government and in the creation of the integrated Lapwai school. He also established the Meadow Creek Presbyterian Church within the Lamatama or White Bird band. Courtesy, Carla High Eagle, c. 1910.

color. They didn't bother to help us. They just assumed that we were handicapped or mentally retarded in some way, that we weren't teachable."

A single parent, twenty-two years of age, said, "At first I never cared about education. I never had a role model in the family to keep telling me to go to school, keep it up. I didn't know what was honor roll. Someone asked me, and I said, 'What is that?' Some kids said, 'That's when you get good grades.' I felt really stupid. My grades were good, but not good enough to be honor roll. Now, I see education is important, being twenty-two years old. I don't have a permanent job. Now, that's what's holding me back. It is so important. You can learn other things and become professional. I don't have that professional education right now. Now, it hurts me inside, working myself up professionally. It's getting hard, the low rate of pay every day, especially trying to raise two children. It's hard. That's one thing I like to see young people do today. Keep going to school, especially for Indian children. It's hard. A lot of white people look at you like you don't have these qualities. Why even try? We need more people in the world to tell the kids to keep going, not to stop, not to look down on each other, not to judge, because a child [who] comes from a bad background . . . gives up easily. It's happening more out there, not just alcohol and drugs; there's more out there. Lots of kids get away from this area. I think it is school's responsibility to prepare kids for that discrimination and racism. That's their responsibility. What's the point in having a school, if they cannot teach history properly? Racism has been taught every day, actually, from the parents to the children. It's the bad part; either you can teach to hate other races, or they can teach it is all right to be around other people than themselves. We should get along with other people from other races to help defeat problems like drugs and alcohol in the world. Edu-cation should go beyond reading and writing or just having a job. Education should give people a quality of life."

A forty-four-year-old mother of two said, "I hope that my children and grandchildren do get a good understanding of the non-Indian way of life. I hope they take the good things from both worlds—the Indian and the non-Indian—and make a life that is compatible for them. I hope they will continue to get an education because I feel like education is where it is at now. I feel that education cannot hurt them; I feel that can only help them in many ways. I have done a lot of work to see that my children have gotten through school, through high school, and my daughter has worked hard in college, and my son is going back to college in January. I hope that they will cope with the things that are out in the world today. There is a change in people; the United States is a melting pot. I just hope that they hold on to their families and hold on to their traditions and their ways that we have."

In the mid-1940s, the University of Idaho Home Economics Department offered home economics classes to women on the Nez Perce Reservation as a community development project through the extension program. The purpose of these classes was to help women to become more independent and to teach them to be better homemakers so that they could in turn teach their families and others in the community. Sewing and cooking were among the subjects taught.

"Education is the only way we can survive with the mainstream of life," said an eighty-year-old interviewee.

The very first Nez Perce woman on the tribal executive council said, "I was involved in all these organizations because I wanted to let the people know that women can do all these things. I didn't have my formal education, so sometimes it is quite a job. I like everybody to be sure and get

7.28. The old BIA building on the Nez Perce reservation. Unidentified students of a home economics class, which was offered through the University of Idaho Home Economics Department. Courtesy, Alta Guzman, c. 1950.

7.29. Lillian Smith and Geneva Stevens (both now deceased) in the old BIA building on the reservation, in a sewing class taught by the University of Idaho Home Economics Department. Courtesy, Alta Guzman, c. 1950.

7.31. From left, Charles Hayes, Chairman of the Nez Perce Tribal Executive Committee; JoAnn Kauffman; U.S. Senator Mark Hatfield of Oregon; Joe Red Thunder; Keith Red Thunder. Courtesy, JoAnn Kauffman. Photographers, Ankers, Anderson, and Cutts, c. 1993.

had also worked as reporter and anchor at KING-TV in Seattle, Washington. She has been a national correspondent for *CBS This Morning* since 1990 and frequently serves as substitute co-anchor for Paula Zahn, as well as contributing to CBS News' *48 Hours* and *Street Stories* and delivering a weekly consumer tip on CBS radio.

Hattie Kauffman has received an Emmy Award for her reporting. She has a unique style of reporting on stories about people and places that often don't make headlines. For example, she reported the human side of the Persian Gulf crisis from major United States military installations.

▲ ▲ ▲ ▲ ▲ ▲ ▲ ▲ ▲ ▲ ▲ ▲ ▲ ▲ ▲ ▲

JoAnn Kauffman, forty-one, talks about her work for the tribe: *"I received my master's in public health administration. After that, I came*

back and worked with the Nez Perce Tribe from 1979 to 1982. My work with the tribe has been primarily in community health. I went into the area of public health because of my concern for the health conditions that I saw that existed for Indian communities. I never pretended to be a person who can actually deal with anything like putting a needle in somebody or opening somebody up. I never saw myself as that, but I wanted to get somehow involved in health and health administration. It proved to be just what I was looking for, to try to help plan and figure out how you get health services to rural communities, how you make it meaningful so that people can make differences in their lives and the lives of their children. So it has been pretty much all my careers have been targeted to Indian Health . . .

"In 1982, I left Idaho and moved to Seattle, where I took a job as an executive director of Seattle Urban Indian Health Program that was fairly comprehensive. It had over 150 employees, a very large budget, and a real opportunity for me professionally, but then I had to leave Idaho; that was a difficult decision. I was there for seven years.

"I worked as a lobbyist for the Nez Perce Tribe in Washington, D.C., for five years and then relocated back to Kamiah. I was representing some other tribes while I was back east, and some of the national Indian organizations. It was fortunate for me that the tribe allowed me to work for them in Washington, D.C. I got to know the tribe in a way that I never got to know them before. I saw people in the leadership positions regularly, executive members of the Nez Perce Tribe Committee would come to D.C. We would talk to them about the issues that they were bringing back, and set up the meeting with the members of Congress, top officials with the Federal agencies, and try to assist and resolve the issues that they bring back. One of the biggest projects I worked on for the tribe was the passage of the amendment to the Nez Perce

National Historical Park legislation . . . that set up these historically significant sites related to the history and culture of the tribe and also the War of 1877, and it provided for the designation of those sites and for the National Park Service to acquire them through purchase of the land. . . . The only problem was that it was 1965. The legislation set this up and restricted the park to the boundaries of Idaho. If you are familiar with the Nez Perce history, that does not cover the true story of the Nez Perce tribe. It is interesting because one of the biggest places of opposition to extending beyond the boundaries of Idaho was from the state of Oregon. There still remains some resistance to even extending through the National Park Service this physical presence of the Nez Perce Tribe back to Wallowa.

"When I first moved to D.C., Allen Pinkham was the chairman of the tribe, and he talked to me about this dream that they made Wallowa [part of the park], where Chief Joseph's father's grave was located. It was being threatened by developers who had purchased land adjacent to the five-acre cemetery site near the lake, with plans for a recreational condominium/hotel kind of development. There is a group of citizens there in Joseph, Oregon, who oppose that. But the wheels of power were turning in the direction where it looked like it was inevitable that was going to happen, so that was a real high priority for the tribe, and I was able to work with the tribe on that. And it took us three years. . . . but it designated sites in Oregon and Washington at the younger Chief Joseph's camp sites in Montana. I think that was the most exciting project that I was able to work on for the Nez Perce tribe while I was back there. I was really happy that finally it worked out the way it did . . .

"I have moved back to the reservation because I did miss the community interaction—being able to be part of the community. I moved to the reservation because I want my children to have a con-

7.32. Julia Davis, member of the Nez Perce Tribal Executive Committee, Lapwai, Idaho.

nection to their peers within the tribe, a real friendship connection, and not feel that they are not a part of the tribe. They need to feel like it is their home, and these are their roots. In my heart, I felt that I had something different. I have work to do here. I am not sure what it is. I am kind of finding [out] what [it] is. I keep working for the tribe in the area of [community health]."

▲ ▲ ▲ ▲ ▲ ▲ ▲ ▲ ▲ ▲ ▲ ▲ ▲ ▲ ▲ ▲

JULIA DAVIS'S EFFORTS on behalf of the tribe are described by JoAnn Kauffman: *"The Nez Perce tribe is really fortunate because they have Julia Davis as their primary advocate on health issues. She is an NPTEC [member of the Nez Perce Tribal Executive Committee], but she is also the chair-*

7.33. Connie Evans in Vietnam. Courtesy, Connie Evans.

man of the National Indian Health Board, so she has a real national role in health. My best work, I think, has been as an advisor to Julia because she gets so much information kind of directed at her. It has been helpful to have someone to filter a lot of thought, to bounce ideas off, and to get some suggestions."

▲ ▲ ▲ ▲ ▲ ▲ ▲ ▲ ▲ ▲ ▲ ▲ ▲ ▲ ▲

"I WAS IN VIETNAM from November 1967 to 1969. At that time, the Vietnam War was not very popular. When I returned, I did not speak to anybody about Vietnam or my experience there. There was a reporter in Kamiah who talked to me shortly after I came back. I think she was the only one I made public statements to, and many people did

not know I was there. It was very difficult for me until about 1982 or 1983, when a book called Home Before Morning was published by a nurse. I read that, and it was very difficult to read because it brought back many memories. It was then that I started working and resolving some of my feelings about it. But now it is a lot easier to talk about it, and I feel pretty good about it.

"I was the only Nez Perce woman nurse who served in Vietnam. I don't know how many women nurses joined the armed forces during that time period. If they had joined, there were very few who went to Vietnam. A majority of the women who were in Vietnam were nurses, since I wasn't the only nurse during that time. . . . I spent my whole year in Vietnam in the recovery room, which meant that I took care of all the people who came out of surgery until they recovered or died. I developed closeness with people I was working with.

"I had a year of nursing school behind, I'd just graduated, and I spent a year in San Antonio, and my experience was in pediatrics, so from there I went to a different area. Initially, I was scared, but then that didn't last long because you did not have enough time to be scared. You have to work, you have to function, and you just learnt as you went along. Everyday it got worse. There were scenes of so many dying every day. Pretty soon you become cold, which was very difficult."

This woman's cousin spoke very highly of her: "She was also a real source of pride for our family because she was a nurse, had a uniform, and she went into the military, and she went to Vietnam. Like, every time Vietnam was on the news, every single night, everybody rushed to see if they are going to see my cousin in there. She had real positive impact on me."

▲ ▲ ▲ ▲ ▲ ▲ ▲ ▲ ▲ ▲ ▲ ▲ ▲ ▲ ▲

"I GRADUATED FROM Washington State University. I have two different careers: one is in my con-

tracting. I contract in construction finish work, painting, wallpaper hanging, decorating. I can assist with selection of art for your home, which takes me into my other career in the off-season, when we are not doing construction: I do art management, and I am a consultant now, right now for the tribe. I am a consultant for the fine art museum for Washington State University. I have been a consultant for the National Park Service on different exhibits, and I am also helping the economic development department of our tribe with our current artists who are either at professional or on the threshold of professionalism in the arts, and that is all the arts: the performing arts as well as the visual arts, the traditional arts as well as contemporary arts. I really feel good about that. . . . [F]or my way of thinking, on the reservation, to bring economics to us, that I don't care if we have 99 percent artists; that is to me very good exposure to the outside world, to think globally. To have the best artists that we can have—that also helps with retaining of our heritage and culture.

"I went into business because I wanted to provide some kind of employment, and I wanted to prove that an Indian woman could have . . . her own business. I also wanted to be a role model for my children. I have four daughters and one son. I thought, in summertime, this could show them a work ethic. I think there is also a problem in our culture, not from 150 years ago, but from three generations ago, when there was no employment. Work ethic somehow slipped away because we were receiving commodities.

"So you could eat, but what about the appreciation of doing the work? Why do it? How do it? You can go out and collect traditionally. You cannot do the contemporary work because there is no work to be done. We got lost there, as far as 'Why get up every day and do something?' But just like non-Natives, as for leisure, that's what we are doing: hunt, collect, or enjoy nature. To Indians,

7.34. Ann McCormack

that was a part of their spirituality, so they need the identification. So, then comes in the lazy Indian. That plays a part in that."

▲ ▲ ▲ ▲ ▲ ▲ ▲ ▲ ▲ ▲ ▲ ▲ ▲ ▲ ▲ ▲ ▲

"I ATTENDED MOSTLY public schools with the exception of a year and a half. I went to Chelaco Indian Boarding School, Oklahoma. After high school, I went to college. I obtained a degree in peace officer training and associate in behavior science, and later I got law enforcement, and I completed a bachelor of science in criminal justice in 1990.

"I kept the concept that I was told by the boarding school that I was not college material. So I went back to the reservation, and I married my high school sweetheart. I had known him ever

7.35. Lucinda Pinkham, in her Wenatchee, Washington, police uniform. Courtesy, Lucinda Pinkham.

since we were small. His family was in up the long house. He was enrolled at Colville, but he was a Palouse Nez Perce. We have sort of been encouraged to marry people of our own kind. He ran into turmoil. We had married in 1971; he died in 1974. He took his own life. He was going through a transition where he could not understand or accept. He was getting out of construction work as an operating engineer and going to go back to Eastern Washington to become a teacher. He already had two years of college in and was going to go back and complete school. This transition was too great for him to bear. He took his life.

"So after that, I found myself with my two children and not having an education. It was very hard to get a job. The first job I could get was as a motel maid. That made it very difficult because I could not support my children on this, and I was not about to go on welfare or anything. We applied for Social Security. . . . But then I felt like the Social Security is not going to last forever, so I felt that I needed to get an education, so when the Social Security ran out, that I would be self-supporting and would be able to take care of my children.

"So I started back to school. . . . I went through the police training at the Lewis-Clark State College and applied to peace officer training. They told me, 'You are eligible for an associate in behavioral science,' so I worked toward that and received both degrees. . . .

"Then, I married my second husband and moved to Wenatchee, Washington. When I worked as a police woman in Wenatchee, I was accepted for who I was there. . . . Today, when I have worked here in Orofino, Idaho, as a police woman, there was a transition there because this is a smaller community. The people have older ideas there. . . . And, for them, seeing a female as an officer goes against their stereotypes of women, especially Indian woman. I had to confront John Wayne in various offices. I had to go above their macho image because I wanted to help in child abuse cases, I wanted to help in rape cases, I wanted to help in spousal abuse cases. I think there have always been places for women there. It's just that they have this male ego, this male image, that they feel that that's man's work.. . . ."

"I worked for six and a half years with law enforcement, but I was a reserve officer. . . . I did that for six and a half years. My husband was a Nez Perce Indian. He had a drinking problem—things got too intolerable. I told him to go to a counselor, or I was leaving. He went to a counselor once and would not return because he had a drinking problem that was in denial, so I left him and went back to college, went back to Lewiston, to Lewis-Clark College.

204

"I started in 1987. . . . I stayed in school, got my bachelor's of science in law and enforcement in 1990. . . . [T]he Orofino Police wanted to hire me, and the Chief of Police kept calling, and finally I told them I would work for them. I worked for them for a year and a half, and my chief had a heart attack. He was the only one who was supportive of me being the only Indian, and the only woman in the area on any department. So after I lost his backing, then I resigned my position. After that, I started as a Research Analyst for the Bureau of Land Management."

▲ ▲ ▲ ▲ ▲ ▲ ▲ ▲ ▲ ▲ ▲ ▲ ▲ ▲ ▲ ▲

"THE FIRST POSITION I was employed at was as a clerk/typist at Northern Idaho Service Unit, located on the Nez Perce Reservation, for five years. My initial duty was as a receptionist. Then, I began clerical support for Administration, Contract Health Services, and other departments at the clinic. I left Northern Idaho in September 1975 to begin classes at the University of Washington in Seattle.

"In 1984, I returned to the Lapwai area and sought employment. . . . I filled in, temporarily, [at the clinic] off and on from December 1985 to September 1986, when Thomas Atkins, D.D.S., hired me full time. I decided to take the position since my father had passed away, and the remainder of his funeral expenses had to be paid. So I decided the clinic would offer more financially. The position offered was on-the-job training, including continuing education stipends through the Northern Idaho Service Unit resources, as a dental assistant, and I believed that this would fit in reasonably.

"In August 1993, I left to return to school at the University of Idaho. I am presently a student at the University of Idaho. My goal is to become a writer. I am taking classes pertaining to writing, for example, creative writing and technical writ-

7.36. Beverly Penney, a graduate student at the University of Idaho.

ing, in addition to computer courses to operate IBM, Macintosh, and the WordPerfect programs. My goal is to become a competent person in attaining some level that is successful.

"As a Nez Perce Indian woman, it is challenging to convince myself that I have capabilities. I realize as a Native American that I was not introduced to building onto literacy as other cultures. Sometimes my dreams to be an 'Amerindian' was my classification as a Native American as fully educated. But the drawback from my background was the emphasis towards social skills as the primary objective rather than exposure and preparation for the outside professional world. . . .

"[T]raditionalism is an important identifying element to a culture. The hindrance is that traditionalism does not qualify a person for technical skills. Acculturation will result in problems substantial to modernization, such as family disinte-

205

7.37. Carla High Eagle, in Nez Perce buckskin dress. Courtesy, Dick Storch.

gration, sociological problems, and limits on technical progress. . . . I am unsure where my pursuits will lead me, but I do hope to contribute in some small way [to modernization]. I dream that my grandchildren will further themselves in their potentials to be useful in life, and my son and his wife will support them."

▲ ▲ ▲ ▲ ▲ ▲ ▲ ▲ ▲ ▲ ▲ ▲ ▲ ▲ ▲ ▲

"I was the president of the Nez Perce Appaloosa Horse Club in 1993. Through this position, I made contact with the Belgium Appaloosa Horse Club. Let's see my role in this. I first received a call about the Belgian Appaloosa Horse Club interest in us going to Europe in March 1994. I followed up with a letter, and we negotiated the number of

riders and costs. In June of 1994, I invited them to Lapwai to see a powwow. Three of them attended. I drove them around the reservation to see Nez Perce Appaloosas and visit the country. They even attended the pipe ceremony at Whitebird battlefield.

"From there, they decided they would like to increase the number of dancers, riders, and singers as well as include an exhibit on Nez Perce history and art. My role then expanded to include all the necessary tasks to accomplish the above. This included organizing an application process, selection criteria, setting up meetings, getting information on passports and Belgium, recruiting artists, meeting with the tribe and the park about the exhibit, including text and photos, meeting the artists, and lots of promotion within the community. Finally, I selected some key helpers, including Joyce McFarland, Cass Kipp, Andrea Axtell, and Ida Ann Wheeler to help me. We then set up a timeline to get tasks done, such as applying for birth certificates, applying for passports, doing an inventory of our outfits and photos for the exhibit. I also contacted the Idaho Department of Commerce for help with export guidelines and rules."

As a result of Carla High Eagle's efforts, some forty members of the Nez Perce Tribe, which has been a breeder of the Appaloosa horse since it was introduced into the United States by the Spanish three hundred years ago, traveled to Belgium to demonstrate Nez Perce singing, dancing, and drumming and to teach about the Nez Perce culture, past and present.

Carla High Eagle spoke about the club's trip in an article in the *Lewiston Morning Tribune* of November 6, 1994: *"I don't want this to be just a one-time thing. I want this to continue. Horses were the mainstay of the Nez Perce culture and they still can be.*

"I feel that by doing all this, the Nez Perce will be seen on an international level as the colorful,

7.38. Group photo of the Nez Perce Appaloosa Horse Club. Courtesy, Carla High Eagle, 1994.

proud, intelligent and friendly people that we are. My role has been and continues to be one of promotion of our culture, beliefs, and [the] generous heart of the Nez Perce people."

▲ ▲ ▲ ▲ ▲ ▲ ▲ ▲ ▲ ▲ ▲ ▲ ▲ ▲ ▲ ▲ ▲

A WOMAN IN HER early thirties gave a description of some of the events which have taken place in her family: "*Another example of just speaking out and standing up for our own selves as women. . . . I had an experience back in September of 1990. The Health and Welfare from Bellingham, Washington, called me and asked me to consider taking my younger sister's children because my sister had lost them through the court at that point, or was going to lose them. She's had problems with drugs and alcohol. . . . [A]nd I said, 'Yes, I'll take care of them, but you've got to give me two or three days to find a reasonable child care center for them because I'm in the middle of school, and I can't take care of them myself.'*"

"*Many people thought that I was crazy to take my sister's children, but if you believe in extended families, as we believe in our Native American culture, it's not unusual for aunts to take in their sister's children—because to us they're our children. It's almost as though they are our sons and daughters. We love them, and we just feel that it's important to have our own family together.*

"*So I was going to take these children as I said, . . . but something happened where the Health and Welfare in Bellingham transferred jurisdiction to the Lemhi Indian Tribe. . . . [D]ue to inadequately trained counselors there on the reservation, they took it upon themselves to be judge and jury, and they refused to let those chil-*

dren come into my home. . . . And I thought at that point, 'That doesn't sound right, nor is it legal.' . . . They knew that I had legal grounds under the Indian Act Child Law, that I had a right to come in to ask for temporary custody of my sister's children. . . .

"So we [my sister and I] went through, we discussed our options with a lawyer, and he helped us with a few details of how to approach our court date. And he advised us not to take in a lawyer, but to defend ourselves, to stand up for our own rights. . . .

"So when we went to court, we went before a woman judge, and she was also a Native American. I stated who I was and told my story, and then she said. 'Why has it taken your family so long to come to get these children? That's what I want to know.' And I told her, 'You know, it hasn't taken very long at all. We were there from the beginning. According to this document that I have received from [Bellingham] Health and Welfare, it shows a statement that we were there from the beginning,' and I was able to quote her a date, and a time, and some of the conversation between myself and the case worker. . . .

"[A]nd the court decided that yes, indeed, I could have the children—that as soon as the prosecuting attorney wrote up a projected plan as to when my sister could be deemed responsible for her children again, to monitor her progress as far as her drug and alcohol consumption was concerned, to provide counseling and AA for her, and to provide counseling for her children . . . I would be able to go over and pick up the children. So I anticipate going over this coming week and picking up my sister's children."

The concerned sister continued, "I would like to say, because of my education I feel that I was more able to express myself and to communicate my desires and the things that I felt were right because I knew they were. I'm not willing to let people tell me how to feel or what to do because I'm able to know better—I know more. So, as I'm sitting here thinking in terms of how monumental that seemed to be, it was very scary, and it was full of obstacles. But I was willing to go through them for my sister's children because of the love that I have for them and because of the love that I have for my sister. . . .

"And I still believe that women have a strong impact, and they have to overcome their fears and use the education that they've got, to be able to overcome things that are not right, but that are important for them, important for their families and for their future. To me, my role was to protect our children because our children are too young to have a voice for themselves. They cannot speak out for themselves, and I had an obligation to speak for them. And that's exactly what I went in and my sister and I did. We knew that we were right, and we had to act."

▲ ▲ ▲ ▲ ▲ ▲ ▲ ▲ ▲ ▲ ▲ ▲ ▲ ▲ ▲

A WOMAN, THIRTY YEARS OLD, who is a single mother of two, said: "It is my opinion the woman is the backbone to life. . . . not only the fact that she gives birth and continues life, but they have always been the rock that holds everything together, the family together. They have an enormous amount of strength. They might be very timid and quiet, they may appear that way, but they have so much strength and so much to contribute, not just only to the family but to the society as a whole. . . . They may not be 'in the spotlight' people, [but] . . . [t]hey manage to keep the culture and traditions alive."

Modern Roles and Problems

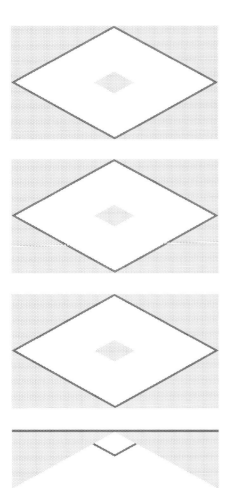

THE TRADITIONAL FUNCTIONS of provider, craftswoman, artist, spiritual guide, medicine woman, social worker, and educator were altered by the introduction of Christianity and agriculture, Euro-American household roles and the single-family household, log and frame houses, and Euro-American clothing and education. Foreign diseases, hospitals, and sanitoriums also affected the roles and status of women, who moved actively from a subsistence to a money economy as they became farmers, worked big gardens, and managed and marketed their grain and produce. Some women sold cattle; others worked for white farmers as laborers. Some women married fur traders, and later, settlers, with little change in their household roles. Others did housework for white women; a few were even their midwives.

In the early nineteen hundreds, jobs on the reservation were limited to work as cooks for the sanitorium. (Some women still frequently cook for senior citizen programs and for Head Start.) During the Second World War, women enlisted as nurses; others worked in war industries as far away as Seattle.

One woman in her thirties said, *"My mother worked in an airplane factory, something that I have never done."*

In December 1952, the BIA proposed a list to the U.S. Congress. Among its recommendations, the list included specific American Indian nations that were recommended to be dropped from federal services and federal jurisdiction of their affairs. Two of the tribes so named were the Nez Perce and Coeur d'Alene tribes. The Termination Act of August 1, 1953, was designed to accomplish this purpose. In 1954, another law placed unterminated reservations under state authority. Then, in 1956, the Relocation Act further diminished federal responsibilities for programs to unterminated reservations, undermining education and health services, and raising unemployment. The Relocation Act also provided funding for moving costs, the establishment of a new residence, and job training to those Native Americans willing to move to one of the federally approved urban centers, such as Los Angeles, San Francisco, Denver, Phoenix, Minneapolis, Seattle, Boston, and Chicago.

The relocation program created many problems, contributing to the development of Indian activism during the 1960s and 1970s. In an attempt to pacify the dissatisfied Indians, the federal government passed the Indian Civil Rights Act of 1968. However, the government continued its relocation program up until 1980, when the urban employment centers were closed down. (Jaimes 1992, 98-100.)

"The relocation programs of the 1950s and 1960s did have tremendous impact on Indian people nationally and then on the Nez Perce Tribe," observed a forty-one-year-old interviewee, offering her assessment of the longer term effects of the relocation program. "I don't think that the Federal government is now actively implementing what's called the relocation program any more because there is a lot of criticism about how the relocation program was handled and the fact that they created these large urban populations without any sort of support system for that population. But . . . , there is still a draw of [skilled] Indian people away from the reservation, away from the tribal communities through education, jobs. And

. . . because of the heritage of the relocation program, you have generations of people who are growing up in those cities related to people back home. To have a sort of a base. Nez Perce people have now a base, [a] family system out there in Seattle or Portland or Los Angeles or San Francisco and other places. The Nez Perce Tribe has a lot of really talented people within the tribe, but there are a lot of talented people who are members of the tribe who are living outside.

For example, Cathy Wilson, granddaughter of Elizabeth Penney Wilson. She is a lawyer. President Bush appointed her Associate Solicitor for Indian Affairs, Department of the Interior. Sounds like an inflated title, but what that means is that she was like a top attorney for the Indian country, getting opinions about Indian law, for example, like the jurisdiction of the tribe's fishing regulations on the reservations. Legal questions like those go up the channels to the Department of Interior's solicitor's office, and her position was head of the Indian Affairs in the solicitor's office. When I lived in Washington, D.C., I was surprised to see how many Nez Perce people there really are out there. We would get together every month or two months or whenever the Nez Perce Tribe sent a delegation back. We tried to organize the Nez Perce people in the D.C. area to come together. About ten, twelve Nez Perces living in the D.C. area are doing really interesting kinds of jobs. Two Nez Perce women are working for the U.S. Census Bureau; another woman, Lauretta Tools, is an attorney, graduated from law school, working for Senate Committee on Indian Affairs in Washington, D.C."

In recent times, women have worked for the county, state, and federal governments. They have trained and received employment as nurses, secretaries, dieticians, and home economists. A majority of those now employed by the Nez Perce tribal government are women. They work for the

Forest Service, Fish and Game, and Wildlife agencies; for road construction companies; and for tribal health and educational programs. Much of this employment is seasonal. The unemployment rate calculated by the Bureau of Indian Affairs for Nez Perce living on or adjacent to the reservation is 65 percent with another 10 percent earning less than $7,000 a year.

Today, there are individual women who own and run their own small or larger scale businesses. There are Nez Perce women who administer national programs, who are teachers, nurses, counselors, U.S. census takers, news anchors, lobbyists, actresses, playwrights, artists, painters, artisans, construction workers, and secretaries. Other women are bus drivers for the school or senior citizens organizations. One Nez Perce woman was honored with an award by the President of the United States for her skill in traditional crafts, and another woman received a lifetime achievement award from Lewis-Clark College for her cornhusk weaving.

A forty-year-old woman said, *"I believe there are more women working for the tribe than men, and they are increasing the responsible roles, for example, two women managers. In the '70s, we had just one. We have more women in NPTEC [Nez Perce Tribal Executive Committee] than before."*

In the modern era, women feel more fortunate than their predecessors to have homes with electricity, running hot and cold water, electric ranges and refrigerators, radios, microwaves, television sets, and telephones. Elderly women recognize that the life of their mothers and grandmothers was much harder without these household aids.

At their work places, women have moved from typewriters to computers. These computers, cameras, tape recorders, and camcorders are being used to preserve data from the traditional past as well as the essential information of the present.

Already, communication between tribes has been improved, and it is widely understood that a good grasp of technology is crucial for survival in today's world economy.

Discrimination was discussed by a Nez Perce woman in her thirties: *"My mother, even in picking raspberries and strawberries and things, would find that there was discrimination in how the bosses would hold the fullest rows with the most berries for a white person and skip us over to a lesser row because of discrimination. My mom would be booted off her jobs because of discrimination. The new laws have been put in . . . they can't discriminate so blatantly anymore. They have to be subtle because of the discrimination laws that they've put out. Even though they are still there, they're more subtle about it now.*

"My mother, . . . as I said, she worked as a seasonal worker, and that means we picked strawberries and blueberries and potatoes and those kinds of things. But I remember the strawberry fields and how she faced discrimination and prejudice. The farmers would hire their wives or their children to be bosses over us, and there are times that I could remember where we'd pick through the field, and then we'd get to the end of the row, and we'd have to contact one of these bosses. Well, if there was an exceptionally full row of berries, so that these vines would just hang down where you could see that we'd make a lot of money if we were able to pick them, but instead of giving us those rows, they would skip us over one or two rows and save those rows for friends, relatives, or whoever.

"That was an example of prejudice or discrimination to us, and had my mother had the education and a voice in the matter, she could have done many things; she could have spoke out and said how unfair she thought it was, or she could have quit the job altogether. Had she had the education, she might not have even had to be working in that situation, but under the circumstances we

had to take what we had, what we could do. So that's one example of what education and the kind of impact a woman could have had, had she had the education and also group senses. She just didn't have the opportunities."

A thirty-five-year-old interviewee said, *"Discrimination, as far as my grandparents and my parents were concerned, they were more blatant then; they were worse then. I suppose I could say that because of the ignorance of that society and of that age, they were more apt to come right out . . . more honest and more clear . . . Because my father was, like I say, half-white and half-Indian. But he was raised Indian. He's been hired on jobs that, as soon as they found out that he was Indian, they fired him. . . ."*

Another woman, in her forties, observed, *"I'm not saying that that's the way the world is . . . that the majority of time I'm discriminated against. I'm saying that it exists. I'm saying that, in spite of it, I still continue on anyway. With my grandparents and my mother and father, they dealt with it as best they could, and they still continue to teach us positive values and optimism about life, in facing our lives. I don't feel that discrimination is so rampant as it might have been before. I feel that, more and more, as Native American people, we are all being taught from a common ground now. We are, whether we like it or not, acculturated. We all are. Yes, we have our culture, and we have what we value, and that's great . . . [T]hat's where my philosophy comes in: where if you can take from all different cultures and philosophies and come out a better person because, in the end, that's what we're going to have to do. We, as a people and as a nation, aren't going to be able to exist unless we work together. And that's what it will come down to, is that we'll learn to work together toward a common goal. And I think that that's happening, even more so now than in the past. I see now that Native Ameri-*

cans as a whole are trying to save what they have left and find what they lost and still hold on to that—and that's good, there's nothing wrong with that. Yet I see them trying to learn and to grow and continue on in the fast paced world at the same time."

Said a woman in her early forties, *"I felt discrimination in a variety of ways. Because I am American Indian, I felt that in some of the congressional offices, from the staff primarily. On the other hand, there are staff members in congressional offices who are wonderful. The discrimination that I felt hurt more was the discrimination within the Indian affairs area because I was a woman. A lot of the lobbyists in D.C. who represent tribes have been white males, law firms who specialized in Indian affairs. To have an Indian woman come on the scene as a lobbyist and compete with other lobbyists in D.C., I think was probably threatening to the non-Indians. It was a competitive, back-stabbing kind of environment among those people who lobby because they're always trying to find more clients so they can make themselves look good. They are always making you look bad. . . . To be in that environment was a little scary at first, I guess. But I developed a rough edge and learnt to be scrappy and protect myself. . . .*

"I worked with the Council of Energy Resource Tribes for four years. It was a good relationship. It was a world of men. I get discrimination from men within my own tribe because I am a woman. They are reluctant to share information dealing with fisheries or those kinds of issues because they want a man to do it or to handle that. I just persevered and kept on it, and one of the things that helped me is just sharing information. That is the best thing that I can do in those kind of situations, where it is clear there is opposition because of my gender . . . is just to get the information as broadly as possible. . . ."

212

"Nez Perce was a matriarchal society because of the way the bands were and the camps were made," a thirty-seven-year-old woman said. "The women were responsible for just about everything to do with the camps. To me, the women are more socially oriented. Even today, they are more responsible to make sure that, economically, things are held together. If you look at both the sides of the family line, the father's side and mother's side, women are stronger . . . Anthropologists never lived here, so they don't know what it is like."

A woman in her forties commented, "I think this society was a matriarchal society to begin with. In my own family background, my great-grandmother and my grandmother were very strong. They made all the decisions. I think that's probably why my sister and I are so strong. We love to have a say a lot in decision making."

Another woman, in her thirties, reflected, "Even when I was a little girl going to church, the women in church would decide. The women who made the decision, 'We are going to have a fundraising here. We are going to have a dinner here, and we are going to do this and that,' and the women got all the food ready, counted for all the money, planned all the activities, carried them all, and it is the same down here in the NPTEC (Nez Perce Tribal Executive Committee). The women, they don't do as much now as they did then. I remember the older women always were the ones who organized the political parties. They are the ones who got on the phones and called people and said, 'We are having a meeting here, and you are invited to come. We want you to share your views if you are running for NPTEC.' But it was the women who did all the organizing and the women who talked to their families and said, 'Well, we had this meeting, and this is who we preferred as candidate, and we want you to let your kids know that this is who they should be voting for.' It was the women who did that."

"Even if women were not involved directly, if they did not like the decisions, they were not afraid. They just left the meeting of the council. I think the reason there are so few women on NPTEC in a leadership role is that the women have farther sight than men do, and the men are in a greater time of transition. Because women still have the family, they still have their children, and they still have their home responsibilities and their financial responsibilities. But the men are in a time of transition from being the hunter, a provider, in the leadership. So how do our men fit into our society? One of the ways they fit in is through this tribal government that we have now as being the elective leaders and the speakers. You talk to any man who served on the NPTEC. They will tell you how much influence their wives have had or the women in their families have had on their decisions they made," remarked a mother of two and a grandmother in her thirties.

"I talk to the young people, and I talk to the women because the Nez Perce tribe basically is a matriarchal society," said a woman, thirty-seven years old. "The women, even though for many years they were not allowed to be on the council, none of them ever voted on that, they still had a large part in the decisions. It happened on the reservation many years ago, the women always formed a group. They had the power to put someone in office. Men and women both were there, but the women pretty much ran it. The women had power. They would tell the candidate, 'We will send you to the tribal council. You have to remember us.' So they would. So that, to me, is social and political independence. They are exerting their authority as voters, organizing and telling the menfolks."

A woman in her mid-forties said, "Nez Perce Indian women were more powerful in the past. Nez Perce women are powerful today; it seems to be a subordinate to kind of a Western culture be-

lief, the male dominance and corporate hierarchy and corporate decision making. I think Nez Perce Indian women as a group were more powerful. I know the stories I heard about; for example, Lewis and Clark camped with the Nez Perce in Kamiah. Then, a lot of decisions got deferred to the women. Let them stay here, or let them not stay here. It was much more interaction and discussion. I think the impact of white culture/patriarchal society/belief system has taken away the power of Nez Perce women. Alcohol was the major impact, mainly in the dynamics between women and men, and the situation in which we have domestic violence and wife battering that I don't think would have been tolerated. The whole issue of whether this is a matriarchal society anymore, like it used to be, and who owns the home, and who owns the possessions of the family and things like that. I think the position of the Nez Perce women is probably [one of] more compromise now than it was then.

"I think the governing system, the process of governing and administering programs and services for the people of the tribe, is based on a Western corporate model that doesn't factor in [the] power . . . of Nez Perce Indian women in a cultural way. On the other hand, Nez Perce Indian women in the tribe are still powerful. They still, through the power of telephone and attending meetings, can have an impact on what happens with the tribe, but it's more behind the scenes, more covert."

It is significant that some of my interviewees think of the Nez Perce as a matriarchal society in the past. In the strict meaning of governance by women, no true matriarchal society is known to have existed. However, the use of this term by modern Nez Perce women for the autonomy and authority enjoyed in their traditional community is quite understandable given the contrast with what they perceive to have been the lowly position of women—the property of men—in traditional Euro-American society. In fact, the status of Plateau women was very high, and they enjoyed economic and social independence.

The division of labor was discussed by a woman who is in her thirties: *"I am glad that in our native society there was a division of labor. I like to think that all the people living within the house were respected. Young were respected; they were the future. The old were respected because they had the wisdom, and the middle-aged people were respected because they were the providers. The division of labor gave everybody the right to existence within the society. That's what women's role continued to be, the definition, and what it is they would be working towards. Everybody has a place within the society. We want just for excellence and achievement to provide better lives for our families and our community. I think, going back five generations in aboriginal life, women had a great deal of independence. They had a great deal of sisterhood, the tremendous friendship and the camaraderie because of the subsistence economy. Because all the large tasks had to be performed in unison so that provided specializing constantly and at the same time independence. I think aboriginal talent and intelligence was greatly appreciated in our tribe."*

One interviewee who was a nurse in Vietnam said, *"It was very difficult, at the powwow, when they had the veteran dance. First, it was difficult for me to go there and dance. No matter where I went, it was difficult. But it is a little bit easier because a year ago, H. Axtell started the pipe ceremony at the Pi-nee-waus [community center] . . . with our VFW [Veterans of Foreign Wars] group, of which I am a member. My post commanders came up to me and said that they were going to have a veterans' circle, with veterans sitting around . . . [having] a pipe ceremony. I was not going to be allowed to sit in the ceremony because*

I was a woman, and this really made me angry. They said I can stay behind the leader, and I said, 'If I cannot participate in the circle, I am not going to participate at all.'

"They started having the pipe ceremony in all of the battle areas. I didn't go to any of them. Not because of that, but because I did not have a lot of time. So when they came to the last one, Bear's Paw in Montana, my post commander came and asked me if I would attend since I haven't been attending any of the others. He said that I will be allowed to sit in the circle. So I did. I went there. As we were gathering at the battle ground to prepare for the pipe ceremony, Mae Taylor came and talked to me. She is also a veteran. She was not in Vietnam, but she served in that time. She told me that, traditionally, women didn't sit in the circle and didn't take part in it, and she didn't feel comfortable. I told her that I was going to sit in the circle because I felt I earned it. I didn't fight combat in Vietnam, but I certainly saved human lives, so I am going to sit in the circle. So he had me sit next to the leader on the left side, and he invited me to join the circle. I was waiting to see if she is going to join, and she did. So there were two women veterans and other male veterans, and then they invited everybody on the council, so other council women joined too. I feel good that they were allowing women, but in the past they never did in the war dances. Women never participated. They stood on the sides. I am glad that they [men] are making the advances again. Women would like to participate. There are lots of women veterans, and I think they have earned that right."*

Said another woman, forty-one years old, "If you go to the memorials and the pipe ceremonies that are held in connection with the Nez Perce War and with the Nez Perce National Park sites, there is a lot of emphasis on men stepping forward, and this is for veterans, and this is for men,*

as if men are the only casualties of war. I think that is the biggest mistake in how the Nez Perce history has been documented, is the attention on men, chiefs in particular, when in fact it is just a cataclysmic event for the whole people: for women, children, and men. That affected our relationships in our family systems and our relationships within our tribe and with non-Indian people for generations after. And, in order to heal from that, we have to understand what happened. We can never do that until we can get past the notion that this was the men's war. It was not a men's war; it was a war that impacted everybody. It's kind of hard to say that Indian women have our place in present society or in our tribal government when we still have not found our place in the history. Until we find our place in history, then we can't get to the discussion of how we get involved today. And, until that happens, we continue to work in sort of a background, behind-the-scene sort of way.

"In the past, Indian women were consulted and were listened to. Now, it is much more informal. . . . Right now, I think Indian women are much behind the scenes. If you look at the General Council and monitor and see what happens there and how people get elected and nominated, Indian women are very much involved. But if you look at the elections, it was not very long ago a woman was elected vice-chairman. I think that's the first time an Indian woman has been elected vice-chairman for the Nez Perce Tribe. I think more needs to be done. Indian women are very powerful in the Nez Perce Tribe today, but they still have so much further to go in the whole area of . . . where money is being spent and where the priorities are—I think children, health care, family issues, things like that, and women are not very high on the priority. . . . [There] seems to be kind of a Western type of mentality within our own tribe about women. I hope someday it will change."*

"Socially, and economically, the roles [of women] have gotten greater to this day so that the majority of the women are socially more prominent than the men, and, even though men do hold some jobs that are leadership roles, it is the women behind them that keep them there," observed a woman nearly forty years old. "And economically, it's women who are the ones who bring home the bacon because a majority of the households on the reservation today seem to be single parent. And, even if they are married, you know, it is usually the woman who does the purchasing and does the buying and things like that; the man plays a secondary role."

"On the reservation, there's a lot of single-mother situations. Indian women are probably, I could say, used to caring and being a provider for her children, because a lot of the time the father isn't there, or, if he is there, then he's not functioning the way a normal society would think. Like, for example, my father hardly worked. He would hunt and fish when he was home, but he was in and out all of the time, and then my mother and father just finally divorced. My mother stayed on welfare and then worked in between and had us work in the summer for these seasonal kind of jobs," said another woman, now forty years old, about her own father and mother.

A young single mother in her thirties with two children said, "My marriage failed because he was a very domineering person. He is a non-Indian. He wanted to be waited on hand and foot all the time. He wanted me in the home and not to go out and work, and I wanted to go out and work. I wanted to work for my own independence, so I could have my own money, instead of him ruling everything. He would get abusive sometimes, and he has problems with alcohol too, so that just compounded it even more.

"Being a single parent and raising two children is financially very difficult. I have to continue to work and hold down jobs in order to take care of my kids and to continue to put money away so I will have something to retire on. I am trying to balance everything the best I can in order to make ends meet. I am trying hard. You know, you get stressed out after a while, but you have to keep on going. You have to. It's a lot of work living here [on the reservation]. In our house, the only source of heat is wood, so you have to stack up all your wood in the wintertime. You are out there chopping wood; you are going to warm up the house for the kids. It's a lot more work living back here than when I was living in Seattle, Washington. The house had all the modern conveniences. Living over here, it's more difficult, it's more physical work, but it's rewarding."

A single parent explains: "I think that the one-parent family has caused a lot of women to become independent by force. I, myself, when my husband died and I discovered that I was the head of the household, this has caused me to change some of my thinking because I have grown up in a society where my father worked. And my mother worked sometimes, but my father was the breadwinner for the family. He was the one who would go out hunting, put meat on our table, and I found myself without a husband, with two children. And I found, to hunt and fish for my children, this is where I started really becoming the person to put the salmon and meat on the table. That's where I started being more self-assertive and learning to become a better hunter and do those types of things out of force almost."

A woman in her mid-forties said, "[As for a] leadership role on women's part, at the same time I feel like somebody needs to take that first step, or no one is going to take that first step. So I push myself out there. Sometimes it doesn't work out good, and sometimes it does. I think that I tried to lead by demonstrating this is how you can do it. I know that there are a lot of women who can do it *a lot better than I could do it, but it's taking risks. That's what's important. People don't want to take risks unless somebody else does it."*

A woman just under forty made these comments: *"I see they [women] are more responsible [than men]. They are more sure that all the needs [of their household] are met and being independent with what they do after that. But a lot of social issues arise that are keeping the women from advancing . . . alcoholism, violence, or sexual abuse. I notice with the younger women, too, sometimes they don't have a role, strong role models, as far as: What does it mean to have financial independence? What does it mean to be a housewife? What does it mean to be a mother? So . . . they are going to their roles, learning 'What is it?' for themselves, and dissolving some of those illusions they thought they would be like.*

"I think that in our generation now, there is more responsibility. It's kind of like a generation of healing—addressing the issue of alcoholism and looking at it with both eyes open, being more aware that our kids are 'do as we do,' and we cannot tell them not to drink, then drink ourselves. We found out that doesn't work. Our kids are more open as far as communicating what their needs are. And to me, it is an important generation, the one we are in now, as far as going down the road of recovery. What is it? What do we want to be? I think that the Nez Perce Nation itself has gone through a lot of turmoil and change in the last 150 years, and it causes us to fall behind in areas that are important to us. But as we develop those areas, it is important that we have input into those areas.

"Being a parent, being a community member, you are involved in these organizations. You have to be on the task force on domestic violence, coming up with a protocol on how the law enforcement agencies will work together; one of the reports received on the reservation, how they will respond, and then what happens to the victims, what happens to the perpetrators. So there is less confusion during those times of crises while you are responding. I am involved with an organization in the school system that has to do with Parents Advisory Committees. We looked at developing cultural curriculum, as well as students tracking system, so that as parents we became more aware of where our students are in the system. If the student is at fault, we want to be there right away, not wait until he/she is down, try to catch them before they fall down. I was involved in a community care team and drafted a resolution regarding the youth and intoxication in our community—a youth rehabilitation program—getting that off the ground so kids who need help can go, as well as parents."

"I would like to see issues discussed at a community level more often than twice a year. You get better decisions, a more involved community. I think the quality of discussion would benefit because of the number of Indian women that would turn out," suggested a forty-year-old woman.

A twenty-two-year-old woman said, *"Sometimes women start fighting among themselves. We shouldn't do that. Women should come together, start planning, teach a program and try to make a success out of ourselves."*

In the opinion of one interviewee in her thirties, *"The money economy has caused a lot of problems for the Indian people because, prior to the money economy, there was a lot of trading done. Men got the meat and fish women needed. They were self-sustained families. When we moved to the money economy, it made it hard because, for men, there were few jobs."*

A single parent and mother of two in her early forties said, *"I think many of the men are not able to find a job. It's not because they are not capable of finding a job, [but] because of the society in the way it was . . . trying to take over the*

217

land . . . and make the European culture the dominant force. They would deliberately undermine men . . . in the Indian culture as the determinant force, as the bread winners, the protectors, as the providers, . . . they deliberately undermined and took that from Native American men as much as possible, and they still do that. So our people would not progress; our family unit could not progress.

"*So it's where Native American women can go into an establishment and can get a job. That's one reason I believe that it's taken us, as women, to have to be potential breadwinners, the dominant providers and care givers: because we are forced into that role as we have taken over. And I think a lot of that is because it's carrying over until somehow or another we change that. It will continue because women are now having to [take] care of their men because they are alcoholic. Some of them cannot do jobs now, whereas they might have been able to do it in the past.*

"*But some of [the men] have gotten addicted to drugs and alcohol to such an extent that they probably can't function in the society, not because they are Indians. I mean that crosses over: all races are now having difficulties with alcohol, but I think as far as our men are concerned, lots of their helplessness was constantly bombarding them with negative things as far as not helping them getting a job and having women like my grandmother, for example. She was our prime bread winner. Grandfather was really ill . . . [S]he had to get out and be creative, be innovative, to get money from . . . making alcohol and selling it to a brewery. She was a bootlegger. . . . She also sold shakes for roofs. They have to go out and take them off the trees on the reservation. My grandma had a lot of land. My mother remembers doing that. She said, 'I was strong as a man because I had to go and do it because I was the oldest child, because I had to go and work alongside of men to get this done so that*

we can go and sell them.' That was part of the money they needed just to live, just for the food.

"*Of course, hunting was the big thing. A lot of the things that men were free to do in their culture before was taken away from them. When horses were taken away from them, the land was taken away from them. A lot of things they knew that was the natural course of events, like to support their family, to take care of them, they could no longer do, and how devastating that could be on our Indian men. . . . [Y]ou hope that people in society don't get the idea that how often the dominant culture would like us viewed as savage or as people who didn't have anything going for them in the first place. They hope that we would buy into that. I imagine sometimes it happens.*

"*It is very unfortunate because we lose the pride and sense of accomplishment, the sense of values and sense of truth as we knew them. We were forced to take on a whole different culture, a whole different value system, and a whole different way of life. We were forced to do it. We had constantly the road blocked ahead of us. We learned how to speak English, we got educated, learned all these things, but that doesn't guarantee that we will ever get a job, or that they will ever let you associate with us. But we have to have you so at least you can talk to us.*"

Said a forty-four-year-old Nez Perce woman, "*I think that the status and role of women have been changed. Some of the things women are doing today in the dance, in drumming areas, is causing the men to lose their identity. Women before among the Nez Perce never used to drum, . . . and it was never part of our culture or tradition. When I was growing up, we would go to our grandfather's house, and he was Nez Perce. . . . He lived in Kamiah, and he would drum. He would bring out the drums. Our brothers would sit around and drum with him these songs. We [women] were not allowed to sit around the drum. We could sit behind them, and our grandfather would put his ear out and try to hear [our] singing and chanting along with them. We were never given a drumstick by our grandpa. We thought that was a man thing to do.*

"*When women are taking on things that are traditionally men's, it changes men's image of women, and it loses it for them. And I see things like this, but [for women] to go and earn a paycheck is something new, something that takes transition for men to get used to. The women have to become more adaptable because we [are] used to doing a lot of hard work. Food gathering is not easy to do when you go out and get huckleberries, and you go out and dig roots. There is a lot of work involved in this, and the women are just used to doing these types of things. It makes it hard for men to understand what their position is when so many women step out of their traditional positions.*"

"*Money started ruling their lives,*" stated a woman in her fifties who is a follower of the Seven Drums religion. "*They had to find paid jobs. In earlier times, it was women who were the providers, and it still is their position to be providers in a lot of, most families because some men are without jobs. Women's jobs like secretarial jobs—there are few men in those jobs, and women have been forced to be the financial provider. They have been forced to get jobs. . . . This degenerated the family social system. Women who should be home providing parenting to the young children have to be at jobs. Jobwise, we have lot of problems in our community. Because of the Indian culture, we have a lot of families who still care deeply for their extended family members. If there is a death in the family, everybody participates and helps. The [non-Indian] community does not understand that. We have people who lose their jobs because they have taken off for three or more days to have a funeral. Society should understand it*

takes three days for all Indian rituals and ceremonies to be performed."

An eighty-four-year-old interviewee told of the cost of living during her childhood: "*Things cost more now than they did at that time, but we did have a lot of chicken. My grandmother and I used to go around gathering eggs. We stored things, and we traded things at the grocery store, and he sold [us] the material, dress material. Sometimes we got that. My mother was a good seamstress, so she made all my school clothes. One thing I wanted from the store was a big doll with long hair. I just used to stand there and admire that. I never did get my wish, but she got me a smaller doll. But I always wanted a big doll. She said, 'That cost a lot of money.'*"

"*When we lived down there, we would go to church meetings, to Craigmont,*" an eighty-two-year-old elderly woman reminisced. "*We'd go, and we never locked our door. When we would come back, we found that everything was the same way. People were very honest; they never touched anybody's things. In my mother's and grandmother's times, when they would travel for months, they would leave things; and, when they returned back, they would find their things at the same place and undisturbed. Now, my storage lock has been broken by someone. My things are stolen from my house. So you see, we don't have that honesty anymore.*"

A woman in her forties stated the following: "*We have a fifth generation of poor self-esteem because we have very little . . . perception about how we should act and what we should do, and it's not a straight path. It makes it difficult. Vision is sometimes skewed as a people, on how we should act and what we should do. Women always have to take care of the household, put food on the table, and take care of the children. So far, that obligation and responsibility [is] having a career, . . . having economic standards that they can main-*

tain. A home, that is positive, that's good; we want that. This shows that we don't want to be on welfare. We were a very rich tribe. I think we want to be again. I don't think that we need to be taking handouts. We just need economic assistance so we can progress and have strong influences."

In the past, interracial marriage was not approved, and some older people still have this attitude, which is not prevalent in the younger generation, however. Today, interracial marriages are increasingly common, although some families still encourage their children to marry Indians only.

According to an eighty-one-year-old interviewee, *"The people never accepted the half-breed. Full-blooded Indians rejected the half-breed. They said they are no good, that their mother was a half [if] their father was a white man and mother was an Indian."*

Said a thirty-five-year-old woman, *"Growing up half and half . . . it was difficult, but it was good to grow up and to be able to enjoy both cultures."*

"When I was living with my grandparents when I was little, there was also a lot of roughness and kind of teasing among our relatives because we are being half Indian and half non-Indian," recalled a forty-one-year-old interviewee. *"There is some discrimination, but my cousin was always very nice to me and never showed any kind of bad words and bad feeling. And it was all very positive, and she seemed to take a special interest in me, and she was always trying to ask what's happening in school and what am I going to do when I grow up and those kinds of things."*

A woman in her forties said, *"I wish my kids could marry now [within the Nez Perce culture] because we are getting so married out, two generations. I wish my kids could marry Indian people. But again, the pool is very small, and I want them*

to have a happy life. So I would hope more that they could choose a person that could make them better as a couple than to remain single. That's more important to me than just that they marry an Indian person."

Like other Native Americans north of Mexico, the Nez Perce neither made nor drank alcoholic beverages before contact with Euro-Americans, early in the nineteenth century (Putnam and Ronnenberg 1983, 10). Liquor was probably introduced to the Native Americans by the fur trade companies (Van Kirck 1983, 26). Observers who find racial differences in alcoholism usually compare stereotypical "drunk Indian" behavior with idealized Euro-American upper- or middle-class forms of social drinking, rather than considering the actual drinking patterns of the frontier which were brought to the Indians along with the liquor (Dorris 1989, 83-84): the behavior of fur traders, trappers, and, later, prospectors, cowboys, and loggers.

An elderly woman, age eighty-two, shared this experience: *"We lived in the mission way up on the hills. At one time, we were going to Lewiston in a horse and buggy. Instead of coming down, I don't know why, we were going over the hills till we got to Lewiston. There were livery stables at that time. That's where we put our horse, and we got a room in a hotel. And my father came, and he kept crying. I thought he was sick. I guess he was drinking. I didn't know anything, what went on up in the hills. I asked my mother, 'What's he crying about?' 'Because he is drinking, that's why. It makes him cry when he drinks.' I whispered, 'Then, he better quit that.' I thought, 'It is easy to tell him to quit.' But a lot of men, when we used to come down from the hills to churches, a lot of them on horseback, they were drunk. They didn't gallop away, and I thought, 'Why are they doing that?' 'Because they are drunk,' my mother said, and I said, 'What's drunk?' because I did not know English then, so I did not know what she meant by drunk. She had to tell me. When I was growing up, I spoke Nez Perce. They all spoke Nez Perce until they went to school. That's the way we were raised.*"

Many believe that American Indians share a physical inability to tolerate alcohol, and that, therefore, they behave differently than whites under its influence. This idea is a main component of the "drunken Indian" stereotype. However, there is no valid scientific or clinical evidence to support this theory. One study—which claimed to establish that Eskimos and Indians metabolized alcohol at a lower rate than whites (Fenna et al. 1971)—proved to be flawed, and its results were not replicated in subsequent research. In fact, later studies showed that Indians metabolized alcohol faster than whites (Reed et al. 1976; Zeiner, Parades, and Cowden 1976; Farris and Jones 1978; Schaefer 1981). Liver biopsy studies have found no differences (Bennion and Li 1976), although American Indians have the advantage of more rapid elimination of alcohol from the body. The biology of alcohol abuse seems to be an individual matter and not a specific characteristic of any ethnic group. The need, therefore, is to analyze alcohol use and abuse patterns in other areas, such as social, cultural, and psychological contexts (Bennion and Li 1976; Westermeyer 1974).

A woman in her forties said, "*Well, since the sixties, it's become a full-blown problem for society at large, but, with Native American people, it's a specifically huge problem, mainly because genetically we don't have the extra enzyme to break down alcohol. From a person's first drink or so, they can become addicted. And, traditionally, there were no drugs and alcohol, and so it's new to our system. We've only had alcohol introduced to us at a very [late] time in history. For many years, Indian people were prohibited to drink by law. And it's only been a short while that it's been rein-troduced to our people, and the devastation that it's done to the family structure and to the young as well as the old. When they say that the Native American mortality rate is forty to forty-five years old, that's nothing to laugh at. It's true, because of alcohol and drug-related accidents. Death caused by drugs and alcohol is one of the foremost killers amongst Native American people. And there are numerous tribes that have really made an effort to make a priority in combating and preventing the problem of drugs and alcohol on the reservation.*"

P. A. May, in his 1982 study of substance abuse among American Indians, has countered racial determinism by just such an analysis of cultural and historical factors. He finds that rates of alcohol abuse vary among Indian communities in correlation with the nature of traditional social and political integration and the character of subsequent social and economic changes brought about by modernization. Among the Pueblo Indians in the Southwest, for instance, one finds a lower consumption of alcohol as compared to the Plains tribes, because the Pueblo had a more tightly integrated society and did not suffer as much stress from acculturation. However, all of the Plains tribes suffered greatly from acculturation—the stress induced by high rates of cultural change—the strongest component in the development of alcohol abuse in American Indian culture (May 1982; French and Hornbuckle 1980; Westermeyer and Neider 1985).

Some anthropologists speculate that religious differences which correlate with May's factor of social organization hold the key to these tribal contrasts in receptivity to alcohol. In particular, the Plains tribes' emphasis upon personal visional contact with the supernatural was unlike the Pueblos' compulsive ritualism and emphasis upon priestly knowledge (Benedict 1934). The former could equate the sensations of intoxication with ecstatic or supernatural experience that was

221

a direct source of power and strength, whereas the Pueblo dweller would be uncomfortable with a loss of control and civic identity.

A college graduate and mother of two children offered, *"I feel the problem of alcohol with our people. Alcoholism is related to identity and self-esteem. I feel that the transition that Indian men had to make in today's society, in today's work, has been very difficult for them. Some of them fell through the loops. I hope that our tribe becomes more spiritual. I hope that they reach out each direction to some type of religious foundation to assist them. I think people will come together as a whole. Stop criticizing and being jealous of one another, and start taking care and looking after our brothers, sisters, and children."*

A seventy-year-old interviewee said, *"Alcohol is more accessible to a person than it used to be. When I was growing up, if a woman even drank alcohol or even smoked a cigarette, she was just a nobody. But the men, at that time, they could go out, and as long as they went out by themselves, it was fine, which was the way it was then. It was just the men that were able to go out and drink, and nobody said anything about them. There were a few women that went out at that time, and they were just thought of like being just terrible. But nowadays, a lady goes to a bar or anything else, and nothing has been said. It's just a way of life these days now. Men and women seem equal, as far as going to bars are concerned. It's becoming a real social problem in this culture—drugs and alcoholism."*

"Our mothers never drank, our mothers never . . . They thought more. They'd think of their family . [Not like] in our times. You'd never see their children playing on the street. Never, hu-uh," said an eighty-year-old woman.

A fifteen-year-old girl explained her family's situation as follows: *"Both my parents are Nez Perce. My mom and my dad were separated when I was about two, so my dad has all of us. My mother left because of my dad's alcohol problem. My childhood was really hard. My dad, he was an alcoholic for awhile, and he would leave me with my older sister and with my younger brother. In a way, we've grown up too early. We learned how to do different things at an early age. We stick together. We get into arguments, but we hardly fight."*

Said an eighty-year-old interviewee, *"I wish women, young women, with children, would take care of their children. I know they think, 'Well, I have to work, I have to work.' If they want to work, they should think about their children first, see that they have good care. And, instead of going out and drinking and get into drugs, take care of your children. They're our main resource, and they just, they think, 'Well, if you can do it,' as you grow older, 'If you can do it, I can too.' And I think that's wrong. I think a mother from years back always was with her children; they never left them . . . 'Here you stay with, I'm going to get a babysitter' . . . No! It was either their sister or their mama. If they wanted to go to the store and get something and come right home."*

"And life is not a party," said a young woman in her twenties, who has two children. *"They need to realize that. I think that's one thing that they don't realize. Life is not a party. They can't party for the rest of their lives. They need to straighten up and get an education, or get a job of some type, and raise their family. I even tell that to my boyfriend. I say his life's not a party. Sometimes he gets into his stages, too, where he wants to go out. And I just don't like to do it anymore. To me, alcohol is a turn-off, especially to see women doing it."*

Another young woman in her twenties, who is single, said: *"When my grandmother would come home drunk, it was more embarrassing than anything for me. I felt sorry for her, and I was embarrassed for her, and I see a lot of other Indian* women doing it . . . all ages, is what the sad thing of it is. I think some of it started with the way men would come home and drink, and so now the women do it too, and they get violent with everybody, even with themselves, and something really needs to be done.

"I know for my age group, teenagers, I see my friends get into alcohol. For some of them, they saw it at home. Even myself, I saw my grandmother and other people drinking. And I was really against it for a long time when I was younger. And then, I guess when I was a teenager, I got into drinking a little bit. And then, . . . I watched my friends get into it more, and it became a problem where they were drunk constantly. I just had a good friend, two good friends—they were married. They got into a car wreck. He almost lost his life."

A woman just under fifty years of age remarked, "My own experience, it is related to alcohol. Not so much drugs because my own personal relationship [is] with alcoholism and my ex-husband. It had been dealt on me eighteen years of living under the stress with someone who either was drunk all the time or driving drunk. I know a lot of families that have this now. If you observe, they have alcohol and related problems, the wife drinks, the husband drinks."

According to a single mother of five, "I think when [you have gone through alcoholism] in your life, which I have . . . I have raised all of my children by myself. No help from any man. I did it all on my own, and I worked hard after I sobered up. I have sobered up for fourteen years, but I know how it feels . . . I know how it feels to not have money to buy your kids shoes and socks. I have been there, so when people come and tell me that they are having a hard time, it hurts me. I know how it feels. . . . The main concern is the survival of the community."

A woman in her mid-forties told this story: "My niece goes to kindergarten. She was with me when I went to the grocery store, and I bought a bottle of wine, and she informed me that it is alcohol, and I should not be drinking it. And I thought, 'Oh, my God, she is only five years old, but she is very well aware of what alcohol does.' So I see them educating them in the grade school. We certainly never got education like that. Our education with alcohol was something we saw in our family."

Said a woman who is an Executive Committee (NPTEC) member: "I am a mother of five, a single parent. I returned to the Nez Perce Reservation from Arizona. The motivating factor was the alcoholism that is here, because I went through it, and I know that there are other people that are going through it, and it is affecting those little ones. I worked at the Indian Health Service [in Arizona], and I worked in alcohol programs. I got to learn all the programs with the Phoenix area. . . . I was working at two jobs, going to school full time, and taking care of my kids.

"After awhile, I got tired of it. It just got to be too much, so I thought, 'I will move home [to the Nez Perce Reservation], and I'll go to school up here in Idaho or WSU,' because I could not handle living in the city anymore. I just barely got by sometimes. We did not have anything in the house. We had a roof over our heads, but we didn't have any food. Some of the children did not have clothes. It was just getting too hard, so that's why I moved to Idaho.

"I had been gone for five years, and I wanted to be near my people. I wanted to be home, with my family, my extended family. I thought I would drive back and forth and take care of my kids, but, ironically, when I came home, they were having problems here with the alcohol program. They found out that I had moved home. The director asked me if I could help them out, and I said, 'Yes.' It turned out to be three years, and, in the meantime, I still took classes down here at the Lewis-Clark College while I was still working. I was trying to balance out, but the problem of alcohol and drugs is so big, it is so much work, [that] I found [it too] hard. I had to drop my classes. I was taking night classes. I have kept working with the alcohol program."

Women have set up programs to offer youth alternatives to drugs and alcohol, said one interviewee, thirty-seven years old: "There are a lot of women who started some grass-root children's groups here, on the reservation, in the summer, to take the kids out and do things: take them berrying, fishing, hunting, take them to different places for different activities so the kids have alternatives besides running through town or getting involved in drugs or alcohol. . . . I think they are doing really a good job. I am glad to see that it is happening. There is a problem with drugs and alcohol, but people are becoming more aware of themselves and their culture. I think people are a lot more antidrugs and alcohol than they were before."

A young woman who is the mother of two and a single parent said, "My parents drank a lot, and they fought all the time. My dad used to beat my mom. At night, us kids woke up, and the whole night my dad and mom would be fighting. My dad would be beating up my mom. One time, my sister and I tried to stop my dad from beating up my mom. We got beat up too, when we were trying to stop them. My biggest nightmare was when my dad was all drunk, and he had the nerve to tell me that he was not my real father, when [he] was. . . . He was accusing my mom of sleeping around with different people. My mom won't date. She'd just go out with my dad, get drunk, she'd come home and go to sleep. The only one we had to rely on was my grandpa and my grandma. Now, since my grandpa passed away, we just have our grandma. That's who we turn to. I always turn to my grandma for help."

"I think [women accepted abuse] because a lot of them depend economically and emotionally on their husbands," suggested a thirty-eight-year-old woman. "It's like they have to have a man, and they can't live without him. I would like to see that change. Because what I see happening is that I see them passing the same values on to their daughters. I see the sons see how the mothers are reacting, and so they are going to treat their wives like that. That's the way their mothers reacted to their fathers. I can see a change. I wish that women would take hold of it and make that change themselves. Unless somebody breaks the cycle, it's going to continue. The community has to take some responsibility and not allow it to happen: not say, 'That's his wife, he can do that.' I think it is no longer socially acceptable. Then, maybe it will stop. But I think women have to take some responsibility and try to break that cycle."

A woman in her forties said, "[A]nd I've felt that in the past I've seen other Native American women get battered and put up with it in their life. And I had decided at that moment, at that time in my life, that I wasn't going to put up with that kind of behavior. One thing I would like to add, too, is that traditionally Native American women were never treated that way. They were highly respected in the family structure. However, from the time of childhood to my adulthood, there was a change in the family structure where Native American women were in abusive situations."

"We have many cases of wife battering," a thirty-seven-year-old woman related. "A lot of it goes unreported, and the system fails to listen for their protection, for the treatment of the couple . . . because a lot of time the couple will end up getting together anyway. But, unless they are able to communicate and find out the ways of dealing with conflict, they are back into the same cycle. The reason for wife battering, a lot of it is frustration, a lot of it is a lack of communication, and a

224

lot of it is learned from seeing it in the past—not knowing how to deal with strong emotions and conflict.

"We have child abuse in our communities, too. It has been here for a long time. The reasons are, I think again, the same as wife battering. There are a lot of expectations on our young families of the roles they have to fulfill. When they feel inadequate, feel they are not capable of doing it, and they feel that they are judged for some reason, they strike out. And they strike out at the people who are closest to them because they don't know how to express their hurt and their frustration or their anger in any other way than that. These cases are among different age groups.

"We had a situation with a lady who is in her thirties who was coming to her realization that she had been sexually abused when she was a child by a close family member. When she confronted that family member, they found out that person's wife was of a previous generation and also abused. So this abuse is like a generational thing. It happened, so you have multigenerations of abuse and alcoholism. You combine them together, and it is a difficult pattern to break. It's hard to have all the answers right there in front of you, and you don't know how to deal with them, where they are at, and not where you are at. It's hard to recognize that and deal with it, when you have a court system and a social service system who are not synchronized with each other. They need to get into synchronization.

"Women can take a hold of their life. I have seen so many women who have low self-esteem, who don't feel that they can make any decisions regarding their personal lives, much less the lives of their children or . . . their husbands. They just don't feel like they have any authority to do it. I would like to see that change because they can learn to be assertive and learn to make decisions—especially women—involving themselves. I

have seen a lot of spouse abuse at present, and I see the women accepting this. I see them thinking that 'This is a part of life I have to live with.'"

"My position here on the reservation as a Family Nurse Practitioner with Indian Health Service was very stressful because I am a nurse, female, Indian," a woman in her late forties said. "I did a lot of counseling. The doctors at the clinic were non-Indian. A lot of the women came to me, and I began to do a lot of counseling. There are lots of depressed women on the reservation. There are a lot of problems, and I began to get burned out. I felt like I could not handle it. It was getting real difficult. We were really busy all the time. To me, a lot of that reminded me of Vietnam on a different level. . . ."

A sixty-year-old woman commented: "We had suicide cases in 1989. Six or seven successful suicides within a two-year period. We had a task force come from Albuquerque to study our community. He said that we had all the resources, but we were not sharing. We have to coordinate our services. Once we realized that we need to do more talking and educating about suicide prevention and recognizing the symptoms, [we could] provide some type of effective reporting mechanism. That helps us a lot.

"We are learning to be more interdependent as agencies—the tribe, Indian Health Service, the BIA, the schools, the county, the state, and the federal government—that we need each other to work [together] if we are going to address these problems. It is not just community problems [of the] Indian community; it is a problem at large to grow from each others' experiences."

Said a thirty-seven-year-old woman: "The extended family, the way they used to be, is changing—extended families were involved in child rearing, raising of the children—because of the high turmoil that exists, because of the high unemployment, the young age of our families, and alco-

holism, the need to secure different jobs. . . . The grandparents, uncles, and aunts used to get more involved into 'Where are kids?' and 'What are they doing?' And now we have come to the point we are more [isolated] . . . and I think part of it is based on the government. The nuclear family is the focus: the mom, the dad, and how many kids. If they are having problems, too bad. It's not my problem; I cannot invite into my home; it's too small. Well, before it did not matter if you had a small house or a big house, there was always room for your family.

"I think the other influence is our court system that we have now. Our tribal court, in their child protection meeting, doesn't recognize extended families as much as they need to, because a lot of times those extended families are available if they are aware that there is a problem. Because of the federal guidelines—confidentiality and different things—they are not able to discuss really what's going on. A generation above me, they were raised in a time when kids were moved house to house according to relatives. There was always a home. You wouldn't find kids with no home, and now we have kids with no home. They go to the Tribal Children's Home, which is our new system. It was started in 1984; it is like a temporary shelter, and they can stay there from ninety days to six months. The money comes through a federal government grant. There is a children's home director and house parents. It is working out pretty good. Approximately, we get forty children a year.

"I'd like to see our court system get more into the tribal mode of thinking and the tribal mode of [family] values and get away from trying to copy the non-Indian way of doing it. It doesn't work with our community. For example, different relatives who did different things in the system, like my grandaunt who taught me how to tan hides and my grandma who taught me more of things like sewing, huckleberries, and baking, and my

grandfather taught me lots of things about horses and about driving a car. So everyone had a way of impacting or teaching you something, and we have got away from that. We are putting too much just onto Mom and Dad and not enough recognizing . . . the strength of the extended families."

At present, diabetes, heart disease, arthritis, and obesity are the major health problems. Many of these problems are due to changes in diet and lifestyle.

Mused an eighty-six-year-old woman, *"My parents never had any diabetes or anything. Them days, it seemed like no one had diabetes that I knew of, or everybody was well. . . ."*

A woman, eighty-four years old, said, *"[D]iabetes and high blood pressure and . . . arthritis seems to be hereditary. There's a lot of it in our families. I had one aunt who's just crippled up with, you know, just really bad with arthritis. My mother, she had heart problems, and my dad was diabetic. I don't know about my grandparents, though. They never seemed to be [sick] . . . unless we just didn't know about it; I don't really know. But them days, we used to work, we worked in the garden, and we had healthy foods. . . ."*

An eighty-six-year-old woman spoke of the role of diet: *"Prepared foods, all kinds of foods that you just pop in the microwave or reheat in the oven. Sugared, sugared foods, and everything that is prepared already. Most of it has got a lot of salt on it, and that's a big problem for our . . . high blood pressure problems."*

"We never heard of diabetes. We never heard of cancer either. The only thing we ever heard was tuberculosis and smallpox. That's about it. All the health problems are coming from what we are eating now. The food we eat, now it is treated. They always say on the TV that they spray some kind of spray on them. I don't think we have clean food anymore," an eighty-four-year-old woman said, remembering her grandparents' time.

Health care on the Nez Perce Indian Reservation is a concern of many Nez Perce. A Nez Perce Tribal Executive Committee member notes that many tribal elders go without health care because costs are only partially covered. She thinks the political system in the past has done little to improve health care for Native Americans. As quoted in the *Lewiston Morning Tribune* of November 1, 1992, she warned, *"I think we have some major problems in the U.S. that the new president needs to address, and that is lack of understanding of minority people by the white society."*

Conclusion

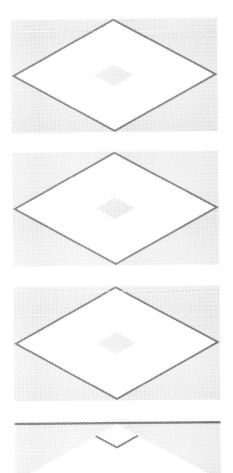

"I HOPE READERS WILL realize that this book is first hand information. We remember something from our great-grandmothers, grandmothers, and mothers to give the overall picture of a family, mother, father, and children, rather than just a man in his regalia," said one interviewee, forty years old.

A forty-one-year-old woman said, *"This work is really important because it focuses on the lives of the Nez Perce women. Seeing them all taken for granted—until you see it all collected in one volume, just the strength, beauty, power, and legacy of so many people. I think [of significant] Nez Perce women in history, the impact of the War of 1877, and how women have provided strength and force for the survival of the tribe as a whole—not just what women did, but how they contributed continuity of everything for the tribe."*

All Nez Perce Indian women have been shaped by their tribal identity and sense of place, yet each has adapted her childhood training and intuitions to a changing world that demands flexibility and the application of acquired knowledge. In the interviews for this book, the women consistently expressed certain major concerns and values which overrode their personal differences.

Nez Perce women today believe that education is the best way to assure the future success and security of their people. They strive to preserve and restore their precious culture by celebrating root feasts and powwows and by returning to traditional crafts, language, and religion, and at the same time they endeavor to provide a broad and technical education for the young.

"It is not a matter of going backwards. It's simply a case of not sacrificing tradition in the name of progress," said a woman in her late forties.

The younger women intend to become more directly active in politics than were their elders, seeing this as a way to bring about constructive change. These women believe that well-qualified Indian women should concentrate their efforts on the solution of the numerous Indian problems, of which, all interviewees agree, alcoholism is the most serious. Spousal and child abuse reflects the kind of problem that often occurs when the men of a household are alcoholic.

"It definitely affects the family and women," observed a woman in her late fifties. *"There are more Native American women that are alcoholic. And it's real difficult to raise big families when you have the problem of alcoholism, because alcoholism just kills anything in its path, including the families. As Native American families, our parents were abused children, and that abusive cycle will continue until we can educate younger children, the youth, about what those patterns are, how and why the destruction of the family came about. There's numerous reasons why there was distancing of family and the breakup of the Native American family home. Primarily, one of them was the efforts toward genocide, or if you will, assimilation. The easiest way that society had chose to break up families was by relocating their children from their homes and requiring from that children be taken off the reservations and separated from their families, thereby breaking the bond of cultural and traditional values so permanent and important in our family group."*

The groundwork for social and personal disintegration was laid when missionaries convinced their converts that Christian life meant giving up all of their traditions and adopting agriculture, Euro-American education, and a money economy. Participation in the market economy fractured the established patterns of kinship obligation and mutual interdependence, as did the introduction of individual land ownership and small dwellings. The resultant insecurity and tension precipitated even more societal breakdown by spawning crime, alcoholism, drug use, suicide, and related social problems such as child abuse and the battering of women.

Although women had long taken strong advisory roles and supplied significant leadership, their responsibilities and activities have only increased in modern times due to the relatively higher incidence of alcoholism among men. They began to see that they had to take more active leadership, or their children would be lost to alcohol and violence.

Nez Perce women's efforts to preserve tradition comes as their own lifestyles are radically changing. Their traditional nurturing role has been substantially modified by participation in the contemporary economy. They are beginning to have fewer children, to work outside the home, and to work at men's jobs. Twenty years ago, few reservation women were wage earners. Now, they are a majority of the tribal administrative work force.

Some Nez Perce women have to take paying jobs off the reservation, where they cannot take advantage of the traditional extended family support in which young children are most often cared for by grandparents. Unlike Euro-American society—which is heavily individualistic and self-centered—Indian culture and Indian society put emphasis on the welfare of the whole tribe. Indian women have tried to continue the Native American strategy of mutual support.

A middle-aged woman believes, *"Nez Perce women are real survivors, and . . . they will be strong people within our structure. And I'm not sure, but I would guess that there are more Native American women than men, and that we have . . . we're going to have a strong voice in how our tribe will be run, and we will have more and more women in the leadership, politically. And I think that, in time, that we will demand economic equal status, and that's coming . . . that's turning about for Native American women."*

A Nez Perce woman in her forties said, *"Women's liberation has let us speak aloud again, but I don't think that Nez Perce women need women's liberation. We were already liberated in our society."*

In their own view, women were liberated in the Nez Perce traditional society until engulfed by a patriarchal, bigoted one. Whites brought the expectation that women should look to men for permission and guidance. And there is little enthusiasm among these women for the current American feminist movement because it appears to them to run counter to traditional respect for the authority of tribal elders. Seniority, not gender, was the measure for deference in the old society. Outsiders rarely glimpsed women's position as advisor to men and their participation in the decision-making process. In public, women wielded their influence quietly, never conspicuously.

The Indian woman is and has been a strong contributor within her culture. Evidence from the women themselves supports this statement, despite teaching to the contrary by missionaries. In their statements here, Nez Perce Indian women typically contradict these passive images, while supporting the view that their role was and is an essential one within the American Indian culture and, as the world changes, within ever widening spheres.

▲▲▲▲▲▲▲▲▲▲▲▲▲▲▲▲▲▲▲▲▲▲▲▲▲▲▲▲▲▲▲▲▲▲▲▲▲▲

Bibliography

Ackerman, Lillian A.
1982   Sexual equality in the Plateau culture area. Ph.D. diss., Washington State University, Pullman.

Anastasio, Angelo
1955   Intergroup relations in the Southern Plateau. Ph.D. diss., University of Chicago.

Aoki, Haruo
1962   Nez Perce and Northern Sahaptin: a linary comparison. *International Journal of American Linguistics* 29:42-4.
1966   Nez Perce and Proto-Sahaptin kinship terms. *International Journal of American Linguistics* 32 (4):357-68.
1970   *Nez Perce grammar.* Berkeley: University of California Press.

Arneson, Kathryn
1993   Nez Perce flat twined bags: a study of symbols. Master's thesis, University of Idaho, Moscow.

Baily, Robert
1935   *River of No Return.* Lewiston, Idaho: Blake Printing Co.

Bataille, Gretchen M., and Kathleen M. Sands
1984   *American Indian women: telling their lives.* Lincoln: University of Nebraska Press.

Benedict, Ruth
1934   *Patterns of culture.* New York: Houghton-Mifflin.

Bennion, L., and T.K. Li
1976   Alcohol metabolism in American Indians and Whites. *New England Journal of Medicine* 284:9-13.

Boyd, Robert T.
1985   The introduction of infectious diseases among the Indians of the Pacific Northwest, 1774-1874. Ph.D. diss., University of Washington, Seattle.

Brown, Jennifer S. H.
1940   *Strangers in blood.* Vancouver: University of British Columbia Press.

Brunton, Bill
1968   Ceremonial integration in the Plateau of Northwestern North America. *Northwest Anthropologial Research Notes* 2 (1):1-28.

Bureau of Indian Affairs
1975   Superintendents' Annual Narrative and Statistical Reports from Field Jurisdictions of the Bureau of Indian Affairs, 1907-38; Roll 51: Fort Lapwai Sanatorium, 1913-15, 1932-35; Fort Lapwai School, 1910-33; Fort McDermitt School, 1910-21. Washington, D.C.: General Services Administration. Idaho Historical Society Library, Boise; microfilm M 1011.

Canfield, Kenneth
1988   Plain abstractions. *Art and Auction: The Magazine of the International Market*, October, 196-207.

Cataldo, J.
n.d.   Sketch of the Nez Perce Indian Mission. Unpublished ms. Gonzaga University Archives, Spokane, Washington.

Chalfant, Stuart A.
1974   Aboriginal territory of the Nez Perce Indians. In *Nez Perce Indians*, edited by David Agee Horr. New York: Garland Publishing.

Chance, N.
1962   *Factionalism as a process of social and cultural change in intergroup relations and leadership.* Edited by Muzafer Sherif. New York: John Wiley and Sons.

Chittenden, Hiram Martin
1902   *The American fur trade in the Far West.* New York: Francis P. Harper.

Chittenden, Hiram Martin, and Alfred Richardson, eds.
1905   *The life, letters and travels of Father Pierre-Jean De Smet, S.J., 1801-1873.* 4 vols. New York: Francis P. Harper.

Clark, Ella E.
1966   *Indian legends of the Pacific Northwest.* Norman: University of Oklahoma Press.

Coale, George L.
1956   Ethnohistorical sources for the Nez Perce Indian. *Ethnohistory* 3:45-55, 346-60.
1958   Notes on the guardian spirit concept among the Nez Perce. *International Archive of Ethnography* 48:136-48.

Collier, John, Jr., and Malcolm Collier
1987   *Visual anthropology: photography as a research method.* Albuquerque: University of New Mexico Press.

Coser, Lewis A.
1956   *The functions of social conflict.* Glencoe, Illinois: The Free Press.
1957   Social conflict and the theory of social change. *The British Journal of Sociology* 8:197-207.

Craig, Wallace, et al.
1963   A human resources survey of the Nez Perce Tribe. Unpublished ms. North Idaho Indian Agency, Lapwai, Idaho.

Crawford, Mary
1936   *The Nez Percés since Spalding.* Berkeley, California: Professional Press.

Crocket, Joy
1923   *The operations of the Hudson's Bay Company in Old Oregon.* Master's thesis, University of Idaho, Moscow.

Curtis, Edward S.
1907-1930   *The North American Indian.* 20 vols. Norwood, Massachusetts: Plimpton Press.

Dorris, Michael
1989   *The broken cord.* New York: Harper and Row.

Dozier, Jack
1963   A Nez Perce homecoming. *Idaho Yesterdays: The Quarterly Journal of the Idaho Historical Society* 7 (3):22-5 (Fall).

Drury, Clifford
1936   *Henry Herman Spalding.* Caldwell, Idaho: Caxton Printers.
1958   *The diaries and letters of Henry H. Spalding and Asa Smith relating to the Nez Perce Mission.* Glendale, California: Arthur H. Clark Co.

Farris, J. J., and B. M. Jones
1978   Ethanol metabolism and memory impairment in American Indian and White women social drinkers. *Journal of Studies on Alcohol* 39:1975-79.

Fenna, D., O. Schaefer, L. Mix, and J. A. Gilbert
1971   Ethanol metabolism in various racial groups. *Canadian Medical Association Journal* 105 (5):472-5.

Fletcher, Alice C.
n.d.   Ethnologic gleanings among the Nez Perce. Bureau of American Ethnology, ms. group no. 4558, item no. 59. National Anthropological Archives, Smithsonian Institute, Washington, D.C.
n.d.   The Nez Perce Country. Bureau of American Ethnology, ms. group no. 677, item no. 57. National Anthropological Archives, Smithsonian Institute, Washington, D.C.

French, L. A., and J. Hornbuckle
1980   Alcoholism among Native Americans: an analysis. *Social Work* 25:275-80.

Gay, E. Jane
1875   *Choup-Ni't-Ki'.* National Archives Microfilm Publications, 22-1635. Washington, D.C.: General Services Administration.
1981   *With the Nez Perce: Alice Fletcher in the field 1889-92.* Edited by Frederick E. Hoxie and Joan T. Mark. Lincoln: University of Nebraska Press.

Gidley, M.
1979   *With one sky above us: life on an Indian reservation at the turn of the century.* New York: G. P. Putnam's Sons.

Gillett, Griswold
1954   Aboriginal patterns of trade between the Columbia Basin and the Northern Plains. Master's thesis, Montana State University, Bozeman.

Gogal, J. M.
1980   Corn husk bags and hats of the Columbia Plateau Indians. *American Indian Basketry Magazine* 1 (2):4-10.
          Rose Frank shows how to weave a Nez Perce corn husk bag. *American Indian Basketry Magazine* 1 (2):22-29.

Green, Rayna
1992   *Women in American Indian society.* New York: Chelsea House Publishers.

Gulick, Bill
1981   *Chief Joseph country, land of the Nez Perce.* Caldwell, Idaho: Caxton Printers.

Gunther, Erna
1950   The westward movement of some Plains traits. *American Anthropologist* 52:174-80.

Haines, Francis
1938   The northward spread of horses among the Plains Indians. *American Anthropologist* 40:429-37.
1955   *The Nez Percés.* Norman: University of Oklahoma Press.
1964   The Nez Perce Tribe versus the United States. *Idaho Yesterdays: The Quarterly Journal of the Idaho Historical Society* 8 (1):18-25 (Spring).

Handy, Henry W.
1948   History of the Roman Catholic Church in Idaho. Master's thesis, University of Idaho, Moscow.

Harbinger, Lucy J.
1964   The importance of food plants in the maintenance of Nez Perce cultural identity. Master's thesis, Washington State University, Pullman.

Herskovits, M. J.
1938   *Acculturation: the study of culture contact.* New York: J. J. Augustin.

Hewes, Gordon W.
1947   Aboriginal use of fishing resources in northwestern North America. Ph.D. diss., University of California, Berkeley.
1973   Indian fisheries' productivity in pre-contact times in the Pacific salmon area. *Northwest Anthropological Research Notes* 7:133-55.

Holder, Preston
1970   *The hoe and the horse on the Plains: a study of cultural change among North American Indians.* Lincoln: University of Nebraska Press.

Howard, O. O.
1881   *Nez Perce Joseph: an account of his ancestors, his lands, his confederates, his enemies, his murders, his war, his pursuit and capture.* Boston: Lee and Shepard Publishers.

Hunn, Eugene S.
1990   *Nch'i-W'ana: the big river mid-Columbia Indians and their land.* Seattle: University of Washington Press.

Jacobs, M.
1934   Northern Sahaptin kinship forms. *American Anthropologist* 34:688-93.
1937   Historic perspective in Indian languages of Oregon and Washington. *Pacific Northwest Quarterly* 28:55-75.

Jaimes, M. Annette, ed.
1992   *The state of Native America: genocide, colonization, and resistance.* Boston: South End Press.

Josephy, Alvin M., Jr.
1955   The naming of the Nez Perce. *Montana* 5:1-18.
1962   Origins of the Nez Perce Indians. *Idaho Yesterdays: The Quarterly Journal of the Idaho Historical Society* 6 (1):2-13 (Spring).
1965   *Nez Perce Indians and the opening of the Northwest.* New Haven, Connecticut: Yale University Press.
1983   The people of the Plateau. In *Nez Perce country: a handbook for the Nez Perce National Historical Park*. Washington, D.C.: National Park Service.

Kessler, Marcia N. L.
1985   The traditional Nez Perce basketry hat: its modal style and cultural significance. Master's thesis, Washington State University, Pullman.

Kirk, Sylvia V.
1983   *Many tender ties.* Norman: University of Oklahoma Press.

Liljeblad, Sven
1957   *Indian Peoples in Idaho.* Idaho State University Library, Pocatello. Mimeographed.

Lundsgaarde, Henry P.
1963   A theoretical interpretation of Nez Perce kinship. Master's thesis, University of Wisconsin, Madison.
1967   A structural analysis of the Nez Perce kinship. *Research Studies* 35:48-77.

Mandelbaum, M.
1938   The individual life cycle. In *The Sinkaietk or Southern Okanogan of Washington*, edited by Leslie Spier. General Series in Anthropology, no. 6. Contributions from Laboratory of Anthropology 2. Menasha, Wisconsin: George Banta Publishing.

Marden, Guy
1983   The northwestern Plateau Indian sweat house. Master's thesis, Washington State University, Pullman.

Mark, Joan
1988   *A stranger in her native land: Alice Fletcher and the American Indians.* Lincoln: University of Nebraska Press.

Marshall, Alan G.
1977   Nez Perce social groups: an ecological perspective. Ph.D. diss., Washington State University, Pullman. Ann Arbor, Michigan: University Microfilms.

May, P. A.
1982   Substance abuse and American Indians: prevalence and susceptibility. *Journal of Addiction* 17:1185-1209.

McBeth, Kate C.
1908   *The Nez Perce since Lewis and Clark.* London: Fleming H. Revell Co.

McGuire, Nancy
1957   An analysis of Nez Perce political organization. Bachelor's thesis, Reed College, Portland, Oregon.

McWhorter, L. V.
1926   Battle of the Big Hole. In *The story of Pe-nah-we-non-ni*. Papers of L. V. McWhorter. Washington State University Libraries, Pullman.
        The last battle, told by Yellow Wolf. Papers of L. V. McWhorter. Washington State University Libraries, Pullman.
1948   *Yellow Wolf: his own story.* Caldwell, Idaho: Caxton Printers.
1952   *Hear me my chiefs.* Caldwell, Idaho: Caxton Printers.

Meyers, Renee
1993   Technology serves traditional values: the Nez Perce Tribe is applying contemporary science and technology to managing its natural resources. *Cultural Survival Quarterly* 17 (1):35-7 (Spring).

Morrill, Allen C., and E. D. Morrill
1963   The measuring woman and the cook. *Idaho Yesterdays: The Quarterly Journal of the Idaho Historical Society* 7 (3):2-15 (Fall).
1964   Talmaks. *Idaho Yesterdays: The Quarterly Journal of the Idaho Historical Society* 8 (3):2-15 (Fall).
1972   Old church made new. *Idaho Yesterdays: The Quarterly Journal of the Idaho Historical Society* 16 (2):16-32 (Summer).
1978   *Out of the blanket: the story of Sue and Kate McBeth, missionaries of the Nez Perce.* Moscow, Idaho: University of Idaho Press.

Morse, Doris C.
1983   Breastfeeding among the Nez Perce Indians from 1977-1981. Master's thesis, Washington State University, Pullman.

Murdock, G. P.
1960   Ethnographic bibliography of North America. 3d ed. New Haven, Connecticut: Human Relations Area Files.
1967   *Ethnographic atlas.* Pittsburgh: University of Pittsburgh Press.

Nielson, Jean C.

1934　　The operations of British fur trading companies in Idaho. Master's thesis, University of Idaho, Moscow.

O'Malley, M.

1915　　Census of Nez Perce Catholics. Master's thesis, Gonzaga University, Spokane, Washington.

Oswalt, Wendell

1966　　*The land was theirs.* New York: John Wiley and Sons.

Park, Willard Z.

1938　　*Shamanism in western North America: a study in cultural relationships.* Chicago: Northwestern University Press.

Phinney, A.

1934　　*Nez Perce texts.* Columbia University Contributions to Anthropology, no. 25. New York: Columbia University Press.

Pree, Donna Marie

1970　　Nez Perce feminine aboriginal clothing. Master's thesis, Washington State University, Pullman.

Putnam, Edison K., and Herman W. Ronnenberg

1983　　Pre-prohibition liquor use by the Nez Perce Indians: and its interaction with Euro-American liquor questions. *The Journal of the Nez Perce County Historical Society* 3 (1):10-16 (Winter).

Ray, Verne F.

1932　　*The Sanpoil and Nespelem: Salishan peoples of northeastern Washington.* University of Washington Publications in Anthropology, no. 5. University of Washington Press: Seattle.

1939　　*Cultural relations in the Plateau of northwestern America.* Publications of the Frederick Webb Lodge Anniversary Publication Fund, vol. 3. Los Angeles: Southwest Museum.

Reed, T. E., H. Kalan, R. J. Griffins, B. M. Kapur, and J. G. Rankin

1976　　Alcohol and acetaldehyde metabolism in Caucasians, Chinese, and Americans. *Canadian Medical Association Journal* 115:851-55.

Riley, R. J.

1961　　The Nez Perce struggle for self-government: a history of Nez Perce governing bodies, 1842-1960. Master's thesis, University of Idaho, Moscow.

Roe, Frank Gilbert

1955　　*The fur traders of the Far West.* Norman: University of Oklahoma Press.

Schaefer, J. M.

1981　　Firewater myths revisited. *Journal of Studies of Alcohol* 9 (suppl.):99-117.

Schlick, Mary D.

1977　　*Design elements in Yakima weaving: a source for learning materials.* Unpublished ms. Virginia Polytechnic Institute and State University Library, Reston.

1980　　Art treasures of the Columbia Plateau. *American Indian Basketry Magazine* 1 (2):12-21.

Schwedge, Madge L.

1966　　An ecological study of Nez Perce settlement patterns. Master's thesis, Washington State University, Pullman.

1970　　The relationship of aboriginal Nez Perce settlement patterns to physical environment and to generalized distribution of food resources. *Northwest Anthropological Research Notes* 4 (2):129-36.

Scrimsher, Leda S.

1967　　Native foods used by the Nez Perce Indians of Idaho. Master's thesis, University of Idaho, Moscow.

Shawley, Stephen D.

1971　　Nez Perce dress: a study in culture change. Master's thesis, University of Idaho, Moscow.

Skeels, Dell

1954　　A classification of humor in Nez Perce mythology. *Journal of American Folklore* 67:47-63.

Slickpoo, Allen P., Sr., and Deward E. Walker, Jr.

1973　　*Noon Nee-Me-Poo (We, the Nez Percés).* Vol. 1. Lapwai, Idaho: Nez Perce Tribe of Idaho.

Spinden, H. J.

1908   *The Nez Perce Indians.* Memoirs of the American Anthropological Association, no. 2. Menasha, Wisconsin: George Banta Publishing.

Spindler, Louise S.

1962   *Menomini women and culture change.* American Anthropological Association Memoir, no. 91. Washington, D.C.

Sprague, R.

1967   Aboriginal burial practices in the Plateau region of northwestern North America. Ph.D. diss., University of Arizona, Tucson.

Thayis, Helga A.

1967   *The Nez Perce trail.* Yakima, Washington: Franklin Press.

Tidd, J. W.

1929   A brief history of the Nez Perce Indians. Master's thesis, Ohio State University, Columbus.

Thwaites, R. G., ed.

1969   *Original journal of the Lewis and Clark expedition, 1804-1806.* Vols. 3, 4, 5, 7, and 8. 1904. Repr., New York: Arno Press.

Walker, Deward E., Jr.

1966   The Nez Perce sweat-bath complex: an acculturational analysis. *Southwestern Journal of Anthropology* 22:133-71.

1967   Mutual cross-utilization of economic resources in the Plateau: an example from aboriginal Nez Perce fishing practices. Laboratory of Anthropology, Reports of Investigations, no. 41. Washington State University, Pullman.

1978   *Indians of Idaho.* Moscow, Idaho: University of Idaho Press.

1985   *Conflict and schism in Nez Perce acculturation: a study of religion and politics.* Moscow, Idaho: University of Idaho Press.

Watkins, I. E.

1935   From a new donor, a Nez Perce Indian woman's dress. *Masterkey* 8.

Watters, Mari

1990   Nez Perce tapes and texts. Unpublished. Upward Bound, University of Idaho, Moscow. Idaho.

Weil, P. M.

1965   Political modernization on the Nez Perce Indian Reservation, 1940-1963. Master's thesis, University of Oregon, Eugene.

Westermeyer, J.

1974   The drunken Indian stereotype: myths and realities. *Psychiatric Annals* 4 (11):29-36.

Westermeyer, J., and J. C. Neider

1985   Cultural affiliation among American Indian alcoholics: correlation and change over a ten-year period. *Journal of Operational Psychiatry* 16 (2):17-23.

Williams, Jack R.

1961   Footnotes to History. *Idaho Yesterdays: The Quarterly Journal of the Idaho Historical Society* 5 (1):14-15 (Spring).

1982   Nez Perce horses: their controversy and their history, part one. *Appaloosa World*, June, 35-43.

Wyman, Anne

1935   Corn husk bags of the Nez Perce Indians. *Southwest Museum Leaflet* 9 (1):89-95. Los Angeles.

Zeinner, A. R., A. Parades, and L. Cowden.

1976   Physiological responses to ethanol among the Tarahumara Indians. *Annual of New York Academy of Sciences* 273:151-58.

Index

Crawford, Elizabeth, 159
Crawford, Mary, 159
Crow Reservation, hostages on, 132
cuk'e·ymit. See pine, yellow
customs, forbidden, 155-56

D

dances, 111
circle, 110, 113
eel, 110
Kihl-lo-wow-ya, 116
medicine, 142-44
owl, 110, 113
powwow, 116
rabbit, 110
prohibited, 116
veteran, 214-25
war, 110
wéyik wecit, 142
women's involvement in, 107
Davis, Etta Moffett, 49
Davis, Julia A., xxi, 115, 201
Dawes Act of 1887, 4
death, 92-93. *See also* burial, cemeteries
demographics of Nez Perce people
at present, 8
tuberculosis, effect on, 180
dentalium, 63
depression, of children at boarding schools, 183
designs, decorative, 45, 58, 63
diabetes, 4, 6, 226
diet, 4, 20, 21. *See also* food; specific types of food
digging stick (*tùk'es*), 12, 15, 17, 65
discipline. *See* children, discipline of
discrimination

against mixed-race people, 220
against Native Americans, 192-96, 198, 204, 211-12
disease, 6. *See also* specific diseases
divorce, 91
Dixon, Josephine C., 159
dogs, 95, 97, 107
domestic violence, 214, 224-25, 230. *See also* abuse
Down-river people, 9, 10
dress, native. *See* clothing, native
dresses
wing, 44, 45, 47, 54
buckskin, 45
See also clothing
drug additctions, 218
drumming
and dances, 110-113
prohibited, 4
return to, 7
songs, passed down through generations, 142
by women, 218-19
See also music; songs; dances
Durr, Mrs. Allen, 31
dwellings. *See* specific types of dwellings
dyes, 4, 61

E

economy, 4, 215
education, 165-208
college, 198
conflicting with sanitorium stays, 171-80
Euro-American, introduction of, 4
funds for, 198-99
importance of, 208, 211-12

modern, 192-208
traditional, 165-67
vocational, 186-89
See also grandparents; Fort Lapwai Indian School; specific colleges
Edwards, Lillie, 49
Edwards, Nancy, 194
eel dance, 110
eels, 27, 28
Ee-u-weehlu-lakh-my. *See* High Eagle, Patricia
elders
respect for, 77
in tribal council, 120
See also grandparents
Ellenwood, Georgia, 48
Ellenwood, Mary, xxvi
Ellenwood, Trulin J., xxvi
elopement, 86
E-luute-Pah-Awh-Yene, 139
embroidery
false, 61
quill, 48
Emmy Award, Nez Perce woman as winner of, 200
employment of Nez Perce women, 109-19
at Fort Lapwai Indian School, 180
at boarding schools, 186
conflicting with ceremonies, 219
in white families, 187
with Bureau of Indian Affairs, 189
in police, 204
See also unemployment; specific employers
Eneas, Helen, 31
engagement, 86
Enos, Hattie, 138, 139-40
epilepsy, as treated by

medicine women, 144-45
ep'ine, 14
Evans, Connie, xxi, 202
E-we-tahnt-my, 101
exile, as punishment for rape, 89
eye contact, between men and women, 81

F

Fairfield, Lizzie, 35
feasts, public, modern, 31. *See also* specific feasts
feather
ornament on braids, 54
symbol of honor, 122
fir, Douglas, 7
fire, maintenance of, 63, 65
firewood. *See* wood
fish, 100
Fletcher, Alice, 5, 6
foods, Euro-American
introduction of, 169
storage of, 69
foods, native
for babies, 73
gathering, by women, 12, 21
medicinal uses, 20
move away from, 6, 67
preparation of, 31
recipes, 28
serving of, 28
storage of, 31-32, 58
wedding trade, use in, 86-88
See also feasts; plants, medicinal; specific foods
Fort Lapwai, 171
Fort Lapwai Indian